Child Development for Child Care and Protection Workers

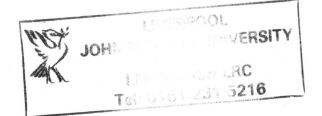

Child Development for Child Care and Protection Workers

*Brigid Daniel, Sally Wassell
and Robbie Gilligan*

Foreword by Jim Ennis

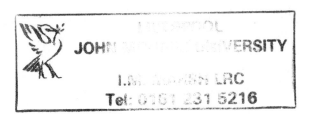

Jessica Kingsley Publishers
London and Philadelphia

First published in the United Kingdom in 1999
by Jessica Kingsley Publishers
116 Pentonville Road
London N1 9JB, UK
and
400 Market Street, Suite 400
Philadelphia, PA 19106, USA

www.jkp.com

Library of Congress Cataloging in Publication Data
Child development for child care and protection workers / Brigid Daniel ... [et al.].
    p.   cm.
Includes bibliographical references (p.   ) and index.
ISBN 1-85302-633-6 (pb : alk. paper)
    1. Child development. 2. Child psychology. 3. Child care workers. 4. Child welfare workers.
I. Daniel, Brigid, 1959–
    HQ772.C44 1998
    305.231--dc21

                                                                98-11672
                                                                CIP

British Library Cataloguing in Publication Data
Daniel, Brigid
Child development for child care and protection workers
1.Child development 2.Child psychology 3.Child welfare
I.Title II.Wassel, Sally III.Gilligan, Robbie
305.2'31'02436

ISBN-13: 978 1 85302 633 1
ISBN-10: 1 85302 633 6

Printed and Bound in Great Britain by
Athenaeum Press, Gateshead, Tyne and Wear

Contents

Authors' Acknowledgements

The book has developed from a collaborative process. However, each author has taken primary responsibility for preparing different chapters. Brigid Daniel was responsible for the overall editing of the book and for Chapters 1, 2, 3, 7 and 8. Sally Wassell was responsible for Chapters 4, 5 and 6 and Robbie Gilligan for Chapter 9.

Jim Ennis was responsible for bringing the writing team together and facilitating the book's development. Elaine Ennis also contributed many helpful comments. We are extremely grateful to the many students attending Dundee University Social Work Department's post-qualifying child protection courses who helped to refine and develop the ideas and kept them firmly grounded in practice. Julie Barclay designed Figure 1.1 and prepared Figures 3.1, 3.2 and 7.1. and Norma Grahame helped with the typing. Thanks also to David Willshaw and Chris Henderson for encouragement and support.

The authors and publishers are grateful to the following for permission to reproduce figures: British Agencies for Fostering and Adoption and Vera Fahlberg for Figures 2.1 and 2.2; Blackwell Publishers for Figures 2.3 and 7.2, from Smith and Cowie *Understanding Children's Development;* Child Welfare League of America for Figure 2.4, from Hartman, *Working with Adoptive Families Beyond Placement;* Routledge Publishers for Figure 7.1, adapted from Meadows *Understanding Child Development;* John Wiley Publisher for Figure 7.3, from Gray, Smith and Rutter *Out of School: Modern Perspectives in Truancy and School Refusal;* Ashgate Publishing Limited for Figure 7.4 from, Quinton and Rutter *Parenting Breakdown: The Making and Breaking of Inter-Generational Links.*

We are grateful to Blackwell Science and the *Journal of Child and Family Social Work* for permission to reproduce material from Daniel, Wassell, Ennis, Gilligan and Ennis (1997) 'Critical understandings of child development: the development of a module for a post-qualifying certificate course in child protection studies', *2*, 4, 209–220 in Chapter 2.

Foreword

Since the launch in 1989 of the University of Dundee's national course programme of Child Care and Protection Studies, the need to build continuing professional learning around a core knowledge of child development has been recognised in course design and development. From the outset, the Certificate in Child Protection Studies, a five module post-qualifying course delivered and assessed at Scottish degree level 3/4, included a module devoted to Child Development. The module used materials compiled in open learning format and the private study of those materials was augmented by direct teaching sessions which sought to help students explore the application of the materials to practice situations.

Early materials were primarily drawn from attachment theory literature focusing on social work practice and did not make extensive use of the vast body of psychological research in child development. Although initially delivered to social work professionals from a wide range of settings, student cohorts very soon included staff from education, law, police, health and other occupational groupings whose role and task included work with vulnerable children. Early delivery and assignment work highlighted the diversity of knowledge and experience across the student range, with even the most experienced and able practitioner professionals sometimes finding difficulty in articulating the theory informing their work.

Routine evaluation of course impact enabled staff to modify, adapt and develop the original materials to better meet the emerging needs of professionals and to provide students with the opportunity to develop a clear theoretical context for learning and practice. In moving towards a major re-write of the child development module materials, course staff recognised that pertinent literature was located in two separate groupings with no readily available text or schema for bringing materials together.

On the one hand, literature focusing on aspects of child abuse often does not refer in detail to normal or healthy developmental pathways and is often written around and based on the extensive clinical experience of the authors in work with children already in difficulty. Although helpfully descriptive in providing detailed guidance for practice, the literature tends either to assume a knowledge and theory base in the reader or provides a level of prescriptive detail that acknowledges its absence. Psychological literature, on the other hand, can often be highly specialised in nature, with researchers concentrating on specific aspects of development. Although texts produced from these sources can often summarise important findings, particularly about healthy development, the material does not always readily translate to the needs of professionals dealing with children in difficulty.

In working to produce course materials that pulled those important strands together, the writing team recognised that they had generated text that would have relevance beyond the requirements of the Certificate in Child Protection Studies. Brigid Daniel, Sally Wassell and Robbie Gilligan's book, *Child Development for Child Care and Protection Workers*, builds on that work. It will be of enormous value to the range of professionals who provide the mainstream response to children whose development has been disrupted by traumatic events or abusive experiences. The authors have produced a text that will help professionals both build a coherent knowledge base about healthy development in childhood and enable them to construct a theoretical understanding of the impact of disruption on development. Perhaps more importantly, they have provided a framework to help professionals to apply concepts of vulnerability and resilience to an understanding of the needs of individual children and, in so doing, have provided an invaluable tool in ensuring that case planning is accurate.

Case examples and other material is used to further the author's hopes of helping practitioners integrate theory and practice. Moreover, it is presented in a way which is illustrative of the writers' own streetwise qualities and will enable readers to know that the book is written by practitioners who understand how difficult the work of mainstream child care practitioners really is. The book will meet a long expressed need among those very same practitioners for a coherent text that will inform the bedrock of their understanding of children's needs and it will provide an impetus towards improved assessment and planning.

There is every reason to believe that, in producing this book, Brigid Daniel, Sally Wassell and Robbie Gilligan will have made a significant contribution to the ability of practitioners to construct helpful interventions in the lives of children in difficulty.

Jim Ennis (Director)
Centre for Child Care and Protection Studies
Department of Social Work
University of Dundee

CHAPTER I

Introduction

This book provides a selection of appropriate theoretical and research material to help social workers in practice. It builds upon a theoretical basis, with the aim of providing a framework for the understanding of developmental issues in general, but also the developmental needs of individual children known to social workers. The book is based primarily but not exclusively upon attachment theory.

Fundamental to the text as a whole is the assertion that to be effective child protection work (for example, investigating allegations of abuse, risk assessment, working with children registered as being at risk etc.) must be informed by the same values as good child care practice (for example, work with fostering and adoption, family support etc.).

Supporting development towards potential

There are some universal characteristics of childhood that can be observed, the most obvious being the complete dependence on others at birth and in early childhood. The psychological and sociological study of children has yielded a vast amount of information about development. Many studies in the literature describe either stages of development or maturational tasks related to age. Those working in child care and protection must have some knowledge of such developmental milestones. However, as Cooper (1993) suggests, 'it would not be possible or appropriate for them to become experts in this wide field but they need an overall awareness of physical, cognitive and emotional development in children' (p.92).

Therefore this book provides an overview of the bounds of *healthy developmental pathways* clustered by age range, and informed by the grouping of practice issues. The material is set out so as to model a process of assessment that considers aspects of social, emotional, cognitive and, where appropriate, physical development (Chapters 6 to 8). To assess where an individual child fits in terms of these bounds practitioners need to be able to gather information from all family and professionals involved and have enough contextual knowledge to make sense of that information. They also need knowledge of the possible consequences of different events and circumstances for a child's developmental pathway (Rutter and Rutter 1993). In essence therefore, social workers need to know what questions to ask, when and of whom.

Throughout the book we will be stressing the importance of considering *each child as an individual*, with a distinct life history, within a unique set of current circumstances. It cannot be stressed too much that individual children vary. The fact that a child has not reached a particular stage that is average for their age may be, but is not necessarily, an indicator of neglect, abuse or trauma.

However, each child is born with *potential* and successful childhood can be seen in terms of achieving that potential (see Figure 1.1). There can be different routes to this potential and different ways to encourage it. Some

Figure 1.1 Each child's potential to flourish in all domains needs to be supported

aspects of adult behaviour will support the development of potential, others will inhibit it and some aspects will have a negative effect. The experience of adverse life events and socio-economic deprivation may also affect development (this idea will be developed further in Chapter 5). The concept of potential is particularly useful when considering children with disabilities.

Thus each child, whatever their physical or intellectual capacity, has a potential which can be promoted. With information about what can be expected at any given age if a child's development is supported and healthy, it should be possible to assess the extent to which an individual child's potential has been undermined by adverse circumstances and events.

However, more is required in practice. Each day, practitioners are faced with children whose *complexity of problems* can be overwhelming. Some presenting problems perhaps have roots going back years, while others are due to current adverse life events and possibly abuse. At the same time the majority of families referred live in situations of extreme poverty and poor housing conditions. The practitioner is then faced with the task of intervening in the life of an individual child, with an distinct life history, within a unique set of current circumstances, while avoiding making the situation worse and attempting to make it better. The key to the social work role in helping to promote potential will be the ability to assess the meaning of those past and current circumstances for the *individual* child.

Further, social workers are faced every day with the complexity of individual *response* to circumstances. It is not uncommon for social workers to know children who have undergone very similar circumstances but whose reactions are entirely different. So, for example, in response to sexual abuse by a step-father, one child may show prolonged problems such as extreme nightmares, clinginess to their mother, fear of all strangers and school refusal; while another child in response to similar experiences may show no ongoing signs of distress at all. Indeed, the lack of any clear-cut relationships between incidents involving children and their symptoms is a major contributory factor in the difficulty of substantiating denied allegations of abuse.

To help with the application of a general understanding of developmental issues to the needs of an individual child two dimensions are used. The first dimension is that of *vulnerability* and *resilience* (Chapter 4). It is proposed that each individual has their own level of vulnerability and resilience to stressful life events developed partly as a result of quality of attachments and other factors like individual temperament. Vulnerability is a concept that should be familiar to most social workers since the classic studies of Brown and Harris on the factors that render women vulnerable to developing depression (Brown and Harris 1978). In children, it is the concept of vulnerability that can help in the understanding of why some children suffer extreme and adverse reactions to negative life events. Indeed recognising vulnerability is an important part of assessing risk in child protection. So, for example, when considering the two children described above, the knowledge that the child showing ongoing problems has an insecure attachment relationship with her mother could go some way to explaining her higher level of vulnerability to prolonged difficulties.

When considering how to assess and support a child's development in the face of crisis, however, a knowledge of factors of resilience is also invaluable. The work of Rutter and others (see for example Rutter 1985; Rutter and Rutter 1993) has shifted the research emphasis towards an exploration of the factors intrinsic to an individual child that allow them to come through stressful life events relatively emotionally intact. So, for example, the child described above who appeared to show little ongoing problems may have had the resilience that comes from a secure attachment relationship.

The second, related dimension is that of *protective* and *adverse* environments (Chapter 5). This dimension allows the range of possible environments and life events to be specifically assessed as either helpful or unhelpful to the child's development. So, for example, whereas living in poverty is an example of adversity, having a secure attachment is described as protective. Similarly, racism is a form of adversity for a black child in Britain, against which the family can act as a protective bastion of defence (Lees 1993).

It is crucial for intervention to be able to assess the interactional effects of the two dimensions. For example, what is described by Bee (1995) as the 'double whammy' of a vulnerable child in an adverse environment is what can lead to the poorest outcome. By the same token, a secure material environment is protective. Thus, taken together, these dimensions can act as a framework for the consideration of the overwhelming number of issues that may be affecting an individual child's development. In particular the model gives pointers to help with the recognition of protective aspects of a vulnerable child's environment and for recognising resilience in a child. The framework is also helpful for the assessment of the situation of a child with special needs. An individual child could, for example, have a disability that renders him or her vulnerable to abuse, suffer the adversity of living in an area where there is inadequate provision for children with special needs, but may have a resilient temperament and the protection of secure attachments.

It is hoped that this approach can rekindle some hope for workers in a profession where it can be hard to retain a sense of optimism about the potential for positive outcomes for some of the children encountered. As Werner (1990) states:

> The life stories of resilient individuals have taught us that competence, confidence and caring can flourish, even under adverse circumstances, if young children encounter persons who provide them with a secure basis for the development of trust, autonomy, and initiative. (p.113)

CHAPTER 2

Developing Relationships

Introduction

This chapter will set out the underpinning theoretical framework for the book. It will explore attachment theory and draw out issues of particular interest for social work practice.

Why attachment theory?

In an exploration of the nature of social work knowledge, Imrie (1984) asserts that 'social workers must know themselves and how to use these selves in *relationships* with other selves' (p.44). She emphasises the importance of relationships as fundamental to the human condition as well as to the helping process.

Knowledge about the nature of relationships is relevant in two ways: first, in terms of the children social workers deal with and, second, in terms of their own working relationships with children and their families. This factor contributes to the decision to select *attachment* theory as the underpinning theoretical model for the book. Several elements of attachment theory as developed by John Bowlby and subsequently Mary Ainsworth can be seen as particularly helpful in understanding developmental issues for social work practice (e.g., Ainsworth *et al.* 1978; Bowlby 1969 and 1988).

(Attachment theory involves the study of human relationships, especially early, formative relationships. (Further, the theory asserts that there is a biological imperative for infants to form attachments and that they exhibit attachment behaviours to promote attachment. In this sense attachment behaviour can be viewed as survival behaviour. The theory relates the quality of such early attachment relationships to emotional functioning throughout life.) That is, it asserts that the development of self as a socio-emotional being is mediated by relationships with other people, which in turn are mediated through communication.

(Attachment theory also relates language, cognitive and moral development to the quality of early attachment relationships. An understanding of the theory of these developmental dimensions should therefore provide a good basis for assessing the possible effects on a child's development where attachment relationships are inadequate.)

Much research based on attachment theory directly aims to further an understanding of the factors that contribute to difficulties in parent–child relationships. For example, the empirical work of Ainsworth described below has demonstrated that infant attachment behaviours can be classified as being indicative of either secure or insecure attachment. Further, an association exists between experiencing secure attachments and healthy emotional development. An understanding of the theoretical and empirical links between patterns of attachment and healthy development should help social workers in assessing the quality of a child's relationships. This directly relates to one of the specific aims of child protection, that is, to protect children from situations where caregivers, who may often be the main attachment figures, cause harm to their children either by commission or omission.)

Finally, the principles of attachment theory are also relevant to a wider and more positive aim of child care and protection, namely, to promote the well-being of children.

(Attachment theory can therefore provide a helpful model for the analysis of the relationship difficulties of families referred to social workers) (Howe 1995). In addition, it can also offer a model for understanding therapeutic relationships because it allows for the potential for change mediated through new and healthy attachments. First, (one of the fundamental elements of effective casework practice is working towards the establishment of positive relationships with children and families. Communication problems can often be characteristic of families in difficulty) (Central Council for Education and Training in Social Work 1991a). These communication problems may be indicative of relationship problems. Social workers therefore need to use their skills in communication for the establishment of relationships and the promotion of change. Second, (social work practice aims to promote a human environment for children that consists of at least one positive attachment relationship.)

Further discussion of the applicability of attachment theory to social work practice can be found in David Howe's book on the subject (Howe 1995).

Activity 2.1

The word 'attachment' is used regularly in practice. There is an assumption that everyone means the same when they use it, is this the case?

1. First note down your own understanding of the concept, then compare this with other people's definitions.

2. What do you think the general population understands by the meaning of attachment?

Fahlberg uses as her definition of attachment, 'an affectionate bond between two individuals that endures through space and time and serves to join them emotionally' (Klaus and Kennell 1976; cited in Fahlberg 1994, p.14). She (Fahlberg 1988 and 1994) notes that attachment helps the child to:

- attain full intellectual potential
- sort out what he or she perceives
- think logically
- develop a conscience
- become self-reliant
- cope with stress and frustration
- handle fear and worry
- develop future relationships
- feel less jealousy.

At its extreme, lack of attachment is associated with problems with:

- conscience development
- impulse control
- self-esteem
- interpersonal interactions
- emotions

- cognitive skills such as understanding cause and effect and using logical thought
- general behaviour
- gross and fine motor control
- personal and social development
- consistent development of different skills.)

The main components of attachment theory

Humans appear to have a basic propensity to make intimate emotional bonds. Bowlby stresses a biological need to seek and maintain contact with others, an impulse to maintain closeness, to restore it if impaired and the need for a particular person if distressed. This process begins in infancy, but continues throughout life.

In order to explain early attachment behaviour Bowlby looked beyond traditional theories that focused on physical care of the infant as the basis for bonding. He particularly drew on ethological theories which stress the importance of considering animal behaviour within the context of the environment. Ethology considers behaviour to have adapted to fit the environment. Thus he considered human development from a biological basis and postulated that emotional bonds have a biological and adaptive basis. This readiness to make these bonds forms a basic component of human nature. In addition, the need to explore the world, which underpins development of understanding is also seen as innate (Bowlby 1988). For the purposes of child protection it is the human environment that is crucial.

Holmes (Holmes 1993) summarises the main components of attachment theory:)

- (The *primary attachment relationship* is not necessarily dependent on feeding the infant. It develops around seven months and the main evolutionary function was protection from predators.)
- (The attachment relationship is demonstrated by the manifestation of *proximity seeking* when the infant is separated from the attachment figure. Proximity seeking can be seen in older children and in adults at times of stress and threat.)
- (A secure attachment relationship creates a *secure* base from which a child feels safe to explore the world.)

- (If separated from an attachment figure, infants and young children exhibit *separation protest* which involves the expression of distress and urgent efforts to be reunited with the attachment figure. Permanent separation from the primary attachment figure can impair a child's security and the associated exploratory behaviour.)

- (On the basis of early attachment experiences an *internal working model* develops which acts as a template for other relationships.

- Attachment behaviour continues throughout life, and develops from *immature dependence* on caregivers to *mature dependence* on friends and partners.)

(Social workers often encounter children who, despite abuse or neglect by their parent or main carer, nevertheless demonstrate strong attachments to them. It is often difficult to fully accept the extent of such loyalty and attachment, especially in cases where the impulse is to 'rescue' them.)However, an appreciation of the instinctual and biological basis for making attachments can help with understanding how deep the ties go. The need for an emotional base is a primary emotional requirement and even the shakiest of bases will be clung to instead of the unknown. If faced with the prospect of separation from parents with little understanding of what may be the alternative, even very ill-treated children can show separation protest and anxiety.

An appreciation of the complexity and depth of children's ties to their caregivers is the main message that can be drawn from attachment theory for social work practice with children. This does not mean that children should never be separated from adults they are attached to; clearly there are situations where this is necessary. It does, however mean that attachments, even apparently damaging ones, must be treated with respect because of their importance to the child.

How does attachment develop?

Attachment develops as a result of the interactions between the carer and the child. These interactions may be initiated by the child and by the carer (Fahlberg 1994):

The arousal–relaxation cycle

When a baby experiences displeasure or tension they do everything they can (either consciously or unconsciously) to let people know, by crying, squirming and so on. During times of discomfort they are too preoccupied to be able

Activity 2.2

Consider the situation of children being looked after by foster carers or in residential settings:

1. How might the above concepts be helpful in understanding some of the range of behaviours shown by such children?

2. What messages for practice can be taken from the concepts?

Hints for answers

Children in care are likely to be living away from the person to whom they have their *primary attachment relationship*. If this is the case, every effort must be made to promote regular and meaningful contact. For a child with no primary attachment relationship intervention needs to be focused on helping them to develop one.

The most obvious manifestation of *proximity seeking* would be running home. Children who make frequent attempts to run home may need support in finding other ways to maintain proximity, perhaps by using a telephone. The level of contact would also need to be considered as it may be insufficient for the child.

The link between the presence of a *secure base* and active exploratory behaviour may explain why some children being looked after away from home are reluctant to take part in what are planned as fun activities. This would indicate that attention should be paid to the child's need for security.

Expressions of grief and anger are manifestations of *separation protest*. They need to be recognised as a natural part of attachment behaviour. (See Chapter 4 for a detailed discussion of separation and grief.)

The theory of *internal working models* suggests that children develop a template for relationships based on early attachment experiences. This pattern may then form the basis for their interactions with others. So, for example, children who are used to making aggressive demands in order to be noticed may transfer that behaviour to carers. This area will be discussed in detail in Chapter 8.

Young people may approach leaving care in different ways. Some may be determined to be totally independent in a way that suggests problems with *mature dependence*. Others may react with the opposite extreme of *immature dependence*. These patterns underline the crucial importance of early planning for a young person's transition to adulthood.

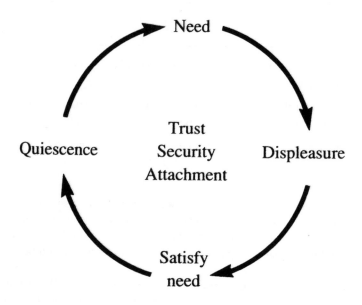

Figure 2.1 The 'arousal–relaxation cycle' (Fahlberg 1994), showing a successful interaction between a caregiver and child, as initiated by the child

to take in much from their surroundings, thus their development in other spheres is suspended. The carer's role is to help meet the need and help the child return to a state of quiescence (see Figure 2.1).

The positive interaction cycle

As well as responding to the child, a carer needs to initiate interaction with the baby. This initiation of social contact must be sensitively tailored to the child. Some children, who are by temperament more shy, do not respond well to loud and sudden adult contact and some babies are happier with physical contact than others. If the adult initiation of contact is appropriate, then a cycle occurs that promotes attachment (see Figure 2.2).

Mary Ainsworth's classic studies (see, for example, Ainsworth *et al.* 1978) on attachment showed, through her 'strange situation' research, that it was possible to characterise different qualities of attachment. She set up an experiment with toddlers which involved them being observed with their mothers; during separation from their mothers; in the presence of a stranger; and on reunion with their mothers. She found that children's responses

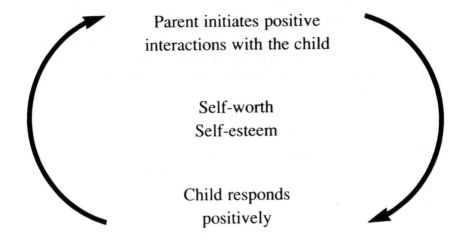

Parent initiates positive
interactions with the child

Self-worth
Self-esteem

Child responds
positively

Figure 2.2 The 'positive interaction cycle' (Fahlberg 1994), showing a successful interaction between a caregiver and child as initiated by the adult

appeared to fall into different kinds that she attributed to the type of attachment between the child and mother. (These studies and the majority of replications have been carried out with mothers only.)

About two-thirds of the children showed behaviour (described below) that Ainsworth described as consistent with *secure* attachment (also known as type B). The others showed responses that indicated *insecure* attachment. She subdivided insecure attachment into type A – 'anxious avoidant' (also known as 'detached') and type C – 'anxious resistant' (also known as 'ambivalent'). Since Ainsworth's earlier studies, a further pattern has been described, type D – 'disorganised/disoriented'.

The different names for the categories can be confusing. However, whatever labels are given, the basic categories continue to be used extensively. Ainsworth's studies were carried out with mothers, as was most of the subsequent work on early attachment. In brief, the categories can be described as follows:

Secure attachment (type B)

Toddlers explore actively when their mother is present and are upset at her departure and stop exploring. They show strong interest in interacting and closeness to her when she returns. They cling to the parent in the presence of a stranger. At home, those securely attached cry the least and appear the least anxious and uncooperative. Typically the mother's behaviour (as observed in these studies) is described as positive, sensitive and encouraging of close physical contact.

Anxious avoidant insecure attachment (type A)

Toddlers show little distress at separation, avoid contact with the mother on her return, some ignore her. They react to a stranger in the same way as to the mother. Typically the mothers' behaviour is described as relatively cold, angry and rejecting.

Anxious resistant or ambivalent insecure attachment (type C)

Toddlers are anxious before separation from the mother, very upset during it, and ambivalent during renewed contact, seeking and resisting contact. At home these children cry more, show more general distress and are negative about physical contact. The mother's behaviour appears warm, but she is less sensitive to the baby's signals, responding at inappropriate times.

Disorganised disoriented insecure attachment (type D)

Toddlers show contradictory behaviour patterns, e.g. gazing away while being held, resistance plus avoidance and unusual expressions of negative emotion.

These categories are commonly referred to in child development and practice literature. However, Downes (1992) describes a type of anxious attachment that is not quite the same as the types described above. In this type, the child has an *anxious preoccupation* with the availability of the carer. It is clearly an insecure type of attachment with anxiety as a crucial element.

Subsequent studies have suggested that insecure attachment is more likely to be demonstrated in children growing up in families in poverty, with a history of abuse or where the mother is depressed (Bee 1995; Cicchetti and Barnett 1991; Spieker and Booth 1988). Such circumstances have the potential to undermine the parent's ability to offer security to the child, but the association is by no means inevitable.

Ainsworth's findings have been replicated many times and the categories she described have been observed in other research settings. Empirical studies are obviously carried out in what can appear to be fairly artificial circumstances. Such careful manipulation of the child's environment is not feasible in practice settings. Individual children can also vary considerably in their attachment behaviours depending on such factors as the amount of contact they have with other adults and so on. However, the distinction between secure and insecure attachments is one that can be very helpful for practice. It provides a basis for assessment of the quality of attachments and for the recognition of areas of difficulty.

Many natural opportunities to observe attachment patterns can arise. It is often points of separation and reunion that provide the most insight:

- Nursery staff, creche workers and so on will often be in a position to observe reunions with caregivers. They will see if a child appears regularly to show no particular interest in the reunion, thus suggesting a possible avoidant attachment (type A).

- Similarly, if a child constantly shows very clingy behaviour during separation and cannot be soothed even in a familiar environment and then shows ambivalence at reunion this would suggest a anxious resistant pattern of attachment (type C).

- Although it can be gratifying if a child is responsive to adults, it can also feel disturbing to encounter a child who seems to be indiscriminate with affection. So, if on a first visit to a family the young child immediately comes to you and sits on your lap it may mean that they are very confident with strangers, but it may be indicative of a less than secure attachment to their primary caregiver.

- Similarly, if a child moves from home to foster parents, shows no apparent distress and immediately transfers their attachment behaviour to the foster carers, this would suggest a lack of a secure attachment.

- Finally, it is important to remember that children encountered in practice may have very secure attachments (type B). Such children will show distress at separation and pleasure at reunion and are likely to take longer to make new relationships.

Activity 2.3

1. Observe the interaction between a parent or significant carer and a child of any age.

2. Note down observed behaviour in two columns, 'behaviour of child' and 'behaviour of adult'.

3. Can you, categorise the type of attachment from the observed behaviour?

Attachment does not depend on physical care

As attachment develops, so by extension does fear of strangers and separation fear. By two weeks babies can show some aversion to strangers and recognise the main carer. They can show upset if cared for by a stranger. By 14 weeks they tend to stare at strangers, by four to five months they can freeze when approached by strangers, sitting very still and breathing shallowly in a way that suggests fear. By eight months babies demonstrate more extreme stranger fear which then begins to fade. This behaviour is less marked in situations where the child is accustomed to being in the presence of larger numbers of people. Fear of a stranger is less when in a foreign environment. Presumably a strange person is less frightening than an unfamiliar place. Similarly, separation anxiety builds up during the first year of life and declines during the second year (Bower 1977).

If it is accepted that separation anxiety is an indication of a strong attachment, then it can be used as measure of who the child is attached to. Bower (1977) cites a number of studies that support the contention that the development of attachment is not dependent on the physical care of the infant, including one in which 20 per cent of the babies observed showed separation anxiety towards someone who took no part in their physical care whatsoever (Schaffer and Emerson 1964).

What does appear to relate to the strength of attachment is social interaction. Babies show a tremendous readiness to communicate and respond to joint play and social interaction. From birth their behaviour leaves openings for communication. If someone sensitively picks up on those openings then a complex pattern of communication develops, which by seven months can be quite specific to a particular pair (Trevarthen 1977). Some argue that it is the role of the adult to pitch communications just in advance of the baby's abilities in order to encourage their development (Meadows 1986). Not only does sensitive communication support the development of attachment, it also provides the infant and young child with skills for communicating about their needs:

> As the secure child continues to try out conversational skills in this atmosphere of open communication, he or she learns that expressing emotions can be a constructive way to get one's needs met. In addition, over time, the child gains further confidence in using language to verbalise goals and feelings. The secure child may also have a greater capacity to attend to the caregiver's signals and goals without fear of a negative response, to accommodate to the wishes and needs of others, and to negotiate about issues and problems. (Feeney and Noller 1996, p.111)

Thus there is an interactional, reciprocal relationship between attachment and social and emotional development. When assessing children in difficulties the quality of their human interactions must be considered.

Effect of child on attachment patterns

So far the descriptions of attachment have focused more on the caregiver's role. However, there is considerable evidence to support the idea that the baby as an individual has an effect on the process of attachment. For example, Fahlberg (1994) notes that premature babies do not always respond to environmental stimuli in the same way as full-term babies and therefore do not promote the arousal–relaxation cycle. Premature babies may also respond differently when lifted, for example, by stiffening and arching away.

There is more information on the effects of different temperaments in Chapter 6, but, in summary, researchers have been able to identify basic temperamental 'types' which will affect the interaction between carer and child. There are two commonly used models of classification of infant temperament. The first refers to particular 'types' of temperament:

- an *easy* child usually seems happy, readily establishes routines, but can also adapt to new experiences

- a *difficult* child, cries a lot, will not settle to a routine and does not adapt well to changes

- a *slow-to-warm-up* child is more passive, negative and less adaptable than the easy child.

The rest of the infants show combinations of traits (Chess and Thomas 1977).

The second model refers to dimensions on which infants can be measured:

- *Emotionality* is the dimension of arousal to stimuli. Those who are high in emotionality tend to respond with strong expressions of distress, fear or anger.

- *Sociability* measures the extent of the tendency for infants to prefer the company of other people to being alone. Those who are high in sociability respond warmly to people and initiate social contact.

- *Activity* level involves tempo and vigour of movement. Some infants are more active, often providing their own energy, others are more passive and need carers to stimulate them to activity (Buss and Plomin 1984).

A mismatch of temperament between the carer and child can be the source of some enduring difficulties:

Imagine a highly-strung parent with a child who is difficult and sometimes slow to respond to the parent's affection. The parent may begin to feel angry or rejected. A father who does not need much face-to-face social interaction will find it easy to manage a similarly introverted baby, but he may not be able to provide an extroverted baby with sufficient stimulation. Parents influence infants, but infants also influence parents. Parents may withdraw from difficult children, or they may become critical and punish them; these responses may make the difficult child even more difficult. A more easy-going parent may have a calming effect on a difficult child or may continue to show affection even when the child withdraws or is hostile, eventually encouraging more competent behaviour. (Santrok 1994, pp.334-335)

It is possible to recognise problems in parent–child or foster parent–child relationships that can be pinpointed to such a 'lack of fit'. Sometimes simply using this form of analysis can help when assessing attachment problems that may have developed from very early on. It can also help explain why a parent may have difficulties in their relationship with one of their children, but not another. This issue is returned to again in Chapters 3 and 6.

Endurance of attachment patterns

There is evidence that a pattern of attachment established during childhood can be enduring and may eventually become a feature of the way the child, young person and adult interacts with other people. In other words, the *internal working model* which develops as a result of early interactions influences later relationships. For example, quality of caregiver behaviour at six months predicts attachment behaviour at three years, even towards another sibling. Children presenting a secure attachment relationship are less likely to show high dependency on the carer in social interactions with other children at four to five years. Those with insecure patterns are more likely to show less positive attitudes with peers and increased behavioural and social difficulties (Sroufe and Fleeson 1988).

There is debate about the extent to which internal models are open to change as a result of later experience. There is also debate about whether it is possible simultaneously to hold different internal models resulting from different early relationships. All of these factors can help with the assessment of the difficulties of children and young people who have experienced troubled family relationships. Often young people's responses to others appear to be the automatic expressions of established patterns, that recreate problematic interactions and serve to fulfil negative self-images. At the same time, the potential for change through therapeutic insight and different experiences of relationships provides an avenue for intervention. There is further discussion of this issue in Chapter 8.

Hazards of uncritical use

Using attachment theory is not unproblematic. Two possible hazards of uncritical use of attachment theory will be described, as well as a description of how the book addresses them:

Sexism and racism

Attachment theory has been the subject of extensive theoretical exploration and multi-cultural empirical research. This has enhanced understanding of the importance of multiple attachments for children's development as well as the extent to which children's emotional needs can be met within different family structures. However, despite these refinements, ideas based on popular misconceptions of attachment theory can and have been used in a way that is oppressive of different cultures and of women.

Bowlby's work has been most influential in the development of attachment theory (see, for example, Bowlby 1969), and it was his original emphasis on the role of the mother as the primary attachment figure that has been used by those who hold women responsible for all aspects of a child's development. Despite Rutter's influential critique of the issue of maternal deprivation (Rutter 1981), which asserts that the quality of the attachment relationship is more important for a child's healthy development than the need for the mother to be the primary attachment figure, this ideology still pervades much child development research.

Further, despite the CCETSW requirement that social workers must be able to 'demonstrate anti-sexism in social work practice' (CCETSW 1991b), it is mothers who still bear the brunt of social work intervention (Wise 1985). As Swift (1995) points out in a study of child neglect: 'In both popular and professional understanding, the mother's quality of attachment and by implication her quality of care are connected to her child's development all through life' (p.97).

Similarly, attachment theory can be linked with an assumption that the 'traditional' nuclear family provides a superior child-rearing environment. This, in turn can devalue cultural and ethnic variety in family structure, despite the evidence that children can develop successfully in many different family structures. The political and majority emphasis continues to be on a Western model of the nuclear family which is not the experience of many children (Gambe *et al.* 1992).

Describing the importance of early close relationships is not the equivalent of prescribing the nature of family structure. Although young children can be seen to possess universal needs for nurturance, these can be met in different ways (Devore and Schlessinger 1987).One study found that children in six different cultures demonstrated the same universal characteristic of dependence, but that the length of time they remained dependent varied according to culture, as did the extent to which those other than the mother met some of their dependency needs (Whiting and Edwards 1988). In summary:

> Although some basic needs are universal, there can be a variety of ways of meeting them. Patterns of family life differ according to culture, class and community and these differences should be respected and accepted. There is no one, perfect way to bring up children and care must be taken to avoid value judgements and stereotyping. (DoH 1989, cited in Gambe *et al.* 1992, p.33)

The aim of this book, therefore, is to draw ideas from child development research of relevance for practice in such a way as to retain the important elements of attachment theory for understanding the development of individual children, without reinforcing the emphasis on the exclusive role of mothers or upon the 'traditional' nuclear family. The book draws from Garbarino's work in asserting that when assessing the emotional development of children the starting point must be the *child's experience* of adult behaviour (Garbarino 1980).

Context of parenting

There is a danger that attachment theory can lead to a crude, simplistic psychodynamic model of family pathology which takes no account of the impact of the wider context upon parenting. Such a model does not match the experience of social workers which daily brings them face to face with the negative effects of poverty and deprivation upon families. Parton (1995), for example, argues that families characterised as neglectful can be recharacterised as families in need once the effects of disadvantage and deprivation are taken into account.

Assessment must explore the layers of influence upon the developing child. While attachment theory can be used as the basis for understanding individual development, emphasis must also be given to the resources and environment within which relationships are established. By the same token, it is essential to explore the extent to which close attachment relationships can mediate the impact and influence of the wider environment on children.

> A framework for the assessment of a child's protective environment will need to acknowledge the part played by the state and society in general, the part played by the community within which the child (or children) live and the part played by the individual family in mediating access to formal and informal resources and supports for both child and carer. (Boushel 1994, p.179).

Social network theory and the ecological approach

Social network theory (Lewis 1994) indicates that there is little data to suggest that a relationship with the mother is the only important one for a child and suggests that rather than looking for a single primary attachment, assessment should take account of the attachment network. For each child there may be a large number of possibilities for attachments. The kind of attachment can be different for different relationships. Lewis also argues that children demonstrate a dual system of needs for both peers and adults from the beginning of life. So it may be better to see peer (and sibling) relationships as developing in parallel with parent relationships, not simply building on a primary relationship. (He points out that most of us 'fondly remember objects and places we were attached to as young children, as well as a variety of people. Can we not each remember someone who was very important in our life other than our parents?) (Lewis 1994, p.49).

This framework enables a broader perspective to be taken on a child's human environment. Historically, it has not always been assumed that mothers should provide full-time care, and women have often been economic providers as well as parents. (Historical and cross-cultural research shows that infant rearing has nearly always been shared with other adults and often with other children) (Goldsmith 1990; Scarr 1990). Children are successfully reared in a huge diversity of situations (Stainton Rogers 1989). Research shows no difference in rates of secure attachment to mothers between infants in full-time day care and those at home (Again attachment is shown to be facilitated by attentive, responsive caregiving, whether by mothers or others (Scarr 1990). Work on fathers' roles has also demonstrated that fathers can have a direct influence on development. One study reported that children brought up in families where fathers stayed at home and took the principal caring role demonstrated secure attachment behaviours in relation to their fathers (Geiger 1996). Dunn's extensive work on a child's relationships with those other than the parents, and especially relationships with siblings describes how even very young children have a sophisticated social understanding and awareness and are sensitive to other people's moods (Dunn 1993).

Throughout the rest of the book, child development is considered within the context of the child's significant relationships including those with:

- mother
- father
- siblings
- extended family
- neighbours
- peers
- school teachers
- hobby groups and club members.

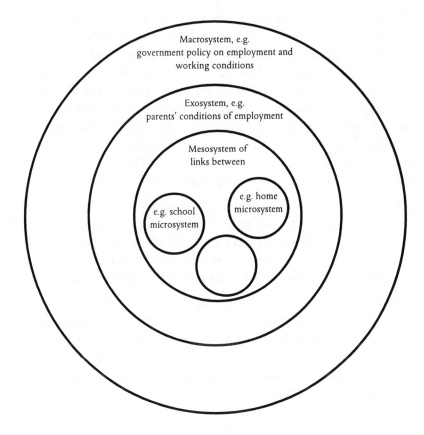

Figure 2.3 Showing Bronfenbrenner's (1989) ecological framework (from Smith and Cowie 1991)

- members of religious organisations
- friends and so on.

(This approach requires that the child never be assessed in isolation and as such is consistent with an *ecological* view of child development as advanced by Bronfenbrenner (1989). It recognises that children do not grow up in a vacuum. Instead each child can be seen to be in the centre of a number of concentric circles (see Figure 2.3).

(Immediately surrounding the child are *microsystems* which comprise family (or alternative family) and others with whom the child has most immediate, direct contact. Attachment networks as described above would be examples of microsystems. In turn, the microsystems are embedded within *exosystems* which have an indirect influence upon the child. Examples of exosystems would be a parent's workplace or the parents' friendships. The *macrosystem*, which has influence over exosystems and microsystems comprises the wider political and cultural context. The economic situation, type of housing, ethnicity and so on, would all be part of the macrosystem.) (All these layers of influence help to shape the child's development, directly and indirectly. Ethnically sensitive practice is entirely consistent with an ecological approach that strives to improve the extent to which the material and social environment meets a person's needs)(Devore and Schlessinger 1987). As stated in a code of practice for race and child protection:

> Ethnicity is a concept which belongs to everyone. All practice should be seen in the context of class, race and gender, which in combination will show the uniqueness of all experience. Ethnically sensitive practice is not a 'sideline' or an addendum – it needs to permeate practice at all times and at all levels. (Baldwin, Johansen and Seale 1989/90, p.19)

The ecological approach to child development suggests that detailed assessment of all aspects of a young person's situation, which includes consideration of all levels, including the wider impact of adversity such as racism and material resources, is essential for the planning of intervention with young people. This assessment must begin with the young person and their past and current experience.

Activity 2.4

Consider a child on your caseload.

Using the social network approach, map out each important relationship the child has. If helpful, use the ecomap provided (Figure 2.4).

1. Note what needs of the child are being satisfied by these different relationships.

2. Consider the implications for the child and adult when only one person is available to meet all the child's needs.

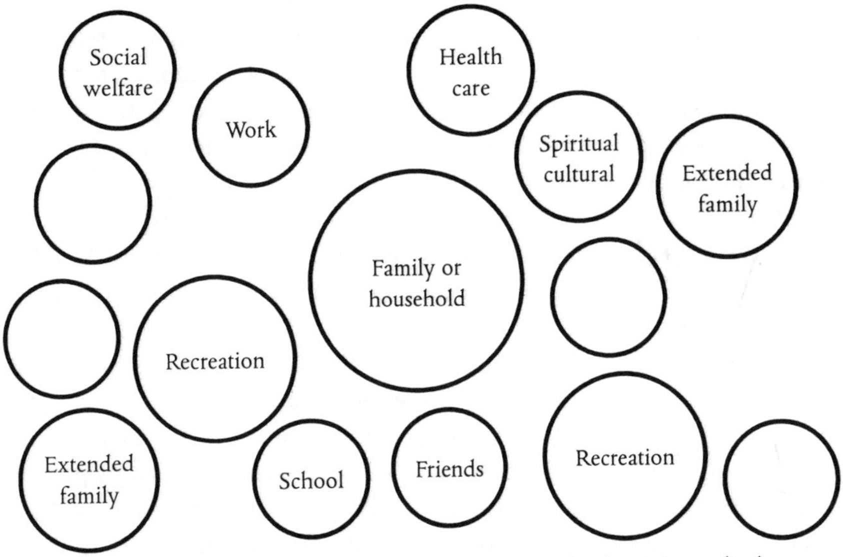

Fill in connections where they exist. Indicate nature of connections with a descriptive word or by drawing different kinds of lines: ———— for strong, ------- for tenuous, +/-/+/ for stressful. Draw arrows along lines to signify flow of energy, resources etc. → →
Identify significant people and fill in empty circles as needed.

Figure 2.4 The ecomap can be a useful tool for mapping out the important relationships in a child's life (Hartman 1984)

Attachment disorders

The issue of attachment disorders is extremely complex and will be revisited in later chapters. Attachment problems can arise from either having an insecure type of attachment to a primary carer, and/or to attachment being interrupted in some way. Fahlberg (1994) cites Bourguigon and Watson's (1987) descriptions of three forms of attachment disorder which may be exhibited in different ways including psychological disturbance, behavioural problems, cognitive problems and developmental delays:

- The *traumatised* child, resulting from serious trauma in an early relationship which leads to a lack of trust or hope of making new attachments.

- The *inadequately* attached child, whose primary attachments were interrupted, unhealthy or intermittent and who has difficulty making new relationships.

- The *non-attached* child, which is the most severe as the child has been deprived of the opportunity to make a primary attachment.

Children who have experienced troubled or distorted attachment relationships will have great difficulty in forming healthy relationships. They may have problems with empathy and with showing affection. They behave immaturely and appear very self-centred. Because it is through early relationships that children learn social emotions, they may exhibit problems with conscience (see Chapter 7 for more on conscience development). Attachment for these children has meant pain and therefore their behaviour may well be aimed at keeping emotional distance in order to prevent further pain) (Fahlberg 1994).

Binney, McKnight and Broughton (1994) have drawn on attachment theory to devise a therapeutic group-work programme for four- to seven-year-old children manifesting 'serious and global relationship problems at home and at school'. The children referred for such help were frequently being cared for by a single mother whose parenting was described as either rejecting or extremely over involved and guilt ridden. The mothers themselves had troubled lives and high levels of stress.

A summary cannot do the programme full justice, but briefly the therapy involves a structured programme that gradually moves from light contact group games through to more intimate activities between mother and child dyads. The groupwork is highly structured and therapists endeavour to act as secure bases for both parents and children. At the first stage group games such as grandmother's footsteps and paired games such as mirroring are used. By the final phase more intense pair games such as face painting and cradling while singing nursery rhymes are used. In addition a mothers' talk group is held to allow the parents to work out their own issues about the child's behaviour and their own experiences of having been parented.

An evaluation of one such programme suggested significant success, with one mother saying

> We loved each other, but he didn't class me as his boss. I was just his [first name] … I feel more like his mum now; before I was more like his sister… I couldn't tell him what to do; he'd just turn around and say 'no way'… He's calmed down a lot since I've been going there. It's amazing. (p.58)

In summary then the above suggests that not only can attachment theory be used to explain particular patterns of challenging behaviour in children, but it can also be used as a basis for intervention. Practitioners should also consider the use of such techniques with other significant adults in a child's life, not exclusively mothers.

Activity 2.5

Read the case study and answer the questions that follow.

Case study

Susan, aged two years, and Martin, aged three years, have been in their current foster placement for 12 months. They were abandoned at the social work office by their mother, Mary, who declared herself completely unwilling and unable to care for them. She has recently stated that she wishes them to be adopted together and that she will support such a plan. She wishes no continuing direct contact, but has offered to provide information for the department to pass on to the new family.

Mary has never actually lived with the children's father, Fraser, and during the early months of Martin's life, struggled with even the basic elements of care. Martin was a poor feeder and slept fitfully. Mary frequently left him with friends and neighbours during his first ten months of life. She says that she never felt close to him and was desperate in the early months of her pregnancy with Susan, fearing the increased demands of another small baby. When Martin was a year old, Mary requested that he be accommodated for the first time and a short placement of three weeks was followed by a return home. He had short periods with two other sets of carers in the ensuing twelve months. All carers found him extremely demanding in terms of their time and energy, principally because he rocked and banged his head and slept only briefly.

Martin's current carers confirm this to be a picture of Martin when admitted to their care a year ago. He was initially almost impossible to comfort when distressed and would go to any adult indiscriminately. He was unresponsive at other times, vocalising very little and stiffening when held. Since then he has begun to talk in short phrases, recognises his primary carers clearly and now expresses both distress at separation and relief at reunion. He is now beginning to explore his physical environment, but only in a tentative way. He panics and screams if separated from carers in an unfamiliar setting and still needs almost constant reassurance.

Martin is, however, also beginning to be reassuringly oppositional and this takes the form of 'nipping' his sister and having screaming tantrums. Susan, by contrast, was described as an 'easy' baby who was cared for little by her mother and was left for most of her first year with a paternal aunt who provided good care but was unable to continue. Not long after she returned Susan to her mother, both children were accommodated together.

The current carers say Susan was anxious and distressed in a healthy way for the first few months but has now made a warm and close attachment to them. She too is going through the stage of challenging and saying 'no'. She is achieving all her developmental milestones.

1.   What would be your assessment of Martin and Susan's early attachments?

2.   Are there any parts of the early attachments that could be maintained?

3.   What advice would you have given the current carers to support them in helping both children develop more healthy attachments?

4.   How might a move from the current carers be planned so as to take account of the individual needs of both children?

Hints for answers

Martin's early life has been extremely disrupted. He has had four care placements in total as well as many changes of caretaker during his first year. The last year has been the longest continuous period with one set of caretakers. Evidently his mother does not feel a strong sense of bonding with him. It appears that he did not have the opportunity to develop a secure attachment for at least two years. He now seems to be developing an attachment to his current carers, but judging by his reaction to separation his internal working model is one of mistrust. He may be developing an attachment to Susan.

Susan's early experience was less disrupted, as she spent a year with an aunt to whom it can be assumed she was attached. The move home from her aunt and the subsequent local authority accommodation will have been traumatic separations for her. However, she now seems to be attached to her current carers.

Although their mother is not expressing the wish to maintain contact, she may change her mind, or agree to some minimal contact. Martin has had a number of carers, formal and informal, and careful assessment will be needed to see if he was close to any of these and would benefit from contact. Susan would probably benefit from contact with her paternal aunt.

Both children have different needs. In some ways Martin appears to be functioning well below his chronological age and needs to be responded to on this basis. He may benefit from structured short separations and reunions within the context of a familiar setting. Both need to keep experiencing the availability of consistent adult caretakers. They also have to continue to learn how to interact with each other.

A further move should only occur if essential as both children appear to be developing close attachments to their current carers. All possible family alternatives would need to be considered, including their father and the paternal aunt who has already cared for Susan. The children should be placed together, although the timing of the moves could be different. Martin, who shows distress at strange places, is likely to need to become familiar with the new house in the company of his current carers. The presence of Susan may also provide him with comfort and familiarity. The prospective carers would need information about the children and about their routines. As language for both is limited, the explanations given to them would have to be in the form of pictures, photos, and stories. Life story information will need to be prepared for both children. There should be arrangements for contact with

Summary

This chapter has set out the reasons for using attachment theory as an underpinning theoretical approach. This does not mean that other theoretical approaches do not have much to offer to practice. For example, Chapter 8 draws from behavioural models when considering conduct disorders. However, the contention of this book is that in social work practice the majority of children encountered have difficulties that can be attributed to attachment issues. Many children have encountered troubled relationships with their main carers and many have experienced loss of important people.

Moreover, attachment theory can offer insights to guide intervention. For children who need to be looked after away from home, attachment theory can help us understand both the impact of separation from important people and the processes involved in making new relationships. Two key messages for practice are:

- Existing relationships are important and must be treated with respect. Even in abusive situations children are likely to have made attachments which have to be taken seriously. Children can always surprise social workers with the extent of their attachment to people who have apparently treated them with extreme cruelty.

- There is great reparative potential in the improvement of existing relationships and the making of new, healthy relationships.

The main components of attachment theory have been set out and the important concept to highlight is that of the secure base. This issue will be returned to in Chapter 3 and underpin material in later chapters.

The development of attachment can either be promoted or undermined. Observation and assessment of adult–child interactions can be sharpened if the operation of the arousal–relaxation cycle and the positive-interaction cycle are understood.

- It may be helpful in some circumstances to describe the operation of the two cycles to parents or to alternative carers with the aim of helping them to promote attachment. For example, some parents and alternative carers feel that children need to be shielded from all discomfort, however, the arousal–relaxation cycle suggests that it is the *soothing* process that is crucial, rather than the attempt to anticipate all discomfort.

The social basis of attachment theory has been stressed, which links with the role that the child plays in the development of attachment.

The message for practice is that it is important to look at *interactions*, rather than simply assessing parenting skills.

- This message, in turn, links with the ecological approach, which stresses the importance of looking at an individual child's development in context.

- Any assessment of a child has to take account of the potential network of important adults and other children in their lives.

Finally, attachment disorders can undermine the development of essential features of resilience, such as security and self-esteem.

- Very careful assessment of attachment disorders is required.

- Even though the early years are important for the development of attachment, it is still possible to intervene with attachment disorders with older children, and the potential for making new and healthy relationships should never be minimised. In other words, it should never be considered to be 'too late' for any child to be offered the opportunity to experience a good relationship with an adult who considers them to be special.

CHAPTER 3

Parenting

Parenting

Parenting is a complex and diverse process and has far-reaching implications. Although the links are complex, research has established associations between childhood experiences and adult health and well-being, with evidence to suggest that much adult distress can be traced to adversity in childhood (e.g. Rutter and Rutter 1993).

'Parenting' need not necessarily be carried out by biological parents. When considered from the point of view of the child, the important issue is not *who* carries out the parenting, but the *nature* of the care received. Although most of the research findings discussed in this chapter refer to biological parents, the messages can be applied to other carers.

As suggested in the previous chapter, there is a potential for attachment theory to be used to support assumptions that the nurturing of children should be carried out by the mother. In fact, a considerable amount of the parenting literature makes an implicit or explicit assumption that parenting is carried out by the mother. This assumption also often permeates practice. For example, in a study of health visitor and social work intervention, Edwards (1998) found that although male figures were often present in the home, they were not included in the discussions about the children. The focus of work was the mother, and both parents were given the subtle message that parenting was in fact mothering. This assumption is perhaps most evident in practice with neglect. Because referral for physical neglect hinges around issues of nurture, it is often equated with mothering and it is mothers who are labelled 'neglectful' (Swift 1995).

The message for practice is that the child needs to retained as the central focus. No assumptions should be made about who is, or should be, the main carer. It may be that one person takes the primary responsibility for the care of the child, but it may be that the tasks are shared. It may be that the mother is the main carer, but equally it could be a grandparent or father. Similarly, open-mindedness is essential when looking for alternative carers for children whose biological parents are unable to care for them.

This chapter will set out research about different styles of parenting as a guide for assessment and to provide pointers for intervention. The chapter will also provide a summary of those aspects of the parenting task (whether carried out by biological or substitute carers) that may be helpful in supporting developmental potential and those that may be unhelpful.

In keeping with the ecological approach which emphasises the importance of seeing child development in context, it is essential to consider the circumstances within which parenting is taking place. Parenting does not occur in isolation and some environments can be more supportive than others. The chapter will therefore explore current material about what kind of parental support is most helpful. It is one thing to know about the style of parenting that may support a child's development, it is another to know how best to promote *changes* in parenting behaviour. Social workers frequently face the frustration of trying to help parents to make changes in what seem to be fixed parenting styles. This chapter will therefore also look at some of the factors that may inhibit such change, including some of the insights attachment theory provides into adult expression of attachment experiences, thus continuing the underlying theoretical theme of the book.

Research into child development and parenting

A considerable amount of research has been done into parenting and its effects on children. However, such research is notoriously hard to interpret. Therefore, some points about interpreting research must be considered.

Much research in child development aims to pinpoint the direct relationships between early childhood experience and later outcomes, for example looking for antecedents for adolescent delinquency, for mental well-being, parenting styles and so on. By its very nature childhood is incredibly difficult to study. The most obvious problem is its length, making longitudinal studies rare and expensive. Children cannot be treated as laboratory creatures and therefore the amount of possible experimental manipulation is necessarily limited. The number of uncontrollable variables is vast, including socio-economic factors, personality differences, differences in social support, education and so on. Naturally, researchers attempt to take account of as many of these factors as possible, but their conclusions must always be interpreted with great caution. In particular, it is vital that when an association is found between factors it is treated as an association only. For example, some studies have shown that being the child of a teenage mother is associated with a range of health and behavioural problems. The temptation is to believe that having a teenage mother directly causes development to be impaired. However, it has been suggested that socio-economic factors are more important for the development of such children than the age of the mother per se (Phoenix 1991). In other words, it is important to ask more questions of any association and consider all possible explanations. This theme is especially important when interpreting research findings about the effect of different styles of parenting.

In addition, even if a direct link is found, the form of intervention is not always obvious, and can depend on other factors. For example, if poor quality child care is found to correlate with cognitive deficits in babies, the response could either be to encourage mothers to stay at home and care for their babies themselves, or to provide better quality child care.

Role of the parent

Even though children's needs can be met by several people, there are aspects of parenting that have been shown to be more helpful than others in supporting the development of a child's potential. The parent (or alternative carer) and child relationship has been described as unique when compared with other relationships because of a number of factors (Meadows 1986):

- because the relationship is an adult–child one there are marked cognitive inequalities between the two, and the gap gradually closes as the child matures
- the interactions therefore tend to be *complementary* and not *reciprocal*, the adult exhibits a greater diversity of interactions and communication than the child
- the 'meshing' of communication is, at least initially, mainly under the parent's control
- the relationship does not involve self-disclosure, particularly by the adult
- the views that each has of the other and of the relationship are very different for the child and adult.

These differences are greater than in any other relationship, they keep changing throughout childhood and the gap closes very slowly. An effective parent or carer has to recognise this change and adjust to it (Meadows 1986).

In practice, social workers often encounter parents who do not seem to fully appreciate the unique quality of the relationship. For example, some parents appear to expect a more reciprocal relationship than is helpful for a young child. They may, in effect treat their child as more of a friend and confide in them inappropriately. In such cases the worker has to help the parent appreciate the difference between child–adult and adult–adult relationships, and, if necessary help the parent find an adult to confide in.

The previous chapter stressed the importance to a child of having a secure base. It is through the adult–child relationship that parents provide this secure base, which, according to Dowling (1993) should include:

> An understanding of the child's wish for proximity, attention and responsiveness, not as naughty, demanding or unreasonable, but as a developmental expression of his or her need. The more this need is rejected, or unmet the more the demand will increase, and eventually it will be expressed in the form of symptoms.
>
> A recognition that the commonest source of children's anger is the frustration of their desire for love and care, and their anxiety commonly reflects the uncertainty as to whether parents will continue to be available. (Dowling 1993, p.406)

The child in turn needs a *coherent story* about early attachment experiences in order to feel secure. This story should be able to incorporate good and bad experiences. Parents need to be truthful with the child about any difficult aspects of their history together so that the child can make sense of their story. The child needs to have a coherent picture of its history. The child also needs *predictability* and needs to be able to make sense of what is happening to them. That is, they need to know generally 'WHAT will happen WHEN and IF…' (p.409).

The concept of a secure base and the extent to which it fosters a coherent story is extremely important. Not only does it seem to be significant during childhood to have a clear account for experiences, but, as discussed later, it is also important in adulthood. Having a satisfactory coherent story for life events depends partly on the internal explanations or attributions for events. Chapters 6 and 7 look at attribution theory in more detail, but, in summary it links the *thoughts* one has about the reason for events with the *feelings* one has about them. So, for example, if a child experiences an upsetting event, such as the death of a grandparent, they may *think* that they are to blame for the loss and, consequently, *feel* guilty and unlovable. An important parenting task is therefore to help the child develop accurate understanding of the reason for events. The links between thoughts and feelings is a theme that will be returned to in other parts of the book.

Parenting styles

Baumrind's (1972) classic work on different styles of parenting has been confirmed as a valid and useful way to categorise specific aspects of parenting that can help provide the secure base that attachment theory suggests is so important.

She described two aspects of parental behaviour, which can be called parental *responsiveness* and parental *demandingness*. Responsiveness (also described as warmth) describes the dimension of response to the child's needs in an accepting and supportive way. Demandingness is the extent to which parents require appropriate mature and responsible behaviour. She also noted that parents vary in the consistency of their rule setting and in the quality of their communication with their children. These ideas have been

---

Activity 3.1

Children who are looked after away from home are often subject to several changes of placement. It is easy to see how such moves can disrupt the security that allows for the essential development of a coherent account for events.

The use of life story books is already established practice with children living away from home. List other ways in which children can be helped to develop a coherent story that incorporates their experiences.

Hints for answers

Examples could include the following.

- Children and the carer/s could be encouraged to make scrap books that include items from outings, events and trips.

- Regular videos could be made in which both children and carer/s talk about any events that seem important.

- Children could be given a tape-recorder and encouraged to record anything about their lives that they want.

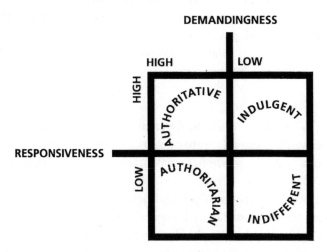

Figure 3.1 Showing the four styles of parenting as developed by Maccoby and Martin (1983) from the dimensions suggested by Baumrind (1972)

developed to illustrate four types of parenting (see Figure 3.1) based on the interaction between the two dimensions (Maccoby and Martin 1983).

These four parenting styles can be summarised as follows (Steinberg 1993):

Authoritative parenting is warm but firm. It sets standards for behaviour, but within the capabilities of the child and matches their level of development. Autonomy is valued, but responsibility is taken for the children's behaviour. Discipline is rational, with discussion and appropriate explanation. Such parenting has been shown to be associated with children who display more psychosocial competence and who are warm, affectionate, altruistic, responsible, self-assured, creative, curious, successful in school and have good self-esteem.

Authoritarian parenting emphasises obedience and conformity. Discipline is punitive and absolute, without discussion. The child is expected to accept rules without question. Independence is not encouraged and their development as an individual is not supported. It is associated with children who are more dependent, passive, less socially adept, less self-assured and less intellectually curious.

Indulgent parenting is accepting of most behaviour. Discipline is passive and there are few demands placed on the child. Control is seen as an infringement of the child's right to freedom. It is associated with children who are less mature, more irresponsible, conforming to peers and lacking in leadership.

Indifferent parenting in its extreme is neglectful. Life and discipline is centred around adult needs. The child's interest is not considered and their opinion is not sought. The child's activities are not routinely supervised. It is associated with children who are impulsive and who show delinquent behaviour.

Authoritative parenting is generally accepted to be the most helpful to the development of potential. However, it should be noted that the characteristics it fosters are those that are particularly valued in twentieth-century Western society. Indeed it has been described as a 'cosy ad-man's dream' by Meadows (1986). Sheinberg and Penn (1991) criticise the emphasis on autonomy, and independence within research on parenting. They also suggest that traditionally it is young males who are encouraged towards autonomy, while this is not normally encouraged of young women. They suggest that the goal of development should not be separation and independence, but an alternating state of both connections and differentiation within the context of ongoing relationships. In this model, maturity would be seen to involve the incorporation of characteristics considered to be traditionally male and those considered to be female. In other words, a more integrated theory of maturity would involve the assessment of inter-dependence, rather than autonomy.

However, within a society that values these characteristics there is no doubt that children who experience poor communication, hostility, low commitment and negative relations within their parenting relationships are likely to suffer social, emotional, educational and employment difficulties (Schaffer 1996; Steinberg 1993).

When thinking about transition to adulthood, the most helpful concept drawn from attachment theory is that of *mature dependence*, as described in the previous chapter (Holmes 1993). This incorporates the need that all people, at all ages, have for connection with other people with the mature ability to make autonomous decisions and function independently.

Helpful aspects of parenting

As described in the previous chapter, it is not sufficient to consider the parent's behaviour alone when judging parental impact, as it is the child's *experience* of parental behaviour that will affect their emotional development (Garbarino 1980). The influence of temperamental variations mean that it

---

Activity 3.2

It can be difficult for some people to appreciate that warmth can be combined with demandingness and the appropriate setting of boundaries. Some people may show considerable warmth, but find it difficult to set limits. Others may exert strict discipline, but in a cold and distant manner.

Set out ways in which the concept of authoritative parenting could be explained to parents who are seeking advice on discipline.

---

would be over-simplistic to be too prescriptive about parenting. Fundamentally, the point of stressing sensitivity and responsiveness as key factors is to underline the importance of the *fit* between the child's needs and the parental response. As stated in Chapter 1, a child must always be assessed as an individual with a particular set of past and present experiences. However, there are some aspects of childhood that seem to require particular aspects of parenting, regardless of individual differences. Cooper (1985) suggests that all children, from all cultures require:

- basic physical care
- affection, including physical and emotional intimacy
- security, which includes consistency of routines, stability and continuity of care
- the stimulation of innate potential through encouragement and praise
- guidance and control
- age-appropriate responsibility
- age-appropriate independence to make their own decisions, tailored to the child's ability and understanding of the consequences of such decisions.

What follows is a brief summary of some basic parenting tasks required for different age groups:

Infancy

The information above about attachment stressed the centrality of the nature of the communication between the carer and the child as the basis for attachment. Although the baby is an active partner in communication and interaction, in infancy the meshing is principally under adult control (see Chapter 6 for more details about pre-school years). In summary infants require carers who offer:

- overt control
- attentiveness
- warmth
- stimulation
- responsiveness
- non-restrictive care.

School age

As will be developed in Chapter 7, during school years children's lives expand socially, emotionally and intellectually. The parenting role therefore requires considerable flexibility and responsiveness. As children move into and through their school years they have a need for:

- Nurturing
- the encouragement of internalised control
- increased use of induction and reasoning
- encouragement with schooling
- consistent discipline
- expression of warmth.

Adolescence

Chapter 8 explores the adolescent–parent relationship in some detail. It also considers the complexities of fostering adolescents. In summary adolescents require:

- empathy
- parents or carers who can see things from their point of view
- constructive discipline, not criticism and constraint
- good communication
- active and warm involvement.

Unhelpful aspects of parenting

In Chapter 5 the damaging effects of some aspects of parenting will be explored as a form of adversity. Such adversity can range from emotional and physical neglect, either with or without intent, to deliberately abusive and cruel acts by those in the parenting role. Several research studies have noted the specific combination of *low warmth* and *high criticism* as a particularly damaging environment for children (DHSS 1995).

The following summary of unhelpful aspects of parenting does not address the intent behind the parenting. There is no doubt that some parents seem to be deliberately cruel to their children. But in many of the situations encountered in social work, parents' ability to appreciate their children's needs is undermined by a high level of personal stress.

Problems in emotional nurturing

- indifference and coldness to the child's needs and interests
- lack of affection.

Problems of discipline

- severe physical punishment
- very controlling parenting
- extreme and arbitrary discipline.

Problems with family relationships

- persistent parental discord
- hostility
- an atmosphere of tension and irritability.

Problems with self-worth

As will be explored in Chapter 7, the beliefs that people have about their own worth and efficacy underpin many areas of emotional development. Aspects of parenting that undermine the child's potential to feel good about him or herself are particularly damaging and include:

- attribution of inappropriate intention
- labelling as bad

- hostility and rejection
- undermining of a positive self image.

Parenting support

Parenting under stress

There is an increasing recognition of the importance of providing the optimum environment for children's growth and development, both for their individual well-being and for the well-being of society in general. Whilst there is a prevailing belief in the role of parents as holding primary responsibility for the nurture of their children, it is also generally acknowledged that parenting is a demanding task. This acknowledgement underpins the requirement in the UN Convention on the Rights of the Child that: 'State Parties shall render appropriate assistance to parents and legal guardians in the performance of their child-rearing responsibilities… (Article 18, 2).

If parenting is demanding, parenting under stress is often very difficult and sometimes impossible. The main demographic changes in Britain, for example, suggest that increasing numbers of parents are likely to be under stress. Since 1971 divorce rates have increased six-fold and the proportion of families headed by lone parents has risen from 1 in 12 to 1 in 5. One in 12 children live in step-families and the numbers of mothers working has risen from under half to two-thirds (Utting 1995). The increase in the numbers of elderly, dependent relatives and the wider dispersal of extended families is likely to exacerbate the stress of parenting.

Moreover, the major stress on many parents stems from poverty. The extent and detail of the increase in poverty for many families has been described elsewhere (e.g. Bradshaw 1990 and 1996). Parents living in poverty, especially women, have to be extremely organised to provide for their children, and frequently go without themselves (Save the Children 1997). The drain on personal resources in coping with poverty can seriously undermine an individual's capacity to meet their children's needs.

Activity 3.3

Using the following chart (Figure 3.2), outline parenting behaviours which, in your view, express a healthy response to each of the child's needs at each age, e.g., affection: cuddling, rocking; stimulation: encouragement of speech by talking to the child.

Parenting responses to children's needs

Age	Physical needs	Affection	Security	Stimulation of innate potential	Guidance and control	Responsibility	Independence
Birth to one year							
Toddler							
Primary Early school							
Middle years							
Adolescence							

Figure 3.2 A table to help guide assessment of parenting responses to children's needs at different stages.

Family support and prevention

The stresses described above can be ameliorated by support, and social workers are often involved in the process of linking families in difficulty with appropriate support projects. Parenting support can involve supporting the *process* of parenting and helping parents as people. Both these elements need to be considered in the support, promotion or development of parenting skills. 'Parenting support can be offered by a range of bodies both professional and voluntary' (Audit Commission 1994). Support should have the aim of offering help at the right time, from the right people and in the right place (Utting 1995).

Pointers about the most effective kind of support can be drawn from a range of research and evaluation of large-scale preventive projects, provision by mainstream agencies and specific parenting projects.

Prevention programmes

At its extreme, poor parenting can be abusive parenting. There is now considerable evidence to suggest that much child abuse is preventable and that family support services should play a major part in preventing abuse (Mostyn 1996; Parton 1995). From their work in Britain in collaboration with parents, Baldwin and Spencer (1993) suggest that effective prevention projects need to focus on the aspects of: *family support*, including practical and emotional support; *social environment*, including safety in the community; and *partnership*, participation and ownership.

Based on reviews of work in the US, Cohn Donnelly (1997) summarises the kind of parenting support that has been found to reduce the likelihood of abuse and improve child outcomes:

- early intervention, either home based or centre based
- a duration of at least six months and possibly up to several years
- support offered close to (or before) the birth of the baby
- intense support, offered at least once a week if not more frequently
- comprehensive input, not just focusing on parenting skills
- help offered by workers whose personality is warm and accepting.

Sinclair, Hearn and Pugh (1997) summarise wide-ranging research into a number of British programmes offering parenting support, run by a large number of different agencies and suggest that successful projects are:

- available

- acceptable

- affordable

- accessible

- accountable

- appropriate

- across-agency.

A comprehensive account of ways in which appropriate social support can be used in a preventive manner is given by Thompson (1995). He stresses the importance of detailed assessment of the kind of support that is needed, because, as he cautions, not all social contact is automatically helpful. For example, for some parents, contact with the extended family may be characterised by arguments, criticism and stress and be undermining to parenting ability.

Because of child protection priorities, individual social workers may not always be in a position to offer directly the kind of intensive support that some families need. The current refocusing debate is questioning the balance of resource allocation within social work and there is an increasing impetus for a shift towards more supportive and preventive intervention (see, for example, Parton 1997). However, workers should have a comprehensive knowledge of all potential sources of formal and informal support available in the neighbourhood and can be involved in linking parents with the most appropriate resource.

Ability to use support

Appropriate non-stigmatising support has the potential to ameliorate some of the stresses of parenting and to reduce the likelihood of abuse and neglect. However, social workers can encounter situations where it seems that no matter how much support is provided, there is little improvement in the parenting the child receives.

In such cases it is helpful to look beyond the immediate problems in parenting and assess the parents' ability to *make use* of the support that is on offer. Crittenden (1996) suggests that families can be categorised according to their ability to assess their own state of need, to seek appropriate services and to make adaptive changes. The categorisation could be a useful guide for assessment when a situation seems stuck. She describes families where parents are:

- *Independent and adequate:* can competently assess needs of the family members, find resources to meet those needs and make changes.

- *Vulnerable to crisis:* are capable of independent functioning but may temporarily need help during a crisis and may need some months of support.

- *Restorable:* are potentially independent but may require two to five years of well-planned support.

- *Supportable:* are unable to make the changes needed quickly enough to meet their children's needs, but can manage if supported with services on a long-term basis.

- *Inadequate:* are not able to offer their children enough to meet their needs even with intensive support.

As an example of how this can be applied in practice it is helpful to look at the case of physical neglect. Many children referred for neglect live in families that seem to have difficulty in making use of support. The parents often feel unable to make changes in their parenting style, and also feel that no one can help them. They

> not only see themselves as powerless, but they perceive everyone else to be powerless. Because they believe everyone is powerless, they believe that effort to achieve goals is futile. Even accepting an offer of a reward for certain kinds of effort ... appears useless if one believes that no one has the power to make things happen. (Crittenden 1996; p.163)

Understanding such attributions should help with understanding why support that is on offer is not apparently welcomed. If people believe nothing can help they will have little motivation to attend a family centre or go to parenting skills classes etc. In these situations the intervention should first focus on enabling people to shift their perceptions of their own ability to change, for example, by starting with much smaller changes like keeping one area of one room clean, rather than the whole house. It is also often the case that children who are neglected are in families that could be characterised as either 'restorable' or 'supportable'. The intervention literature clearly indicates that *long-term* support is needed if real improvement is to be made for children experiencing neglect (Gaudin 1993).

Activity 3.4

Think about cases you have encountered which have seemed to be 'stuck'. Consider whether the parent or parents may have had difficulty in making use of the support on offer. If so, reflect upon which of Crittenden's categories may have been applicable.

What factors can inhibit change in parenting?

If it is established that parents do have difficulty with making use of support, further assessment is required in order to explore why that might be the case.

As described above, effective parenting is characterised by sensitivity to the child and the ability to 'tune in' to the child's needs. In contrast, parents who have difficulty with parenting often seem to have trouble empathising with the needs of the child.

> Specifically, maltreating parents often are characterised by a *lack of understanding* of the emotional complexity of human relationships, especially the parent–child relationship. They have difficulty seeing things from the child's perspective or understanding behaviour in terms of the child's developmental level and the context or situation. (Erickson and Egeland 1996, p.13)

Attachment theory offers pointers in understanding the roots of such problems. The parent's own attachment history appears to influence their ability to promote secure attachment in their child. There tends to be an association between a parent's recall of their own attachment experiences and the pattern of attachment in their children (Main and Goldwyn 1984). A study of 65 mothers in Germany showed that 80 per cent who recalled secure attachment experiences had securely attached infants, while 80 per cent of the mothers who had experienced insecure attachments in childhood had children who showed insecure attachment to them (Grossman *et al.* 1988, cited in Howe 1995).

So, it does appear one's own attachment experiences can influence parenting style. Specifically, it has been suggested that there may be a link between inner working models and the capacity to feel empathy for the child's needs. Thus, if a person has developed an insecure inner working model that characterises relationships as anxiety-provoking and unsatisfactory it is harder for them to be sensitive to the child's messages (Grossman and Grossman 1991, cited in Howe 1995). So, for example, when a baby expresses distress by crying, a parental response in line with the arousal–relaxation cycle would involve an attempt to understand what was wrong and appropriate soothing (see Figure 2.1). However, for a parent with an insecure internal working model the baby's crying will lead to anxiety, with the parent experiencing personal emotional distress. This personal distress then dominates the interaction and undermines the parent's ability to soothe the child.

What adds to the complexity is that having an insecure inner working model of relationships appears to inhibit the ability to take in information that might facilitate change (Feeney and Noller 1996). In other words we tend to selectively perceive events in line with our inner working model. An example would be the case of a woman who had experienced a rejecting upbringing. She expressed great distress because of her belief that her young son did not need her since he would not look at her. When their interaction was carefully observed it became apparent that whenever she handed an object to the child she looked down and away from him and missed seeing him looking at her. It is easy to surmise that she looked away to avoid seeing what she anticipated would be a rejection, thus missing the very information that could have shifted her belief. When the interactions were videoed and she was able to observe both that her child did look at her, and that she was looking away she was able to start making changes to which the child responded with delight.

However, there is not a simple relationship between childhood experience and parenting style. Instead, the most important factor seems to be the *sense* that adults make of their childhood experiences. Adults can overcome difficult childhood events if they can account for their experiences in a coherent way. The *coherent story* that is so important in childhood therefore remains important into adulthood. So, although inner working models of relationships will develop on the basis of childhood experience, they are open to change and development. They can be modified with reflection, so that it is not necessarily the quality of an experience that matters, but how that experience is made sense of (Main and Goldwyn 1984).

Feeney and Noller (1996) explore the factors that contribute to the stability of internal working models and those that contribute to change. An understanding of these factors can help both with assessing why parents are not able to make the necessary changes and also with creating the opportunities for facilitating change.

Stability

- People tend to select environments that are consistent with their beliefs about themselves.

- The internal working model can be self-perpetuating as it affects perceptions of people, for example, those who believe that others cannot be trusted are more likely to notice behaviour that supports that conclusion.

- People's responses, especially in times of stress, are often involuntary, and spring from the automatic triggering of typical response patterns.

- Internal working models can be self-fulfilling, for example, those who believe that no one cares for them will approach people defensively and thus are less likely to elicit caring responses.

Change

- Significant life changes can lead to changes in experience that lead to changes in the internal working model. The experience of a satisfactory intimate relationship is one of the main contributors to a change to a more secure internal working model.

- Conversely, an experience of an insecure relationship can undermine a secure internal working model.

- Making sense of previous attachment experiences, perhaps with the help of therapeutic intervention, can lead to a change in internal working models.

There are a number of ways in which this framework can be used in practice.

The fact that changes of the inner working model can come about through healthy relationships suggests a focus for intervention with this issue.

- Parents who are in a relationship may welcome couple-counselling.

- Those who are not, or who find that they make unsatisfactory relationships, may benefit from a chance to explore ways in which they may be repeating unhelpful patterns of behaviour.

It is clear that parents with insecure inner working models would benefit from the opportunity for *reflection* upon their own attachment experiences.

More specifically it would be important to help people develop a coherent story for their own childhood.

- It may be appropriate to adapt the kind of life-story work that is done with children for work with adults. This could involve making contact with family members to locate photographs, going back to see where they grew up, visiting childhood haunts, schools etc.

- Similarly people could be encouraged to tell their story, in other words to talk about their life in story form. An example of one way to do this comes from the work of Martin (1998). She describes a technique called direct-scribing in which young people tell the story of their life and their words are typed verbatim on a computer as they talk. In this way people can see the story unfold and can be actively involved in modifying what is written. The story is printed out so that they can keep a copy of it.

- The use of video, as described in the example above, can enable parents to get direct feedback of their interactions with their children. Video has to be used sensitively; it can be very undermining for some people to observe themselves, and could be counterproductive if they only look for actions that confirm a negative view of themselves as parents.

Summary of developmental issues and considerations for practice

It is not possible to cover all aspects of parenting in one such chapter; however, some of the key issues that relate to practice have been presented.

The first point to stress is the importance of looking at the issue of parenting in context, without preconceptions and assumptions.

- Retaining the focus on the child and his or her needs should help with this.

The next and related issue is that of the complexity of the role of the parent.

- The message for practice is that some parents may benefit from the opportunity to step back and reflect upon the unique quality of the parent–child relationship.

The key concepts of secure base and coherent story run throughout this chapter and indeed the whole book. They underpin resilience as will be explored in the next chapter.

- The priority for practice is to assess whether the child has the kind of security that facilitates the development of a sense of coherence and continuity. Children need to be able to make sense of events, both good and bad, and practitioners can play a crucial role in checking that this is happening.

The research on different styles of parenting provides pointers for practice about what to look for when assessing family situations.

- The main message that is helpful for both practitioners and parents is the importance of the *combination* of warmth and appropriate expectations.
- The list of helpful and unhelpful aspects of parenting can be used as a guide to assessment.

Parenting can be undermined by stress and financial and material deprivation. Such stress can be ameliorated by appropriate support.

- The main messages from the support literature is that parents themselves need to feel involved in the process, support is not something that is done to parents. Instead, a variety of non-stigmatising services need to be available with the acknowledgement that *all* parents may need some help at some time.

Some of the most challenging cases for practitioners are when it seems clear what needs to change, when support is offered, but the changes do not occur. In these situations the research suggests that it is helpful first to assess ability to make use of support on offer.

- If it is clear that someone cannot make effective use of support the focus of intervention may need to shift to assessing what is blocking their ability to use support and what therapeutic help is needed to overcome such a block.

In conclusion, it should be evident that parenting is a complicated and challenging task. When there are problems of parenting they are often not solved by simple attention to parenting skills. Instead, it is important to remember that parents are people who have their own attachment history and their own needs. Effective intervention must take this into account and consider the whole parent within their ecological context.

CHAPTER 4

Resilience and Vulnerability

Introduction

In the course of the exploration of various factors which influence both the vulnerability and resilience of individual children, key themes emerge which it is helpful for the practitioner to bear in mind throughout.

1. It is the *impact* of the event or set of life circumstances which dictates the way in which a particular child is likely to be affected.

2. Whilst the chronology of events is of importance, of even greater salience is the age and stage of development at which these events occurred, as the child's responses will be influenced by their cognitive capacity to make sense of these events.

3. It is the particular coincidence of individual personality factors, the nature of supportive relationships available to the child or young person and the relative vulnerability or resilience at the time, as shaped by the influence of past history, which is most likely to inform the child's need for support.

4. We should be not only providing what each child needs at the time, but anticipating what they might need in developing for themselves the coherent story of life events and circumstances at later stages of development. This can be invaluable in influencing parents' and carers' preparedness to identify and support the child's later needs for additional help.

An overall framework for identifying the focus for intervention in individual cases

This chapter invites you to explore what is currently known about vulnerability and resilience in children and young people as a basis for examining the impact of particular stresses and life events which may challenge healthy development. The focus will be on identifying and harnessing particular strengths and advantages in an individual child's situation in order to reduce vulnerability and build their resilience in the face of adverse circumstances.

This chapter concentrates on identifying key factors and circumstances in the life of an individual child which may be of particular relevance for practitioner intervention. The chapter explores these considerations within a particular framework. This framework is designed as a simple tool to facilitate an assessment of the developmental progress of individual children and young people with whom we work. These children may be living in a variety of circumstances, many of them at home with one or both parents, some in newly constituted families with additional half-siblings, and others in substitute family care either fostering or adoption, or in a residential setting.

The chapter overall focuses on particular effects of stress and adversity in children's lives and their likely effects on the individual child's development. There are four key terms which will be used throughout this and the following chapter. These are *resilience, vulnerability, adversity* and the *protective environment*. We offer a working definition for each of these concepts under the different section headings and go on to explore key findings from research which illuminate what is currently known about their significance for development.

We will explore the significance of resilience for our work with pointers for the recognition of protective factors within the child, their family and community resources which may act as a buffer against stress. We will offer a definition of vulnerability and examine once again factors within the child, family circumstances and community supports which may render a child more vulnerable to developmental interruption or delay.

We will consider the significance of particular life events and circumstances, for example, the key issues of separation and loss and various kinds of abuse, and we shall look at protective factors in the environment. The challenge for practitioners is first to identify the degree of vulnerability and the nature of adverse circumstances in order to focus on how resilience may be developed or promoted, and protective factors introduced into the

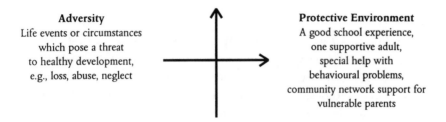

Resilience
'*Normal* development under difficult conditions'
e.g., being female, secure attachment experience, an
outgoing temperament, sociability, problem-solving skills

Adversity
Life events or circumstances
which pose a threat
to healthy development,
e.g., loss, abuse, neglect

Protective Environment
A good school experience,
one supportive adult,
special help with
behavioural problems,
community network support for
vulnerable parents

Vulnerability
'Those characteristics of the child, their family circle and wider
community which might threaten or challenge healthy development'
e.g. disability, racism, an 'unusual' temperament lack of attachment
network or any community supports

*Figure 4.1 Framework for assessing the vulnerability of an individual child,
elements of adversity and focussing on supporting resilience and harnessing
protective factors*

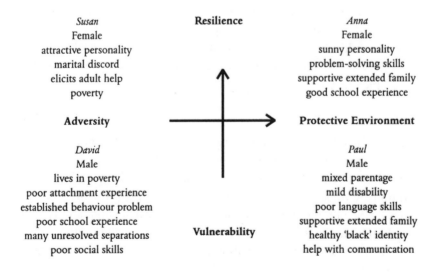

Susan
Female
attractive personality
marital discord
elicits adult help
poverty

Resilience

Anna
Female
sunny personality
problem-solving skills
supportive extended family
good school experience

Adversity

Protective Environment

David
Male
lives in poverty
poor attachment experience
established behaviour problem
poor school experience
many unresolved separations
poor social skills

Paul
Male
mixed parentage
mild disability
poor language skills
supportive extended family
healthy 'black' identity
help with communication

Vulnerability

*Figure 4.2 Examples of children's circumstances illustrating the degree of
vulnerability and resilience and the level of adverse and protective factors*

environment to support the most vulnerable children. Case examples will be offered in addition to recommended reading in order to expand and develop the potential significance of stressful experiences for children and young people. Figures 4.1 and 4.2 illustrate the basic framework.

Anna

From Figure 4.2 we can see that Anna is likely to have the best chance of healthy overall development. Not only is the fact of being female in itself protective, as boys are generally more vulnerable to stress, but also if Anna has a sunny, responsive personality and has learned social problem-solving skills, she will be well equipped to survive life's stresses. If she has additionally taken a healthy degree of responsibility for a sibling who perhaps has a disability, but does so in the context of a supportive extended family who are responsive to her needs, this may also be advantageous. If additionally she has had a good experience at school, this will stand her in good stead should she face other life stresses.

Therefore, she has the advantages of a resilient personality, learned skills which equip her to face adversity, and a protective environment which ensures that her needs are met.

Susan

If we consider that, although Susan may face the adversity of living in poverty and additionally in a household full of marital discord, if she is an attractive child who can elicit support from adults and children alike, this will be a buffer against the long-term effects of stress. Therefore, she has advantages which help her significantly in adversity.

Paul

Paul is of mixed parentage, and, living in a predominantly white community, he may be vulnerable to the effects of racism. If he also has a mild disability which has affected significantly his development of language, he may be additionally vulnerable. However, if he lives with supportive members of his extended family who build his self-esteem as a black child, and resources have been found to focus on building his effective communication skills, his vulnerability may be reduced. This is dependent on the protective factors in his environment.

David

David is clearly in the most vulnerable position as regards potential interruptions to his healthy development. He is the most obviously disadvantaged child because of a combination of stressors. If we imagine that not only is he vulnerable because of poor attachment experiences, but he also has long-standing behavioural problems, is falling behind at school and about to be excluded, we can see that he is already at risk of suffering from developmental delay or interruption.

If he has additionally experienced adversity in that he lives in poverty and he has experienced numerous unresolved separations, we can see how his vulnerability might be increased. Not only is he more vulnerable but he has therefore also experienced many negative life events which are also likely to increase his vulnerability.

In identifying ways in which we can build his resilience and reduce his vulnerability, for example, by offering him a warm attachment experience and increasing his social skills we may reduce his vulnerability.

Additionally, we may be able to consider whether any of the circumstances of adversity can be reduced or removed and protective factors in the environment either harnessed or introduced which may be protective. For example, with an appropriate school placement and supportive adults managing his difficult behaviour adeptly, these forces may combine to help him to develop problem-solving skills and higher self-esteem.

The level and nature of intervention will therefore depend upon the degree of vulnerability and levels of adversity balanced against the resources in his family community and professional support system which can be harnessed to address them.

When considering the key concepts of resilience, adversity, vulnerability and protective factors as they are illustrated throughout the text, issues of relevance may emerge in relation to an individual child or young person with whom you are working which may help to clarify the focus of intervention.

Here we see the often powerful interaction between vulnerability and adversity as it may be that the more vulnerable a child, the more affected they may be by adverse experiences. Equally, the greater the persistent adversities, the more likely they are to render a particular child vulnerable.

Resilience

Definition of resilience

Fonagy *et al.* define resilience as: '*Normal* development under difficult conditions' (1994, pp.231–257).

When we meet a child in stressful circumstances it can be helpful to be aware of those factors which act as a buffer, strengthening the child to help them withstand difficult life events, such as separation from loved ones.

We shall examine those factors within the child, their family circumstances and community support which may be harnessed in our work to the child's benefit. For practice purposes, identifying those children who are less robust at an early stage can help us to identify the additional supports they may need.

What follows is a summary of factors identified by Emmy Werner (1990). Werner explores, from an examination of international research, key factors in the child, the family and community and wider context which have been found to promote resilience.

The following three domains are in line with an ecological approach to development (see Chapter 2).

Resilience factors within the individual child

INFANCY

Werner comments (1990), 'Resilient infants tend to have predictable temperamental characteristics which elicit positive responses from other people, (p.100).

They:

- are active, affectionate, .cuddly, good-natured, responsive, easy to deal with and have a capacity for self-expression
- have experienced a secure attachment and learned to trust in its availability
- have a supportive family member
- have a pronounced sense of autonomy and social orientation
- are described as alert, cheerful, responsive, self-confident and independent
- are advanced in communication, mobility and self-help skills
- are more advanced in social play than vulnerable toddlers

- have developed a coping pattern that combines autonomy with an ability to ask for support when needed
- these characteristics are also predictive of resilience in later years.

PRE-SCHOOL YEARS

Resilient pre-schoolers have/are:

- well-developed communication and problem solving skills which the child is able to put to good use
- sociable but also independent.

MIDDLE CHILDHOOD

Stress resistant primary schoolers are:

- well liked by peers and adults
- reflective rather than impulsive in thinking style
- feel they can influence their environments positively
- are able to use flexible coping strategies, including humour
- are adept at recruiting surrogate parents, even if not blood relatives
- resilient *boys* are emotionally expressive, socially perceptive and nurturant
- resilient *girls* are autonomous and independent
- resilient *children* display flexible coping strategies which promote mastery over adversity rather than reactions in a rigidly sex-stereotyped manner
- overall, *girls* are generally more resilient to stress and trauma than boys.

ADOLESCENCE

Resilient young people are those who:

- are more responsible and achievement oriented
- prefer structure in their lives and have internalised a positive set of values
- have more positive self-concept

- are more appreciative, gentle, nurturing and socially perceptive than their more vulnerable peers
- are characterised by pronounced social maturity and a stronger sense of responsibility
- have belief in their own capacity to control their fate
- by pre-school stage were healthily autonomous with an ability to enlist support
- have repeated successful experiences of overcoming stressful situations (often with support of others)
- have a sense of self-efficacy and confidence
- can select what they need from their environment and make good use of it
- change or restructure a situation
- are optimistic and hopeful.

Resilience factors within the family

We shall now consider those factors in the family setting which may be protective against stress and adversity. Resilient protective families provide:

- an opportunity to establish a close bond with at least one person who has provided stable care and adequate and appropriate attention (secure base) in the first year of life
- affectionate ties with alternative care givers, e.g. grandparents, who may support parents and provide the child with alternative nurturing
- involvement in sibling care giving, either as the giver or the recipient, which can be a major preventive factor for vulnerable children. (The availability of some supplementary support from an adult is a crucial determinant of whether older siblings will help or hinder younger ones.)

SOCIALISATION PRACTICES

Key characteristics of the home environment have been identified in respect of boys and girls as particularly protective of healthy development.

Resilient girls are reared in households combining:

- an absence of over-protection
- an emphasis on risk-taking
- reliable emotional support.

Resilient boys are reared in households combining:

- greater structure
- rules
- parental supervision
- the availability of a male as healthy role model
- encouragement for emotional expression.

REQUIRED HELPFULNESS

Productive roles of responsibility for the child, associated with close family ties, are protective.

FAITH

A belief in a broader value system can help the child to persist in problem solving or in surviving a set of challenging life circumstances.

A sense of 'coherence' in their experience gives the child a feeling of rootedness; the conviction that life has meaning and an optimistic focus.

Resilience factors in the community

FRIENDS

The capacity to make and sustain friendships is protective, a source of comfort and support.

SCHOOL

Even if not gifted, resilient children can put their abilities to good use. School is often an effective refuge for children under stress or those who have experienced abuse. Teachers can shape both academic attainment and positive self-concept and esteem.

FOR GIRLS

The nurturing and fostering of responsibility builds strength and resilience.

Activity 4.1

Focusing on your work with an individual child or young person, please consider, in the light of Werner's framework, the following questions.

1. How might you decrease the child's exposure to key risk factors and stressful life events?

2. Identify potential strengths in (a) the individual child; (b) the family context; (c) the wider community.

3. Outline suggestions as to how these might be harnessed to support the child.

FOR BOYS

Structure and control helps them to develop an 'internal locus of control' which fosters social and intellectual development.

Summary

Rutter (1985) identifies three key factors associated with resilience:

1. a sense of self-esteem and confidence

2. a belief in own self efficacy and ability to deal with change and adaptation and

3. a repertoire of social problem-solving approaches.

Intervention

An important focus for work may be:

- to decrease exposure to key risk factors and stressful life events and, wherever possible, additionally

- to increase the number of available protective factors e.g. building competencies and social support.

Resilience factors in the parent–child relationship

In Chapter 2 key ideas about the importance of attachment relationships for children and young people have already been explored. The idea of a secure base as a focus for promoting and sustaining the development of a feeling of security and well-being underlines an examination of a child's attachment relationships as highly significant, both in assessment and in work with individual children and adolescents either remaining at home, placed with foster families or in residential units.

Throughout the research literature, the nature and strength of the attachment relationships available to an individual child are clearly identified as being of key significance in promoting resilience. Factors include (Reder and Lucey 1995):

- Parents' feelings towards the child – the greater warmth and pleasure in the relationship the more the child is protected against adversity.

- Parents demonstrated concern or interest in the well-being of the child, this builds the self-esteem and confidence of the child and links with the positive interaction cycle (Fahlberg 1994; see Figure 2.2).

- Parents' capacity to empathise with the child's perspective on experiences, in other words to connect imaginatively with the child's age-appropriate way of experiencing events.

- The parents' ability to view the child as a person in his/her own right.

- Their ability to respect the child's needs and give them primacy over their own wishes/needs.

- The parents' ability to anticipate the child's needs, e.g. for protection/comfort in distress for example, support in strange situations.

THE IMPORTANCE OF THE PARENTS' RELATIONSHIP TO PARENTING

- What are their feelings about being a parent? Are they positive?

- Do parents accept responsibility for their own behaviour and are they aware of the impact on the child?

- Is the parent clear that the child is not responsible for his/her own protection and do they take steps to offer this?

- Where there are concerns, does the parent acknowledge that there may be problems and that change is needed?

These are often some of the crucial points to establish where there are significant problems. A refusal to acknowledge the impact upon the child of carers' actions, of failure to act in correct ways, is crucial to establishing a real partnership. The way the parents themselves view any problem will be critical in informing the way in which resources may be structured to help them.

INFLUENCES FROM THE FAMILY CONTEXT

- Does the parent have an awareness of the impact of their own parenting experiences on the ability to parent?

Howe (1995) underlines the value of a parent's capacity to *reflect* on their own experience in providing empathy with the child's experience.

- Meaning of child to parents – what does this child mean to these parents? For example, replacing a lost child or resembling another loved person.

Reder and Duncan (1995) explore this issue in depth proposing that some children have 'a special significance to their parents and, as a result, were at greater risk of harm than other children in the household' (p.39). This led them to appreciate the importance of building a picture of the psychological meaning of a particular child when undertaking assessments.

- Is the child involved in dysfunctional family relationships, such as marital discord, or abuse? If so, what role does the child take, e.g. as protector, comforter, all to one parent against another, focus for marital arguments and/or violence between parents?

- How do they cope with relationship stresses and do they have a variety of healthy responses, e.g. capacity and willingness to seek and make use of support?

CONTACT WITH EXTERNAL WORLD

We might ask ourselves the following questions about the parents' links outside the family.

- What is the relationship between parents and informal support network, do they have anyone to whom they can turn? If so, do these people confirm or challenge punitive or abusive styles of child management?

- In terms of their relationships with professionals – are they able to cooperate? For example, what is the evidence of responses to previous attempts to support, has it been seen as useful in the past?

- How sensitive is this family system to stress and how do they cope, for example by use of alcohol, violence?

Reder and Lucey (1995) explore various key components of parenting assessments which help to focus attention both on causes for concern and also on protective aspects. Vital issues are considered here such as the importance of a careful and sensitive awareness of critical components of a family's cultural and racial background.

The importance of sibling relationships as a factor in resilience

Whilst not denying the security dimension of healthy attachment relationships with carers, Dunn (1994) expands our understanding of the broader world of the child's close connections.

The relationship between brothers and sisters holds potential for support under stress, but also for additional isolation and rejection for a few children who experience themselves as outsiders or scapegoats within a sibling group (Kosonen 1997).

For example, practitioners are familiar with children who appear more closely attached to siblings than to anyone else. We meet children who care for one another or who are even the main caretakers for a sibling group. Although we often view this scenario with concern, the caretaking role may bring some advantages to a child despite the early burden this represents.

We strive wherever possible to make and maintain joint sibling placements so that we can minimise any further stress of separation. Day or foster carers and residential staff need to be sensitive to the fact that this caring role, however inappropriate it may seem, may well be central to the child's current sense of self-esteem and identity within the family. Care should be taken to encourage the child to relinquish this in a gradual way, with a clear acknowledgement of the child's caretaking instincts.

Some children are clearly the scapegoats within a sibling group, constantly criticised and undermined by their parents' attitudes and responses. Rutter and Rutter (1993) comment upon the particular predicament of such children as they regard them as more vulnerable in a family where all the children suffer some neglect or abuse. They quote Dunn and Plomin (1990) in suggesting

It may matter very little whether children are brought up in a home that is less loving or more punitive than average whereas it may matter a great deal that one child consistently receives less affection or more criticism and punishment than his brother or sister. (p.49)

Dunn and Plomin further found in their studies that, 'Those children who received less affection and more control than their siblings tended to show more problem behaviour' (p.48). Clearly, this is a particular group of children we need to identify, support and monitor with special attention.

PRACTICE POINT

What emerges as especially significant is the *rejection* experienced by a child, particularly when they live with the constant daily comparison of their carers' more positive (or merely less negative) behaviour towards a sibling.

A second factor of major impact and significance is the experience of not mattering to anyone, having no one in their lives to whom they are of importance.

Some children who are not naturally *persistent* in their attempts to reach out to adults in the hope of their needs being understood and met may 'give up' and hide their own needs. These children, especially if they are compliant and 'easy to manage' or keen to please, may hide their needs even in placements away from home, and practitioners need to be aware of underlying neglect and its potential longer-term impact.

There is a very useful practice tool called The Sibling Relationship Checklist (DoH 1991) which provides a practical framework for exploring the different features of particular sibling relationships. This can be helpful in identifying the focus for intervention when practitioners are wishing to concentrate on building and supporting positive elements of a sibling relationship. It can also be used to clarify the strength and nature of sibling attachments also a vital issue in planning accommodation or longer-term placements.

Practice points

The careful assessment of factors of resilience in individual children, in their family relationships and wider community networks is important for shaping intervention. Care is needed in making sure that avoidance of dependency relationships, an attitude of 'I'm fine, I don't need anyone' or a persistent tendency to be self-parenting are not mistaken for resilience from a basis of healthy dependence. Some children and young people develop skills in keeping adults at a distance by learning to mask and cover up their underlying distress. Their needs are more likely to go unnoticed, especially if they have siblings who are very demanding or whose behaviour signals their needs more explicitly.

Given that one of the most helpful areas for intervention with individual children and young people is that of building healthy resilience, it is useful for the practitioner to have a framework from which to begin to consider strategies for work with the individual child.

Practitioners are frequently engaged in work which builds strengths in the child and it may merely be a question of giving added emphasis to this work and involving the child or young person themselves in developing the ideas which may add to the impact of positive strategies. It may be helpful to question the assumption that the social worker is always the person who offers all the direct support as other adults in the child's life may be better placed to sustain these efforts over time. Recruiting someone already known to the child or a befriender to act as a mentor can be an alternative way of offering continuity of concern and interest and tracking progress and success and mastery. Gilligan (1997) identifies six key areas of focus which can form the basis for clarifying initiatives for work:

- Encouraging purposeful contact with family members and other key adults from the child's past.

- Encouraging positive school experience.

- Encouraging friendships with peers.

- Actively fostering interest, involvement and talents in sport, music, hobbies or cultural pursuits.

- Helping the child to rehearse, dissect and discuss problem-solving and coping skills and strategies.

- Promoting pro-social qualities in the young person. (pp.7–8)

Vulnerability

Definition of vulnerability

Vulnerability can be defined as those innate characteristics of the child, or those imposed by their family circle and wider community which might threaten or challenge healthy development.

KEY FACTORS

Factors that might render a child vulnerable to abuse and neglect and/or to not weathering ordinary adversities and veering off a healthy developmental path can be separated into:

1. some intrinsic characteristics in the child which might render them more vulnerable

2. those vulnerabilities imposed by parents' views or expectations of the child.

Alongside these general factors, the particular age of the child and developmental stage may render the child particularly vulnerable.

BABIES AND INFANTS

1. Intrinsic characteristics of the child

- the child who is born too soon – in particular the child who is premature
- the child who is born with developmental difficulties, in particular various sorts of disabilities
- the child who is arrhythmic, i.e., the child who cannot be helped to settle into any predictable rhythm or routine
- the child who cries and cannot be comforted
- the child who cannot sleep or disturbs the parent frequently, waking during the night in particular
- the child with an unusual temperament – especially the child who is either very active or very passive, and the child who will not accept being held.

2. Those vulnerabilities imposed by parents' views or expectations of the child

- the child who is born of the 'wrong' sex, i.e., where the sex of the child disappoints parental expectations and hopes
- the child who resembles a hated partner or spouse.

Alongside these general factors, the age of the child and developmental stage may render the child particularly vulnerable. Babies can be particularly prone to all kinds of abuse and neglect because of their total dependence on adults and their vulnerability to specific physical trauma, e.g. shaking injuries.

The child who is between 6 months and 18 months is especially vulnerable to effects of separations because they have 'selected' or identified their primary carers and therefore experience their loss in a pervasive sense.

The child between these ages who experiences multiple caretakers may well be especially vulnerable to a difficulty in establishing a secure base.

What is clearly protective for a child at this age and stage is to have experienced at least one good attachment in their early years.

PRE-SCHOOL STAGE

1. Intrinsic characteristics in the child

- At the pre-school stage, the child is likely to take on some sense of responsibility and personal connection with negative life events, particularly if they are separated at this time. They are more likely to attribute blame to themselves and this will render them more vulnerable to the effects of future separations and may threaten their confidence in their 'secure base'.

- The fact that the child at this stage will be challenging authority figures through healthy autonomous behaviour, may render them at risk of physical abuse or emotional abuse.

- The child who feels unsafe to explore and insecure in their attachment may cling or follow the carer in an irritating manner, provoking abuse.

- If the issues of autonomy and independence are not well managed at this stage, they may well re-emerge in a salient way in adolescence. However, this then provides an opportunity for re-working these issues in a healthier manner.

2. Those vulnerabilities imposed by parents' views or expectations of the child

- The child at this stage of development should be exploring his/her environment – therefore if they are either under-protected or over-protected at this stage, their development may suffer.

- The lack of healthy boundaries.

THE SCHOOL-AGE CHILD

1. Intrinsic characteristics in the child

- The child who is subject to developmental delay and the child who needs special help at this stage, especially to enter school, may be particularly vulnerable. Therefore the child who is sensitised to separations may not manage this milestone well.

- The child who is aggressive or who has persistent behaviour problems.

- The child who makes no demands for their emotional needs to be met, i.e. is passive and unresponsive, as they do not enlist adult support.

- The child who is slow or unable to learn, who has particular learning difficulties which are not identified.

- The child who is struggling intellectually at school, as this has particular knock-on effects in terms of their social and emotional development as well as their intellectual functioning.

2. Those vulnerabilities imposed by the parents' views or expectations of the child

- The child who is isolated as part of a closed family system.

- The child who is scapegoated, in particular the child who is the focus of negative responses and initiatives from parents amongst siblings who are more clearly valued.

1 and 2

- The child who is different in any way. For example, in particular the child who may be identifiably different in racial terms within a predominantly white society, particularly those children who are of mixed parentage.

ADOLESCENCE

1. Intrinsic characteristics in the child

- The young person who has learned no planning or problem-solving skills may well be vulnerable as they are unable to protect themselves or ask for adult support in a healthy manner.

- The young person with established behaviour problems which have not been addressed and/or patterns of disturbed behaviour, especially conduct disorder in boys. These children have often already encountered difficulties in nursery settings as well as in primary and secondary school as their behaviour sets them apart from their peers. They are more likely:

- to have trouble in making and keeping friends
- to find it hard to develop a pattern of learning
- to gravitate towards other children or young people in trouble partly as a reflection of their view of themselves, as well as attraction to the excitement this peer group offer
- to be more vulnerable to disruptions in schooling which is a setting invaluable for providing resilience in late adolescence and in the transition to adulthood.

- The young person with poor self-esteem or sense of self-efficacy.
- The young person who is part of an under-achieving or anti-authority group with limited choice of other peers.

2. Those vulnerabilities imposed by parents' views or expectations of the child

- The young person who is disapproved of or blamed for family problems: the scapegoat may believe there is no point in trying as they cannot affect any improvement in their circumstances.
- The young person who is pressed to take on too many family responsibilities, in particular the 'parental' child.
- The child who has no support for their developing independence.
- The child who is not nourished in terms of their questions and confusions about their sexual identity and orientation.
- The young person who has no continuity of confiding relationships at a stage of development when the 'secure base' is particularly necessary once more.
- The young person who is frequently separated from important people, their attachment figures, their peer connections, and their school links, with no support in addressing these moves and changes, and no help in making sense of the continuity and coherence of their own life story.

Parental factors

Certain factors within parents' own experience or relationships and circumstances may add to an individual child or young person's vulnerability:

- The child who lives with parents who are depressed or have significant long-standing psychiatric problems which affect the parent–child relationship or safety and nurturing of the young person. This is especially significant if long-standing mental health problems remain unidentified.

- The child who witnesses long-standing marital discord with no resolution.

- The child who lives in a household where there is domestic violence. It is vital to know the *predicament* of the individual child within their family.

- The child whose parents separate, especially if these separations are unpredicted and repeated.

Continuing friction between parental partners post-separation and a poor post-separation environment for the child or young person are especially significant as are tensions or even violence or abuse in contact arrangements after divorce. The child of:

- parents under particular long-term stress may be additionally vulnerable

- a parent with no warm, confiding relationship themselves

- a parent who was poorly nourished themselves in emotional terms

- a parent who had a particularly difficult time at the developmental stage which their child has now reached

- a parent with poor knowledge of child development and therefore unclear expectations will need help to learn what it is reasonable to expect of a child and what stimulation and opportunity the child needs

- the parent with significant intellectual limitations who has no support with the parenting tasks

- the parent with significant drug or alcohol dependency which negatively effects their emotional availability

- the parent who themselves has poor problem-solving and planning skills who may be devastated by every setback

- a parent who is caught up in a violent relationship or series of relationships with violent partners.

Absence of community supports

The availability of certain community supports may be invaluable in building resilience and providing some protection for an individual child/young person within their family setting. Particular issues are seen as especially significant:

- the absence of any extended family support; this is particularly exacerbated where there is active disapproval from family members
- poor housing, which places stress on adults and children
- money worries or significant poverty
- a lack of support groups for the parents within their local community with no relief at all for the parent from the strains of the parenting task
- the lack of available early intervention services within the community
- poor mental health diagnosis and treatment of parents' problems or individual child's depression or other psychiatric problems
- racism within the local community where the child is either black or of mixed parentage
- isolation from ethnic community supports which might be preventative in terms of building the strengths of parents, children and young people in combating racism
- unhelpful conflicts within different support systems surrounding any particular family. This is especially unhelpful in situations of abuse and/or neglect where the helping systems may mirror the conflicts within the family.

We see many situations in our practice which may call into question the degree of emotional nurturing available to an individual child within their home setting. We may, for example, observe a parent shouting loudly at a child, or treating them physically in a rough manner. What remains to be explained is the often surprising variability in the effects that this kind of treatment has on individual children. This might lead us to wonder how we can identify most readily those children who may be particularly vulnerable to the negative effects of life's stresses. For example, marital violence, separation, maternal depression, etc.

Research can tell us something about combinations of stresses which are likely to render a particular child more vulnerable. However, in terms of intervention, there is no substitute for detailed, careful observation of the effects of a particular environment and all its influences on a child and a sensitive awareness of that child's experience of their environment and relationships. If we can identify those children who are particularly vulnerable as early as possible, it is likely that we can then focus intervention more precisely, so as to harness any potential for resilience within the child and within his or her close environment.

Activity 4.2

In relation to a specific family with whom you are working:

1. Identify particular vulnerabilities within (a) the child, (b) the family (c) lack of community supports.

2. Can you identify other factors of vulnerability not mentioned?

3. What resilience can you identify (a) in the child, (b) within the family (c) within local community supports?

4. How could they be harnessed to build resilience and protection for this child or young person?

Disability

How might children and young people with disabilities be particularly vulnerable to abuse/neglect? Watson (1989) identifies six factors which may render a child with a disability more at risk of abuse.

CULTURAL FACTORS

The way in which society's prejudices act to discriminate against those who are different may place considerable stress on individual families. This may change the way the family is seen in the community and may lead to rejection and scapegoating of the child.

ABUSE–PROVOKING CHARACTERISTICS

Some children with disabilities have characteristics which place additional stress on parents. For example, aggression, hyperactivity, whining or withdrawal. Moreover, those children who are emotionally disturbed in addition to their original disability may provoke physical abuse through the stresses that their behaviour imposes.

Further, those factors which may draw physical abuse may be present in the behaviour of children with disabilities to an unusual degree and for longer than with non-disabled children. For example, there may be incontinence, violence, poor feeding and sleeping patterns alongside unpredictable behaviour.

EXTRA STRESSES ON CARE GIVERS IN THE FAMILY SETTING

The stress of caring for the child with a disability may be immense for example, because of the lack of sleep, profound and unusual degree of dependency in the child, or physical demands such as incontinence or lengthy feeding processes. Families may feel extremely isolated and may see little progress or indeed little response from the child.

Importantly, the more a child is helpless, the more they are vulnerable to exploitation in all its forms, for example, sexual abuse. Difficulties in communication in the child render them less able to seek help.

INSTITUTIONAL ABUSE

Techniques for behaviour management, alongside medically invasive procedures may be tantamount to abuse for the child with a disability. At times, undue restraint is used or medication is overused.

There may be significant neglect of the social and intellectual development of the child, or failure to allow them choices in the decisions made about their futures. There may be a lack of privacy afforded the child or young person and deprivation of ordinary rights, such as the right to contact with important attachment figures.

LACK OF TREATMENT OR OPPORTUNITY TO LEARN

These factors may constitute neglect of the child which is in itself a form of abuse. For example, Tom was 18 months old and had been abandoned in hospital by his parents. They had been told that he had several severe physical disabilities alongside numerous intellectual impairments. He was not expected to live and was left in the hospital for more than 12 months.

However, he did survive and was ultimately placed in a foster home. In this environment, it became apparent that he had the capacity, not only for enjoyment of adult and peer contact, but also a considerable ability to learn. Ultimately, although his parents were not able to care for him themselves, Tom was placed with an adoptive family who were happy for his parents to maintain contact. Additionally, when his mobility increased, largely as a result of the stimulation he received, medical staff reviewed their decisions to offer operative procedures which increased Tom's mobility and most significantly, his ability to communicate.

THE DILEMMAS OF THE PARTICULAR DISABILITY

Children with particular disabilities, for example blindness or deafness, may be especially vulnerable to abuse because of problems in identifying a perpetrator. Any kind of communication difficulty is likely to increase vulnerability.

Different stages of development are likely to leave the child open to particular forms of abuse, for example, the teenager who requires intimate physical care may be especially vulnerable.

How can we help?

Watson (1989) outlines two aims:

1. protection

2. empowerment.

He identifies three means by which these two aims may be achieved.

COMMUNICATION

This issue is critical in terms of detection, teaching, counselling or support to children who have special needs. The child may or may not have the capacity to use all of their speech. Any communication may need to be consolidated by the use of concrete images.

The skill is determining how this child communicates and the particular mode of communication with which the child is most skilled and comfortable. Therefore, the principles of good assessment of any child hold true for work with children with disabilities. We need the expertise of those particularly skilled in work with children with a range of communication problems in order to facilitate our understanding of the individual child's communications.

OPENNESS

The care and protection of the child with disabilities may well raise sensitive and difficult issues. The child is more likely to be kept safe if there is a network of people with whom the child has contact. It is essential that they communicate with one another and plan the care of the child in an open way, consulting with the child themselves. The involvement of friends, or links with self-help groups, or indeed the use of an individual who acts as advocate for the young person, may be additionally helpful in providing a protective environment for the child which is preventative of abuse.

EDUCATION

Particular attention needs to be paid to ways in which the individual child may be helped to learn. This should include issues such as sexual development, which may need to be presented in a rather different way, as the child with the disability often does not have access to learning processes available to non-disabled children, both formal and informal. Additionally, it is helpful to be clear that it may well be possible to teach the child about safety from potential abuse. Although the methods may have to be very specific, the idea of using normal teaching routines to help children seek help, is sound (Elliott 1995).

Experiences of separation and loss

Experiences of separation and loss are, as we know, very much part of human experience as even developmental progress involves, not only gains, but also losses associated with what is known and familiar. Some losses are inevitable in the course of development in our culture, e.g. leaving home as a five-year-old to go to school, leaving primary school to move on to secondary school. However, those children whom we are meeting daily in our practice have often been subjected to multiple separations from, and sometimes the permanent loss of, those people who are of greatest significance in their lives. Thus their sense of a 'secure base', however tenuous, is threatened. Some children are, of course, more vulnerable to the effects of separation than others and it is our assessment of the potential or actual *effect* on an individual child or adolescent which informs our interventions. For example, a

---

Activity 4.3

Considering one child under five with a recognised or likely disability:

1. How far do you regard the network of support has been clearly made available to the family?

2. What additional local support groups and key professional services might be offered to build family strength in coping with the demands of the child's special needs?

---

child who is sensitised to separations and anxiously attached to carers may need particularly thorough preparation for a move away from home.

The way in which we understand children's experience of loss will shape not only any preparation for an anticipated move, but also vital elements of reparative care they may need following planned or unpredicted separations.

In reflecting on separation and loss we shall address a number of areas which may be of significance, namely:

- understanding the process of grieving in children

- considering key variables which may affect a particular child's adjustment and recovery

- an awareness of the psychological tasks which confront the child or adolescent

- reflection on the additional tasks facing children who have been placed apart from their families of origin.

Understanding the process of grieving in children and adolescents

Jewett (1984) explores in some detail the normal healthy process of grieving in children. In many ways this parallels the experience of adults, one obvious key difference being that children at different ages will have varying capacities to process and understand the experience of separation and loss. The three key stages of grieving explored by Jewett may be summarised broadly as follows.

First stage: early grief

SHOCK AND NUMBING

She describes the typical emotional withdrawal of the child which is often accompanied by somewhat mechanical behaviour, as if the child is behaving without deliberate intention but almost on 'automatic pilot'. The third characteristic behaviour she notes is the possible outburst of acute panic in the child. This might show itself as apparently unprovoked signs of anxiety with an acute need for immediate reassurance.

ALARM

Behavioural reactions which commonly accompany this feeling in the child are numerous bodily reactions including an increased heart rate, signs of tension, sweating and other reactions associated with anxiety, including the relaxation of bowel and bladder functions leading to bed wetting and soiling on occasions.

Typically at this stage also many children find it hard to sleep and there is frequently a characteristic, unusual proneness to infection. Fearful behaviour especially at night and generalised increased anxiety may become apparent at this stage.

Other typical signs of distress and anxiety including nail biting and the child picking at his/herself or pulling out hair are not unusual.

DENIAL AND DISBELIEF

It is very common at this stage of grieving for children to feel a need to deny the loss of the loved one. Commonly this is accompanied by a refusal to acknowledge the facts of the loss. Equally the child may deny the feelings accompanying the loss, for example it's not at all unusual for a child to say 'I don't care about him/her anyway' or 'I don't want to go home'. Frequently we may hear the child making rejecting or deprecating statements concerning the lost attachment figure and it is important for practitioners to be aware that this is very typical at this stage of grieving and there may be a significant change in the child's feelings at later stages of the grieving process.

Some children refuse to believe that the lost person is no longer available to them. For example, one child commented following separation from home circumstances of extreme rejection from her parents 'I'm going home tomorrow, my mum wants me home'. Many children show signs of extreme over-activity as if they need to keep physically active in order to make sure that the painful feelings are kept at bay.

BARGAINING

A typical feature of the behaviour of children separated in the care process is that of *bargaining*. In their struggle to cope with the pain of the loss, the child may well begin to construct ways of thinking which protect them from painful feelings and act against the powerlessness which characterises the grieving process. For example, commonly children encountered in the care system go through a process of constructing ways of thinking to defend themselves against the reality of the separation. For example, a child might think 'if only I hadn't been naughty/difficult I would not have been separated and if I am good, I can return'. Therefore bargaining as a form of denial can lead to or reinforce existing self-blame and therefore can also impact on the self-image of the child.

SUPPORTING A CHILD IN THE EARLY STAGES OF GRIEVING A LOSS OR SEPARATION

Children and young people need a great deal of comfort at this stage of the grieving process and a real recognition by carers that something very significant has happened for them. If we see denial in the early stages as an understandable, and indeed healthy, part of the grieving process and if we can move close to the child to comfort and reassure them, there is every chance that they will progress to the next stage of the grieving process.

However, some children we meet in our practice can get stuck at this stage and it may well be helpful to try to tune in to the way in which the child is beginning to make sense of the loss in terms of the bargaining process and the way they explain to themselves, explicitly or by implication, the part they have played in the separation. Supporting the child and clarifying misconceptions about the reasons for the separation and teasing out a realistic picture of the child's involvement can prevent later difficulties in moving towards the acute stage of grieving.

It is not uncommon to meet children who remain fixed at this stage of the grieving process in relation to a specific loss or separation. These children may need much more help in moving into the next stage of grieving. For example, we may meet a child who one week will be acknowledging the separation and the reality of the loss, and only the following week denying that anything significant has happened. If the denial persists over weeks and months, the child is likely to need more active support from the worker and/or parents and carers in order to help them take on the painful reality of the experience. Jewett (1984) explores a range of methods which practitioners might use to begin to talk with the child or young person about their experience. She stresses that the most critical element is the environment of care within which there is recognition that there is nothing more important to the child than the acknowledgement of the feelings around the loss.

Second stage: acute grief

This is the phase in which many of the most powerful feelings about the loss begin to come to the surface. The first part of this phase is often characterised by elements of yearning and pining in the child. We often see children also searching for the lost person and wishing for the restitution of the relationship.

This stage is characterised by a conflict between the need to let go of the person and a wish to hold on to the relationship. This can be very tiring for children and they are frequently emotionally labile at this stage. These mixed feelings can cause not only exhaustion and fractiousness in the child but also in some children, regression to an earlier stage of development.

Some children may become aware of an element of relief if the pre-separation experience has been very difficult for them. However, it is all too easy for practitioners to assume, for example, when working with a child who has been severely abused, that the ceasing of the abuse is the most important factor for the child. The child's experience may be very different, and the experience of separation may be the worst pain that the child could think of in terms of a consequence of action by social workers or other professionals. This can be very complicated in cases of abuse where a child has decided to disclose, in a purposeful fashion, and may explain why, once the separation has become apparent, they regret and begin to retract the disclosure.

Some children literally search physically for their lost loved one and may even return to a previous home. They may appear completely preoccupied with the loved person and imagine that they see them in a crowd in the street. There is frequently a sense of suspension of the child's ordinary activities whilst he or she waits for the restoration of the lost person. This is often accompanied by extreme restlessness.

We see in the middle of this stage of grieving the emergence of strong feelings. Some of the commonest feelings that children experience when grieving a loss are sadness, anger, guilt and shame. The expression of these feelings may be direct or indirect and the child/young person may appear overwhelmed by these feelings at times. There may be no apparent trigger to outbursts of aggression or sadness and commonly it may be more acceptable in some cultures than others to express either sadness or anger. There may be great pressure on a young person, for example, not to reveal the vulnerability implied by tearfulness and open expressions of sadness. It may be much more acceptable in the young person's culture to express anger. Therefore, if this is taken at face value, the young person may experience very little relief over time from the expression of anger and adults need to be sensitive to the possibility that other, commonly conflicting, feelings may lie underneath.

Jewett (1984) stressed that it is often the mixed feelings that children have about an experience of separation or loss which complicates the grieving process.

Following, or even accompanying, this expression of powerful feelings comes a sense of disorganisation in the child's emotional life. They often appear to lack energy, to be completely unfocused in their activities and to exhibit an atypical lack of concentration. They may find it very difficult, for example, to retain any information at school and may in fact experience the loss of familiar skills which they thought they had mastered. This can be extremely frightening not only to a young child but also to an adolescent, and workers and parents can help by being sensitive to the fear that this temporary loss of competence engenders in the child or young person.

Children at this stage of grieving often find it very difficult to retain information effectively and may in fact lose hold of the detail of the reality of events. It may well be helpful at this stage, not only to encourage in a very active way the expression of feelings, but also to check out once again the child's perception of the process of events. This is a good opportunity to clarify the child's understanding and to prevent potential long-standing problems of guilt or self-blame.

DESPAIR

This can be the most frightening stage of grieving in the child and for the adult working with them. The child may exhibit complete loss of interest in everyday life and a strong pessimism about the future. This is the stage at which a child may be vulnerable to suicidal thoughts and it is important to tune in to adolescents in particular as they may be especially prone to para-suicide attempts, or indeed suicide at this stage.

The loss of energy in the child and the feelings of hopelessness may be very difficult for adults to tolerate. This may be particularly true if the child remains in a household where other family members have very different feelings about the loss, or indeed are at a different stage in the grieving process. A child or young person is especially vulnerable to unresolved grief if their own feelings are denied by those on whom they are dependent for their care. For example, it can be very difficult for a child who has lost an adult who is perhaps significant for them whilst being hated or rejected by the child's parent.

At this very painful stage, there are additional opportunities for parents or carers to establish a very close, caring link with the child. Comfort and reassurance are once again necessary at this stage as with the very early stages of grieving. Time needs to be allowed for the child or young person to begin to recover their energies at their own pace.

REORGANISATION

Gradually the child begins to emerge from the grieving process and to experience a slight increase in self-control. The emotional energy returns which allows the child to begin to invest in relationships and to let go of the preoccupation with the loss. This then allows the child to begin to look to the future and sets the stage for the integration of the loss and grief.

Third stage: integration of loss and grief

When the child's energy returns this may be very slow but we may notice the recovery in increased physical energy or psychological robustness. Gradually the child will begin to feel better about themselves and to be able to replace the pain of the extreme loss with a more reflective attitude. It then becomes possible to help the child to concentrate on regaining competence and mastery in the current setting, e.g. school and clubs or hobbies, and to begin to contemplate looking towards the future.

This is a crucial chance for parents or carers to offer valuable support to the child in restructuring their activities and regaining their skills. If this is accompanied by an acknowledgement that grieving is important emotional work for children and they are offered support in regaining lost ground, there is every chance that the child will make a good recovery and also that the existing attachments with the supportive adults may be significantly strengthened.

Timing

The time it takes a child or young person to go through the grieving process varies greatly in individual children as it does in adults. We need to be particularly aware of children who have not had the benefit of any emotional support in their grieving. They may take much longer to move through the stages of grieving or may indeed be 'stuck' at one stage.

For example, some children, because they are not supported by adults, may continue to deny the reality of the loss or may appear to have begun to experience the strong feelings associated with the acute phase only to return to denial as a form of protection from the painful feelings.

Lack of positive integration

Any one or more of the following signs in behaviour indicate that a child may be struggling with unresolved feelings about an important loss:

- prolonged anger and depression
- an inability to express feelings – helplessness, giving up
- lack of ability to become involved with others
- blocked development
- unusual vulnerability to new separations
- difficult to control
- marked impairment of self-esteem
- discounting of self and others
- destructive behaviour towards self and others.

Practice point

Many of the children we work with, either in their own homes or in substitute care, have had repeated, unpredicted experiences of separation from loved ones. Some children and young people have complex feelings of loss. Frequently at the time of the loss, they have not been offered the kind of emotional support which would help them experience the grief process in a healthy way. Typically, we might find they have come 'stuck' at one particular stage of the grieving process, unable to progress further without additional support.

Further losses, in the context of existing unresolved losses may only serve to confirm this survival strategy. However, if we are aware of significant losses in the past, new losses may represent an opportunity to support the child to reflect and express confusions and misperceptions of previous losses.

Activity 4.4

Consider a child with whom you are working who has experienced a significant loss, either recently or in the past. Reflect on the following:

1. Are you able to describe the process of grieving experienced by this child, including specific behavioural reactions?

2. Maybe this child has become stuck at a particular point in the grieving process; if so, at what stage?

3. Who is available in their close environment who may offer support?

Key variables affecting recovery from loss

Particularly significant variables have been identified by Fahlberg (1994) as potentially relevant in affecting the nature and extent of difficulty in resolving an individual loss for a particular child or young person.

AGE AND STAGE OF DEVELOPMENT

For example, very young children are especially vulnerable to feelings of self-blame following a loss or a separation. However, many adolescents also display clear signs of having internalised the responsibility for losses they have experienced.

THE NATURE OF THE CHILD'S ATTACHMENT TO PARENTS/CARERS

Generally speaking, the more secure the attachment, the more receptive the child will be to accepting comfort following a loss. Because the child has experienced emotional support and response he/she is more likely to believe that adults can offer comfort. Conversely, the child who has rather ambivalent relationships may be not only less trusting of the availability of support but also more burdened with complex, mixed feelings about the lost attachment figure.

THE NATURE AND DEGREE OF BONDING

Commonly experiences of separation are more challenging for children whose parents have bonded with them less than securely. The child may for example be 'anxiously attached' (see Chapter 2) and therefore particularly preoccupied with the loss of the attachment figure.

THE CHILD'S PERCEPTION OF THE REASONS FOR SEPARATION

The separation of children from parents who have resisted reception into care may be more difficult to resolve, engendering a confusing and preoccupying conflict of loyalties.

THE DEGREE OF EMOTIONAL NURTURING AVAILABLE IN THE ENVIRONMENT THE CHILD IS LEAVING

The poorer the quality of emotional nurturing available to the child in their family setting, the more support they are likely to need following that separation. This is likely to shape the child's expectations of, and indeed ability to make use of, additional support in the new setting.

THE PARTING MESSAGE

Children may be preoccupied for many years with the parting message given to them by important attachment figures. This may be true despite nothing having been said to the child. A child may read a particular parting message into the circumstances surrounding the separation; for example, a child whose parent kills themselves may believe that this action in itself constitutes a message to the child that they were not sufficiently lovable to make the adult's life worthwhile.

THE POST-SEPARATION ENVIRONMENT AND DEGREE OF EMOTIONAL NURTURING AVAILABLE

Much can be offered to individual children and adolescents following a separation which may contribute to their healthy recovery from the loss. This may be particularly true for children who have experienced numerous unpredicted separations with no opportunity to grieve at the time.

THE CHILD'S TEMPERAMENT

The individual child's temperament and particular vulnerability or resilience to life stresses will shape their capacity to face and survive healthily the current separation, and individual children vary considerably in their style of response to losses.

THE SUPPORT AVAILABLE TO THE CHILD IN DEVELOPING A COHERENT STORY

The life story approach is only one example of a range of techniques used in direct work with children and young people to help them to clarify their misperceptions about losses and build a coherent understanding of the

---

Activity 4.5

Thinking of a child you know who has recently suffered a loss:

1. Do you recognise any of the above signs in their thinking and/or behaviour?

2. What support has or might be offered to help the child or young person gain healthy information of the experience?

---

process of their lives. The emphasis in effective work on the 'coherent story' is helping the child to express, identify, name and direct feelings about the experience.

AVAILABLE CONTINUITY OF RELATIONSHIPS OR ENVIRONMENT

Following a traumatic loss, practitioners often attempt to maintain as much continuity in the child's environment as possible. The availability of attachment figures in supporting the child after the separation may well be critical in facilitating healthy grieving.

Rutter and Rutter (1993) argue that in order to understand the effects of loss and to develop effective modes of intervention, it is important to examine specific features which may modify grief reactions. They argue that four particular factors would appear to make things more difficult for children:

1. an ambivalent or unduly dependent relationship with the person who is lost (i.e., where the mixed feelings experienced by the child complicates the grieving process)

2. an unexpected or untimely death

3. the coincidence of the death with other stresses or crises, for example, family discord or loss of employment

4. the experience of previous losses especially when they have been incompletely resolved.

Conversely, they argue there are four features which seem to be associated with less disturbed grief reactions:

1. the availability and effective use of social support from family friends and others

2. the re-establishment of life patterns

3. the development of new intimate relationships

4. the provision of crisis intervention.

Rutter and Rutter (1993) argue additionally that consideration of the key factors involve two interlinked components: (1) the loss of a loved one, and (2) the lack of a love relationship. The pain of the former is, they argue, intensified by the fact that it leads to the latter. Therefore the presence of one or more close confiding relationships and the development of a new love relationship help to mitigate the grief.

The psychological tasks which confront the child or adolescent

Goldman (1994) identifies four critical tasks in the child's psychological adjustment to loss:

UNDERSTANDING

This is the first psychological task of dealing with loss. Children need to make sense of the experience. This is particularly true of a death and we need to remember that children's understanding of death changes as they develop. Children perceive death differently at various childhood stages and their perception has a predictable influence on their grieving. Young children in particular are vulnerable to misunderstanding losses.

Understanding affected by magical thinking

Young children feel responsible for what happens in the world around them. Therefore when a child experiences a loss, not only a death or significant separation, they commonly believe that they have caused the loss themselves. If not helped to understand the circumstances they may live with overwhelming guilt for many years to come.

Understanding blocked by common clichés

Common clichés and euphemisms can interrupt the grief process. We need to give honest answers to questions about loss, not only death, using simple and direct responses. Facts need to be presented accurately. Children will find out in time, and telling the truth now will create an atmosphere of trust and confidence. We have to be careful how we explain loss, as young children often take and believe what we say literally, for example:

- Albert 'lost' his mother
- Dad 'went on a long trip'
- it is God's will that the important person died
- the lost person 'went to sleep' last night

It is obvious the ways in which children can misunderstand these kinds of statements, taking them literally because at this stage of development they are concrete thinkers.

GRIEVING

Grieving is the second psychological task for children who have experienced a significant loss. Anger as well as grief must be dealt with and many times anger is less acceptable to parents, schools and friends. Children's grieving is an ongoing process, often continued and reworked through to adolescence.

Behavioural symptoms

Symptoms include sleeplessness, loss of appetite, crying, nightmares, dreams of the lost person, sighing, listlessness, absent-mindedness, clinging, over-activity, withdrawal from friends, verbal attacks on others, fighting, extreme quietness, bed wetting, excessive touching and excessive hugging.

Thought patterns

They may show an inability to concentrate, preoccupation, difficulty in making a decision, self-destructive thoughts, low view of themselves, confusion and disbelief.

Feelings

Feelings include anger, guilt, sadness, mood swings, depression, hysteria, relief, helplessness, fear, loneliness, anxiety, rage, intense emotions and feeling unreal.

Physical symptoms

Physical symptoms include headaches, fatigue, shortness of breath, dry mouth, dizziness, pounding heart, hot or cold flushes, heaviness of body, sensitive skin, increased illness, empty feeling in body, tightness in chest, muscle weakness, tightness in throat and stomach aches.

COMMEMORATING

This is the third task of grieving. Children need to establish ways to remember the person they have lost. It is important to find formal and informal ways of commemorating the significant person. The child's own creative ideas are an essential part of this process. For example photographs, videos and other personal mementoes can be invaluable in keeping alive for the child their memories of the lost person.

Thinking again of a particular child, how might you help them to remember and commemorate the lost person/place by, e.g., use of rituals, photographs, drawings, tapes, posters?

GOING ON

The last psychological task for children experiencing significant loss is one that emphasises looking forward to the future. Children can begin to risk loving again and enjoying life. This does not mean forgetting the person who has gone; it means developing a readiness to participate once again. Sometimes it signals the release of some deep guilt that is often felt, especially by young children.

Summary

Understanding, grieving, commemorating, and going on are important parts of a child's processing of loss and change. Listening to the communications from the child about the loss is often helpful. Recognising these tasks can create a picture of where the child is in the grieving process. Caring adults can see if the child is stuck in one particular task and help him or her to work with the grief.

Our intervention may be more effective if we use an analysis of the degree to which these tasks have been completed to inform a focus on creating opportunities for these missed areas to be addressed: for example, by creating a personal ritual within which a child can commemorate their loss of someone important.

Additional tasks facing children who have been placed apart from their birth families

Littner (1975) identifies the particular vulnerability of this group, facing as they do unusual stress, often repeatedly through failed rehabilitation attempts, he describes four forms of psychological scarring that often come from separation and placement:

1. the freezing of personality development

2. excessive mistrust of people, based on the expectation that love is inevitably followed by loss

3. self-defeating behaviour (e.g., driving carers to reject; what the child most fears, they appear forced to provoke)

4. in the longer term, a tendency to repeat with one's own children the separation scenarios of the past (e.g., the adopted child who then, as an adolescent, has a baby adopted in impossible circumstances).

Littner sees the tasks of the placed child in four phases.

MASTERING THE FEELING AROUSED BY SEPARATION FROM OWN PARENTS

These feelings may be very complex depending on the nature of the child's attachment relationship, the nature and degree of bonding from parents and the circumstances of the separation.

MASTERING FEELINGS AROUSED BY PLACEMENT WITH NEW FAMILY

The new placement may trigger painful memories of family life and arouse poignant feelings in the child. Some children are more ready and able than others to accept support with what are often complex mixed feelings; for example, guilt and relief.

DEALING WITH SUBSEQUENT SEPARATION FROM NEW PARENTS

Having already experienced a highly significant separation, these children are vulnerable to difficulty in dealing with even brief subsequent separations from their new carers. For example, they may become very clingy when separation is threatened or withdraw emotionally in order to protect themselves from pain.

MASTERING THE THREAT OF CLOSENESS TO THEM

The particular pattern of attachment experienced by the child in relation to key attachment figures is likely to determine the degree to which closeness and intimacy with new carers is experienced as threatening. Downes (1992) explores ways in which substitute carers of adolescents can promote increased feelings of trust in children who have had distorted or unhealthy early attachment experiences.

Effective purposeful contact as an aid to healthy adaptation

A useful summary of the benefits of maintaining contact with members of the birth family for children separated for whatever reason, principally in local authority accommodation, can be found in DoH (1991).

In order to maximise the benefits of contact for each individual child, it is most helpful to focus on the *purposes* of the contact. Well-planned and well-managed contacts can maximise the possibility of the earliest possible successful return home for the child. As most children who are in out-of-home placements are likely to return home, maintaining effective contact is of prime significance in planning for their care and well-being.

Even for those children who are unable to return home, work which actively supports their positive contact with their birth families can be of significant long-term benefit.

Exploring the purposes of contact

Fahlberg suggests that there may be several clear purposes behind the structuring of contact arrangements for children separated from both parents in local authority accommodation, either in foster or residential care.

ASSESSMENT

Particularly at the early stages of work with a family, it may be important to structure contact in order to build a picture of the relationships which exist between parents, siblings, extended family and a child in order to assess the potential for rehabilitation. Well-managed contact can facilitate an assessment of the nature of the child's significant attachment relationships and this can shape the focus of future work.

SEPARATION WORK

It may well be that contact can be used to help a child and/or the adults to work towards an effective separation. It may also be important to facilitate the child's grieving work on previous losses or changes within the family system in order to facilitate later reintegration. This can help to build a 'coherent story' for the child which may be protective to their emotional well-being in the long term, whether or not they return home.

PLANNED FAMILY WORK

It may well be that contact sessions can be used purposefully to involve the child with the whole or part of the family system in order to work on particular identified family difficulties. Family systems therapists favour the involvement of children directly, often in whole family sessions, so as to gain a clear picture of the role that the child takes within the family. This may be particularly helpful in work with the child who is, for example, carrying distress for other family members or other unexpressed feelings such as anger, and particularly for the child who is scapegoated.

REINTEGRATION INTO THE FAMILY

Contact may at a particular time be focused on preparation for the child's return to the family unit. For the child who has been away from home for any considerable period, it may be that there have been changes within the family. These can be acknowledged and explored in family contact sessions, and the family can then renegotiate room for the separated child. If this is managed in a planned and sensible way, problems should emerge more clearly and effective intervention is then easier.

HELPING WITH IDENTITY FORMATION

For children who are living separately from their families, their developmental tasks can be particularly complicated. The key area is the formation of a secure identity: in other words, answers to the questions 'who am I?'; 'why am I here?'; 'who am I like?'; 'what will I be and what will I do?'. Even for those children permanently separated from their families, contact which is clearly focused on meeting this purpose can benefit the child in the longer term. The experience of direct contact rather than a hazy idealised picture of the parents can facilitate secure identity formation, particularly in adolescence.

SHARING INFORMATION

Additionally, for those children separated permanently from their families, it may be important at particular stages of the child's development to reconnect with family members, even if contact has been lost, in order to clarify misperceptions about the past, reasons for separations, to reallocate responsibility for negative life events. It is possible then also for the child to be updated in terms of changes in the family structure.

TRANSFERRING GAINS IN BEHAVIOUR

In order to maximise the possibility of a successful return home for a separated child, it may be very important to use family contact time to work at identifying, confirming and transferring established gains in behaviour from the substitute care setting. The more explicitly families are helped to understand what changes have occurred, and how these have been achieved, the more readily they may be able to take on these gains and transfer them to the home setting.

WORK ON LOYALTY ISSUES

Commonly, children who are separated from their families feel bound up in conflicts of loyalty. It may be of particular value when working with parents in direct contact with their child to release the child from these conflicts where possible. Frequently, the child is receiving covert as well as explicit messages from birth family members that they do not have permission to be in their placement and to do well. Releasing the child from this stress, even minimally, can maximise the child's potential in using the substitute placement, whether residential or foster care.

ATTACHMENT WORK

Underlying this purpose in the contact may be the effective maintenance of existing, significant relationships for the child and communicating the continuing concern of significant people in the child's life. The child may be building relationships with new family members or renewing a key link with previous carers. Clear purposeful contact can be a major benefit in preparing a child to maintain and transfer attachments.

Clarifying the purpose of the contact often helps to shape decisions as to where, when and how the contact should happen in order to meet the interests of the child. It is important to note however that the developing child may have a greater potential for emotional health than a parent, therefore we need to be continually aware of the child's changing needs for contact (Hess and Proch 1993).

Activity 4.6

Think of a child or young person separated from their family in an out-of-home placement.

1. What are the precise arrangements for contact?

2. Does the frequency and shape of the contact reflect the purposes it is intended to serve within the context of the plans for the child or young person?

3. What are the purpose/s of contact with attachment figures whether direct or indirect contact?

Important aspects of putting together a plan for contact

Hess and Proch (1993) lead out key elements of the visiting plan which need to be considered and reassessed as the placement unfolds. The visiting plan should reflect the purpose of contact and should specify the following:

- frequency, venue and length of scheduled visits
- if and how visits are to be supervised
- who is to participate in the visits
- tasks that are to be accomplished during visits
- agency and parental responsibilities related to visits. (p.29)

It is important to remember to brief in full any supervisor of contact. Are they to be concerned, for example, merely with the safety of the child, or primarily with the careful observation of interaction. If the latter is the case, what aspects will guide and structure the supervisors' assessment?

Contact after divorce and separation or after abuse
DOMESTIC VIOLENCE AND CHILD CONTACT

One particularly difficult area of work in terms of maintaining contact between children and their separated parents is that involved in the structuring of contact after domestic violence. Hester and Radford (1992, 1996; Hester and Pearson 1993) explore the impact of domestic violence on the negotiation of contact arrangements for children after parents have divorced or separated.

Their observations result from a comprehensive study in Britain and Denmark. Two central issues in this research have been the safety of women who have experienced violent treatment from their male ex-partners and concerns for the welfare of their children.

Of significant concern from the study was the absence of clear linking between the safety of women and the safety of their children in the professional plans of organising contact between children and their separated parents. Underlining these worries appears to be a lack of clarity in terms of the links between domestic violence and child welfare.

The fear is that children may well suffer emotionally and psychologically from having lived in a violent situation and additionally that the whole process of establishing arrangements for contact in these circumstances is more complex and may be fraught with risks for the mother and for the child.

They sum up their views in the following three points.

1. The lack of regard for women's safety amongst professionals and legal personnel, and the effect of this on the welfare of women and children.

2. The misguided belief of professionals and advisors that to face visiting contact with an abusive father is *always* in the best interests of a child.

3. The difficulties which professionals and advisors have in considering the actual, rather than hypothetical, needs and views of a particular child. (p.103)

They argue that professionals need to consider whether or not direct contact with the absent parent, following domestic violence, can necessarily be assumed always to be in the child's best interest. In fact, their observation is that rather than the child's' interest being paramount, it might appear from their recent research that it is contact that is now viewed as paramount.

Not only may the mother be at risk of further violence or intimidation directly from the abusive ex-partner, but there may be significant risks to the children themselves within the contact arrangements. These risks may not only include the possible kidnapping of the child but also physical, sexual or emotional abuse during contact visits.

A further risk may be the child either witnessing or being implicated in the further violence or abuse of the mother. It is argued that, even in cases where physical or sexual abuse of a child has been established, there was a worrying tendency on the part of those structuring contact with a father to challenge the child's reluctance to see him and structuring arrangements which potentially leave the child additionally at risk. Many of these arrangements involve court welfare officers and their safe management is dependent upon the level of awareness and a degree of understanding of domestic violence the individual professional holds.

Furthermore, the availability of advice and support for women and their children in terms of listening to their worries and concerns is very uneven. Mama (1989) notes that the availability of resources and legal advice are especially critical for black women as institutionalised racism in the provision of such services leaves these women particularly vulnerable in contact arrangements.

The Report of the Association of Chief Officers of Probation (ACOP 1992) makes recommendations for probation officers and court welfare officers. It suggests that workers:

- Take domestic violence into account by looking carefully for evidence of abuse and by asking women about their past histories.

- Advise victims of domestic violence that they have the right not to attend joint meetings.

- Employ techniques of conflict management, rather than mediation. (Hester and Radford 1996, p.113)

The conclusion from the research was that this report had had little effect on practice by 1993.

The provision of effective supervision for contact in these circumstances can be problematic. For example, accommodation may be scarce, and the resources to provide effect supervision, not available. For children who speak two languages and who come from violent homes, it may be vital to ensure that supervisors of the contact can understand what is being said to the child in contact in order to prevent emotional abuse, or manipulation of the child.

Of real importance is the way in which children's views are heard in relation to organising contact. In this context ascertaining the child's wishes becomes a very complex task and takes time. Hester and Radford (1996) note:

consideration needs to be given to what children actually say, to what they do not say, to what they indicate non verbally, and to whether they are under any undue pressures to voice a certain opinion. Children may need some time to say what they really want. (p.115)

In circumstances of domestic violence it will be important that the practitioner is aware of the position of the child in relation to any violence, and to consider the age and stage of the child and that parent's ability to keep the child's needs for protection in 'mind' in the context of the visits may vary.

The authors advocate the availability over time of a sensitive practitioner trained in communicating with children in circumstances of domestic violence and/or child abuse so that a relationship of trust can be developed with the child through which a child's changing needs and wishes for direct contact with the absent parent can be monitored and evaluated with care.

Practice points

- Practitioners need to be aware of the inter-relatedness of domestic violence and child abuse. (Kelly 1994)

- Children may not initially be able to speak about what they want and need time to develop a relationship with an adult with regard to their wishes.

- Some women, having been in a powerless position in a very violent relationship may need help and time to see the risks for the children.

- Women should be listened to about their wishes and asked about their experience of violence as they may not volunteer this information.

- The meetings, and especially the handover, need to be managed in a way which protects the woman and her child.

- As in other circumstances, ask the questions:

  - why is the contact happening?

  - will it/can it be safe and beneficial for the child, both are important in this context.

- Concerns about safety *must* inform the careful planning of effective supervision of contact where this is thought necessary.

- Black women, or those from other minority groups, are especially vulnerable where there is ignorance of their particular predicament and where resources available to them are likely to be meagre.

- Focusing on the predicament of the child as well as that of the child's mother in relation to past experience of proven abuse, will be crucial in informing:

  - whether or not face to face contact is in the child's interest

- the nature of support which will need to be made available if it is to be safe for the child.

- Some abused children, still living at home, need to be protected from the possibility of further abuse or distress occasioned by contact with the abuser.

Smith (1995) suggests:

> We must have clearer guidelines on the exceptions to the rules of good practice which promote contact. Recognition of the different situations in which children enter the care system is needed. Often the child's history of abuse is such that continued contact is not in the child's best interest and could possibly be dangerous. (p.98)

She adds a note of caution in the context of the broadest assumptions that generally speaking, practitioners should be working to preserve family links. In discussing what is helpful to children who have had abusive experiences, she argues:

> We need to ensure that we try to promote healthy attachments, to disrupt previously unhealthy attachments (by which I mean very sexualised and abusive contact) and to facilitate the transformation of unhealthy attachment into healthy ones. (p.98)

She argues caution in promoting contact where children in these circumstances are anxious about a parent still at home, as this can sometimes interrupt the child's recovery and reinforce the unhelpful pattern within the family of the child parenting the parents.

In summary, it is vital when practitioners are involved in considerations of this kind, that care is taken to build a trusting relationship with the child in order to establish their wishes in very difficult circumstances and to do this with sensitivity to the child's particular predicament.

Childhood depression: The relevance of attribution theory

Zimmerman (1988) explores the significance of understanding processes at work in children who have experienced many moves and losses and who frequently manifest symptoms of childhood depression. Although her article focuses on working with foster children in a care setting, there are useful ideas in her theoretical formulation which may be adapted to work with parents as well as with substitute carers. Zimmerman explores the connection between repeated experiences of moves and separations beyond the child's control with the phenomenon of 'learned helplessness'. The learned help-lessness theory was first explored by Seligman and Peterson (1986) and was derived from animal learning research in which dogs were subjected to electric shocks. When the dogs were subjected to repeated shocks, initially with no possibility of escape, they became more and more passive in the face of the shock stimulus. Thereafter, when means of escape were available, the dogs did not take advantage of them. In more recent research with human beings, the model has been developed to attribute depression to the perception of an inability to influence outcomes in one's life or the inability to avoid negative outcomes. In addition, this theory takes into account the individual person's interpretation of the causes of the uncontrollable event.

Developmental implications

The model explores three explanatory dimensions which an individual must face when dealing with either positive or negative events in order to explain the cause of those events.

The first concerns whether the cause is internal or external to the person, that is, whether the cause is due to something about the person or their behaviour or about the situation and other people.

The second dimension concerns the persistence of the cause, whether it is stable or unstable. For example, in the stable explanation, the cause is seen as continuing over time, while in the unstable explanation the cause is viewed as transient.

The third dimension deals with how pervasive the effect might be; in other words, how many outcomes the cause will affect. It may be thought to affect a variety of consequences, i.e. the global explanation, or it may be thought to affect just one outcome, i.e. the specific explanation.

Where a child is thought to believe that the cause of the negative event lies with themselves, i.e. is internal, this pattern of thinking is believed to lead to a loss of self-esteem. Where the explanation focuses on an external source of bad events, the individual is more likely to feel anger towards the external source. The combination of interpretations across these three dimensions which is believed to be most often associated with depression in individuals is that of an internal, stable, global explanation, i.e. 'it's my fault, it's going to last forever, and it's going to affect everything I do' (Petersen and Seligman 1985).

This style of thinking associated with depression has also been confirmed to exist in children. Rutter, Tizard and Reads (1986) found that depressed children aged eight and over often have an attributional style in which bad events are seen as caused by internal, stable, global reasons. Good events, however, are seen as external, caused by other people, unstable, unreliable, and specific to one event, not to be generalised to events in the future.

Children in foster care often develop patterns of thinking which mirror these patterns. Zimmerman argues that depression in foster children is often an overlooked explanation for behavioural problems.

Very often, behavioural and emotional problems are seen as isolated entities resulting from poor early training or from the effects of separation. An undue focus on the behaviours themselves can lead to a failure to assess the whole child and to a failure to look for emotional cognitive, motivational or somatic components that would serve to confirm a diagnosis of depression.

Furthermore, this kind of focus can also lead to a failure to recognise, and attempt to alter, the environmental factors inherent in the care situation which promote feelings of helplessness and depression. Often these children may not view themselves as responsible for any action or able to produce any good effect. They may additionally hold themselves responsible for events which, in reality, could have had little to do with them. Zimmerman argues (1988) 'These cognitive distortions in turn limits their interpersonal problem solving skills and impair their ability to learn from new experiences' (p.43)

Practice point

Children need help to reflect on what consequences, both good and bad, can realistically be linked with their own behaviour and what can be attributed to other people's behaviour or to particular circumstances. This kind of sifting out also needs to be done in relation to time dimension, i.e., confirming that what happened in the past but doesn't necessarily have to happen in the future. Additionally, help needs to be offered in relation to the pervasiveness of effects, the fact that things happen in specific contexts but are not globalised.

In day-to-day care the child needs to experience an environment which is structured consciously to permit them to experience desirable outcomes as a result of their own actions, that is, to be in control of good results. It is also useful if negative outcomes are experienced in an environment that helps the child to explore how far his or her own actions may be linked to the specific negative outcome. If they are responsible for the negative outcome, support can then be offered in order to explore other ways of behaving which might produce a different outcome. The provision of good experiences, she argues, is protective for children of all ages.

In addition to circumstances involving the trauma of repeated separations, experiences of abuse or neglect can lead to patterns of thinking or attribution in the individual child which need to be understood if help is to be geared to the very specific needs of each child.

For example, the degree to which an individual child or adolescent blames themselves for complying with sexually abusive experiences will vary considerably. Whereas one child may blame themselves and believe 'I deserve this because I am dirty', another child may blame a non-abusing adult in preference to blaming the abuser. It is important that practitioners are aware of the thinking of the individual child and the way in which this is influenced by the particular unique circumstances of the abuse. What the child has taken from the experience by way of a view of themselves will be vital in informing therapeutic work.

THE VERY YOUNG CHILD

Basic accomplishments like riding a bike, throwing a ball, learning to dress oneself are all fundamental competencies which can result in the child feeling effective and receiving positive feedback.

THE PRIMARY SCHOOL-AGE CHILD

Children at this stage can be encouraged to learn how to make a friend, how to protect themselves when under stress, how to please adults, how to focus on learning tasks. Zimmerman puts a particular focus on managing in school, both academically and socially, as this is of powerful significance to children at this stage of development (see Chapter 7).

THE ADOLESCENT

Giving adolescent foster children appropriate involvement and control over particular aspects of their lives, and working in whatever placement, either at home or in foster care or residential care, to ensure that they develop social, occupational, and self-care skills are all means of mitigating against the helplessness they may feel. Certain factors for children separated from their families seem especially significant.

The possession of an 'age-appropriate understanding of the reasons for placement reworked according to the child's age and stage of development to

---

Activity 4.7

Think of a child or young person with whom you are working who has experienced many moves and negative life events.

1. Focusing on how they think about themselves in relation to their responsibility for these events, do they see the cause of negative events as internal or external to themselves?

2. Does the child see the internal or external causation of negative events as being stable over time or transient and linked with particular circumstances?

3. Does the child or young person believe that negative events will always happen, that is, the global explanation, or related to one negative event, that is, the specific explanation?

4 What opportunities may be created in the child's current living situation to challenge their habitual way of thinking about negative events in their lives?

5. What attempts have been made to help the child to put together for themselves a 'coherent story' about their lives to date? How might this be done and by whom is it best carried out?

---

accommodate cognitive changes as well as changes in circumstance' is essential. Zimmerman argues that these explanations are a must to prevent the child blaming themselves for negative life events.

The involvement of older foster children in pre-placement visits and allowing them an appropriate voice in determining their living arrangements can also be viewed as preventing the development of learned helplessness.

Involving the child, particularly the older child, in negotiations over the planning of family contact can mitigate against the feelings of powerlessness occasioned by the separation.

All areas of choice and consultation allow the young person to know that they can have a voice which will affect the people who control major aspects of their lives. This in turn, develops self-efficacy, an important feature of later resilience.

Summary of main issues and considerations for practice

Key themes

1. When formulating assessments of family functioning in relation to a child 'in need' or at risk of 'significant harm', it may be helpful to take an overview of salient factors which clarify the current *predicament* of the individual child.

2. It may be helpful for practitioners to focus on eliciting strengths and capacities, problem-solving skills and coping strategies within the child, the family and family supports so as to maximise these and harness them in the way in which support may be structured and offered.

3. The process of identifying vulnerabilities within the child, their close family setting, and their extended family and community support can help in focusing attention on the most vulnerable children.

4. Such an analysis can be used as a basis for building partnerships with the children themselves and with their families and the overall framework offered can be shared between professionals to enhance multi-agency cooperation.

5. Sibling relationships have great significance for individual children and their contribution to the development of both younger and older siblings needs to be taken seriously in the work with individual children and with the sibling group as a subsystem of the family.

6. An appreciation of core factors influencing the *impact* of adversity on the individual child is vital in structuring effective intervention.

7. The powerful negative impact of carrying the role of scapegoat within the sibling group needs to be viewed with the utmost seriousness by professionals.

8. The experience of loss in all the different forms is a common adversity and the process of grieving in children needs to be understood if helpful resources are to be offered to families and to the children themselves.

9. The framework of attribution theory has much to offer the practitioner in building an understanding of the dilemma an individual child carries as a result of negative life events.

10. Contact after divorce, abuse and following a child's removal from the home to local authority accommodation may reflect complex considerations and the *purposes* and *benefits to the child* should be vital determinants of the way contact is planned and supported.

Messages for practice

- When working with complex situations, practitioners may be helped by the use of the simple framework offered in this chapter to isolate key variables of resilience and vulnerability in structuring an analysis of information about a child at the assessment stage and in formulating interventions, often in partnership with other agencies.

- This framework can be used to set broad targets, e.g. building upon the resilience of family support systems or of key abilities and strengths in a child and to monitor progress.

- A key question here may be 'how will we know when things have improved/developed?' The framework may help practitioners to tease out from a mass of information and description, an analysis of the *impact* and *meaning* of events or circumstances in the life of an individual child. For example, how might the loss of a key family member affect the balance of safety and well-being for a particular child?

- An emphasis on resilience can enable workers to tap into the child's skills and strengths, an advantage seen in particular methods of work, for example, focused brief therapy.

- Work which focuses on resilience-building strategies with individual children and young people can increase feelings of security, self-esteem, and self-efficacy, all of which are important for later resilience.

- Friendships, schooling and experience in problem-solving and pro-social activities involving empathy may be as important as placement security in work with children unable to live in their birth families, as well as for those at home in less than ideal circumstances.

It is the impact and meaning of experiences of separation and loss which determines the degree to which the child may be interrupted in their healthy developmental progress. Age and temperament, the nurturing relationships and the emotional support available to the child before, during and after key separation or loss experiences are highly influential in recovery.

It is the sense which the child makes of the loss through support in the emotional and cognitive working through of the coherent story which can be helpful in clarifying misperceptions and in reducing self-blame. Repeated losses experienced without emotional support, can lead to feelings of powerlessness resulting in reduced self-efficacy and even depression.

- Strategies which focus on challenging the negative messages which the child may have taken from these losses/disruptions and providing opportunities for assertion and involvement in decision making can challenge negative patterns of thinking.

- A sensitivity to these patterns of thinking, as explored in attribution theory, may be as useful when applied to the effects of abuse and/or neglect as to experiences of separation and loss.

- Clarifying the *purposes* of post-separation contact in a variety of circumstances can be helpful in structuring plans *in the child's best interest.*

Whilst it is generally recognised from the research that direct links with carers are of value to separated children, some circumstances may further distress, interrupt a child's development or even leave them open to abuse.

- The careful interpretation of distress in a child is a core skill informing key decisions about contact and placement.

The support from parents, carers or workers to the child in developing and reworking at later stages of development a 'coherent story' of life events and circumstances is likely to be highly influential in building the child's strengths and future resilience.

Understanding the child's coping skills and survival strategies helps workers to make sense of puzzling 'bizarre' or 'difficult' behaviour following traumatic events. This, allied with an understanding of the messages the child has taken from these events, all help to inform sensitive strategies for work with individual children, be they family, group or individually based.

CHAPTER 5

Adversity and the Protective Environment

It is helpful to reflect upon the factors which constitute adversity for an individual child. As already suggested in the consideration of vulnerability, there is often a clear relationship between past adversity and increased future vulnerability as a consequence of that adversity. In this chapter, we shall explore the implications for children's development of the experience of various forms of adversity including maternal depression, marital discord and domestic violence. We will also consider the effects of emotional/psychological abuse, physical abuse and sexual abuse. We will not be examining in detail the therapeutic work but will be exploring the importance of an awareness of the impact of various types of abuse.

Definitions

Adversity

Adversity is the experience of life events and circumstances which may combine to threaten or challenge healthy development.

Protective environment

This comprises the factors in the child's environment that act as a buffer to the negative effects of adverse experiences.

Examples of adverse and protective factors

Racism

When working with individual children, the worker must be aware that racism is endemic within British society and that it is not 'if' but rather 'how' this impacts upon the individual child, affecting the child's sense of identity and self-esteem. McDonald (1991) suggests that all workers need to be aware that they must:

- take care to inform themselves of the cultural and ethnic origins of the families and children with whom they work and remain sensitive to the significance in their work of their own origins
- strive actively to combat racism in their work at all levels, whether with groups of clients or with individual families or children.

The practitioner should begin from a position of building on the strengths and achievements of black children. This is entirely consistent with a resilience-based approach to work with children but, unless the worker starts from an awareness of the prevalence and pervasiveness of racism, vital skills which the child needs to combat this may be overlooked.

The Children Act 1989 and the Children (Scotland) Act 1995 define a requirement for social workers to consider the multi-ethnic and multi-cultural diversity of our society when assessing and providing services to meet children's needs. However, what will be vital in making a real difference to the experience of the children and their families will be the degree to which a sensitive awareness on the part of practitioners and managers is translated into practice at all levels, from the assessment of overall need in devising children's service plans in individual authorities, to the work with each child. Ahmed (1991) comments:

> Not to take account of racial, cultural, religious and linguistic needs of a black child within his or her individual needs is tantamount to extracting the child out of his/her social reality. (p.ix)

Being a child who is black or of mixed parentage will add a dimension to the child's experience of negative life events, for example, physical or sexual abuse, neglect or rejections. Once again, however, assumptions should not be made as to how an individual child will have made sense of their own experience, but rather, care needs to be taken to 'tune in' to the *meaning* each child has put together for themselves. From this the worker can assemble a picture of the dilemmas *this* child is left with and this will shape future work, whether family focused, individual or group support.

We know that children who are of mixed parentage are especially vulnerable to periods in local authority accommodation. As quoted in the DoH publication (1991) current research emphasises this high risk factor.

> (There was) a remarkably high overall admission rate for children of mixed parentage... in all age groups but particularly amongst pre-schoolers... When the authorities' figures for admission of mixed parentage children are examined individually, interesting differences can be seen. In areas with large black populations... mixed parentage children accounted for less than half of black admissions to care. But in authorities where black people account for a smaller proportion of the population, the majority of black children admitted to care proved to be those of mixed parentage. (p.15)

Young children of mixed parentage are also the most likely to have multiple admissions to local authority accommodation. Their readmission rate was more than twice that of young white children in the Child Care Now sample (Rowe, Hundleby and Garnett 1989) and the implications are that an alarmingly large proportion of youngsters who have one white parent and one parent who is black or from a different ethnic group will experience multiple admissions during their childhood.

Practitioners need to be active in preventative work with parents if we are to avoid those unnecessary repeated separations for young black children in particular. Sensitive approaches to work with both black and white parents of these children is vital if we are to meet their needs for support:

> Ethnic monitoring is an essential prerequisite to the provision of services for black and minority ethnic children, families and carers. It should be carried out routinely and translated into policy, service design and practice which should in turn be monitored.
>
> Special attention should be directed toward the situation of mixed parentage children who are at present in care in disproportionate numbers and at risk of multiple admissions to care or accommodation.
>
> The cultural backgrounds of children's families and the influence of this on their family relationships need to be better understood. Cultural issues should receive more attention both in the provision of services and in direct work with children and their families. (DoH 1991, p.34)

McDonald (1991) urges workers to challenge their departments about the range, quality and appropriateness of services offered to black children and their families. She urges us to consider our assumptions in the assessments of black families, using two possible models, the 'deficit' and the 'empowerment' model.

Whereas the 'deficit' model emphasises problems and dysfunction, the 'empowerment' model, by contrast, emphasises strengths, abilities, the

---

Activity 5.1

How far do you consider your own agency to be addressing these issues in provision for black children and those from other ethnic groups in your area?

---

capacity to solve problems and overcome obstacles. The latter model seeks to identify resilience within the family system which may be harnessed to manage current stresses and crises.

Phillips and Dutt (1990) explore the vital differences in approach in full. In the assessment of black families, two added dimensions are stressed from the family's perspective:

- their own experiences of racism and its effect on the assessment situation and interaction, and

- the personal and institutional stance of the worker and agency on anti-racism. (p.7)

McDonald (1991) further agrees that practitioner assumptions about families influence assessments by shaping:

- the information asked/not asked for

- who is routinely included/excluded from assessments

- perceptions about family lifestyles

- what interventions/services are necessary. (p.49)

An open-minded, curious and respectful approach is more likely to be successful in obtaining the information as to how *this* family functions than an approach based on stereotyped assumptions and a 'deficit' model. More sensitive family support could significantly reduce the number of black children who are accommodated.

When thinking of factors which render children particularly vulnerable to developmental interruption or delay, or to psychological disturbance, three key adverse factors emerge as being of real significance: (1) maternal depression, (2) marital discord, and (3) the effects of domestic violence.

Maternal depression

Much has been written about the increased vulnerability of children experiencing the adversity of having parents suffering from depression. Cummings and Davis (1994; see also Cummings 1987) summarise much of the research about the effects of maternal depression on child development. They note that children of depressed parents are found to be two to five times more likely to develop behavioural problems than children of non-depressed parents. However, Rutter and Quinton (1984) state that:

> For the most part, parental mental disorder does not give rise to an increased risk for the children that is independent of the family's psycho-social circumstances as a whole, rather it should be seen as one of several psycho-social risk factors that are more damaging in combination, than in isolation. (p.866)

More particularly, Rutter and Quinton (1984) articulate several of the possible pathways relating parental depression to child disturbance. In addition to the consideration of genetic transmission, they suggest other possibilities:

- Depression can have an indirect effect on the child as it may well influence the quality of the parent–child relationship.

- Parental depression may lead to family disruption and specifically to separations for the child which in turn may lead to psychopathology;

- Marital discord, often correlated with depression of a parent, is known to lead to psychological problems in children. (p.75)

Extra-familial factors

Living with a parent who is depressed may impact in a negative way on the child's relationships with others outside the home. As Cummings and Davis note:

> …a primary responsibility of parents is managing their children's interpersonal activities and support networks. Ideally, parents provide their children with opportunities to develop positive relations with peers and adult role models. (p.87)

Other researchers note that there is evidence that depressed parents are less willing to encourage their children's social activities and assimilate their children into social groupings and events outside the immediate family.

> …this may prevent children from developing adequate extra familial support network of extended kin, neighbours, peers and even friends.

Familial isolation may therefore leave children of depressed parents more vulnerable to psychological difficulties. (p.89)

Practice points
PARENTAL SELF-EFFICACY AND SENSE OF CONTROL

Several researchers have concluded that depressed mothers have relatively little confidence in their caregiving abilities and low levels of perceived parental efficacy. Cummings and Davies note that, in comparison to parents with high perceived competence, parents with low perceived competence reacted to unresponsive and uncontrollable children with substantially higher levels of withdrawal, unassertiveness, negativity and physiological arousal. In summary therefore, a reduced sense of efficacy which is common amongst depressed parents, may place them at increased risk for responding unhelpfully to the problem behaviour of their children. Depression has frequently also been associated with impairment of the parent's management techniques for dealing with the child's behaviour. It may also interfere with the development of secure attachment relationships, therefore potentially undermining the fundamental quality of the emotional bond between parent and child.

Much emphasis is placed on maternal depression in the literature with a corresponding dearth of studies into the effects of paternal depression. Feminist theorists would argue that in a male dominated society where the contribution of women is underrated and where male abuse of power is condoned, women are disenfranchised. The assumption, all too readily available, is that the woman should take responsibility for the nurturing and well-being of the child. An emphasis on individual pathology is invidious, protecting, as it does, the absent fathers.

We might ask, what help does the parent want at this point? She/he may need respite or shared care if energy is low. This points to the advisability of considering intervention in these circumstances on a number of fronts. It would be all too easy to fail to identify the depression in a parent and to adopt an assumption that mothers in these circumstances are 'to blame' for the difficulties in their children's behaviour and in their relationships with their children.

It is vital, first to identify the depression and help the parent to seek medical help. Second, active support in effective child management techniques may well prove preventative and protective of any abuse or a deterioration in the relationship and ideally avoid the kind of separation to foster care or residential care which may lead to later difficulties for the child.

Resources within the extended family or within the community may be offered, to allow the parents some recovery time from the depression and before enlisting them in a supportive network to provide the parent with at least one 'warm confiding relationship' which may be protective, not only immediately, but also in the longer term. All too often, however, a depressed parent may be bombarded with offers of help, all of which imply a need to make new relationships just at the point when emotional energy is low.

Marital discord

Child development research abounds with references to the significance of marital conflict in contributing to children's difficulties. Cox *et al.* (1987) found that marital discord was more closely related to disturbances in mother–child interactions than maternal depression alone. Particular features of marital discord appear to be of significance.

Anger and aggression

Interparental aggression is linked with child maladjustment. Children from maritally violent homes are four times more likely to exhibit psychopathology than children from non-violent homes. Witnessing verbal and physical anger between parents is linked with severe internalising and externalising problems in children, i.e. this leads to children being likely either to blame themselves severely or to externalise their anger towards others in a persistent way.

Conflict resolution

Cummings and Davies reflect that the way in which conflicts end and specifically whether or not there is a resolution to parental battles, may also be of real significance for the impact on the child. Cummings reported that unresolved quarrels, continued fighting, 'the silent treatment' elicited more anger from children than partially resolved disputes, which in turn resulted in more anger than resolved conflicts (apology, compromise). Therefore the resolution of conflict significantly reduces its impact on children's emotions and behaviour. This points to the importance for intervention of working actively with the parental conflict itself and building parental strategies for conflict resolution.

Explanation

It is highly significant that parental explanations absolving the child from blame in the conflict buffer the child from feelings of fear and responsibility. Explanations that imply or attribute blame to the child as the cause of the marital dispute only increase children's feeling of shame and distress.

Parental divorce and remarriage

Rutter and Rutter (1993) in exploring the findings of longitudinal studies of divorcing families by Hetherington (1989) pull together six main points of significance.

1. The studies confirm that long-term psychological disturbance is more likely to follow parental divorce than parental death.

2. The psychological disturbance often precedes the divorce which is suggestive of a link between marital discord and strife and the disturbance rather than the marriage break-up itself.

3. Psychological disturbance is found to be as frequent in non-divorcing families where there is marital discord, which confirms point 2.

4. The disorders themselves tend to be conduct disorders including aggression, the poor control of impulses and disturbed peer relationship rather than depression. This does suggest once again that the link is between the stresses of family discord and its effect on the child rather than the grief of the loss itself.

5. Disorders in children following divorce tend to arise more often if parental conflict continues. This is particularly relevant if the parenting following the divorce is less than adequate or if the parent who has custody is depressed or in other ways not managing.

6. It seems clear that these effects may have an increased impact on boys who are already temperamentally difficult.

Hetherington also found that on the whole, in terms of remarriage, boys tend to benefit more from their mother's remarriage whereas girls tend to show more psychological difficulties. Also, in terms of age, younger children are more likely to benefit than adolescents. Girls who had a warm close relationship with their mother before remarriage, are more likely to have a conflicted one afterwards.

Additionally, where step-fathers attempted to exert some control over children's challenging behaviour at an early stage in the relationship, this is associated markedly with poor step-father–child relationships.

This parallels the finding from Dunn and Kendrick's study of siblings (1982) where they found that a girl with a close relationship with her mother before the birth of a sibling was more likely to be hostile to her young brother or sister afterwards, as if some jealousy or rivalry reaction were operating.

Practice points

Identifying and addressing not only depression, but also, importantly, any additional marital conflict is a key consideration for the practitioner.

This leads to an acknowledgement of the potential significance of building children's own networks and supporting parents in promoting these as a potential protective factor for the child's security and well-being.

It may be critical to support depressed parents in helping the child to engage in age-appropriate tasks, i.e. the maturational tasks appropriate to their stage of development.

The development of positive self-concept and healthy peer relationships may well be protective in buffering children from the effects of depression in parents.

Parents' own supports are vital in combating the effects of depression.

The inference for practice would appear to be that step-fathers need to build a positive emotional relationship with the child before expecting their right to act as disciplinarian with the child to find any acceptance.

Activity 5.2

Considering an individual case in which you have been involved, which of the above factors may have been particularly relevant to your work with the family where there was either maternal depression, marital discord or both?

Which of the identified areas of potentially fruitful protective intervention were/are relevant in the case you are considering?

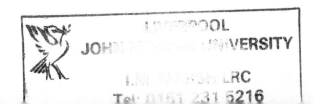

The adverse effects of domestic violence

NCH Action for Children (1997) summarise much of the research into the prevalence of domestic violence in Britain. Amongst other observations, they note the following:

- Domestic violence comprises more than 25 per cent of crime reported to the police in Britain

- In 90 per cent of those incidents involving domestic violence within families, children were either present when the assault was occurring, or in the next room and able to overhear the conflict

- One-third of children who witness abuse do make attempts to protect their mother (Stark and Flitcraft 1985)

- On average, women are beaten 35 times before they ask for help (McGibbon, Cooper and Kelly 1989). The severity and frequency of domestic violence often escalates over time (Dobash and Dobash 1984)

- In 1993 it was found that 21,000 children were currently living in refuges in England and Wales (Women's Aid Federation Annual Survey 1993).

The NCH Study (1997) highlights a number of factors which affect children's responses to the violence they witness.

- The frequency and severity of violence children have witnessed being inflicted on their mother, either through overhearing or observation.

- The length of time children have been exposed to such violence.

- Issues relating to race, culture, age, gender, disability, sexual orientation and socio-economic factors.

- Whether the child has any outside support from extended family, friends or community.

- The nature of external interventions from agencies or community, for example, a sympathetic teacher, while not able to prevent domestic violence, can do much to boost a child's self-esteem.

- Whether children blame anyone, including themselves, for the violence.

- Whether children perceive violence as a way of getting their needs met.

- Whether there is inconsistent punishment from the mother or father.

- Whether the abusive man manipulates family relationships.

- The quality of the mother's relationship with her child. (pp.15–16)

Practice point

This again emphasises the need for the practitioner to be aware of the details of the particular circumstances of the individual child in order to assess vulnerability to negative effects.

The researchers consider a range of effects which witnessing the domestic violence may have on individual children. These include:

- feelings of guilt, shame, powerlessness, anger and responsibility for their mother's suffering

- feelings of fear and anxiety that may result in low self-esteem and self-confidence

- nightmares, disrupted sleep patterns, bed wetting and eating disorders

- depression, withdrawn behaviour, passivity, aggressive and disruptive behaviour

- disruptions to schooling due to a range of factors such as injury, caring for siblings and moving

- experience of suicidal and self-harm feelings

- isolation from peers, children may be violent or act out violence towards their peers and siblings

- in cases where mothers take the side of their violent partners, children may experience betrayal

- running away from home and leaving home prematurely in adolescence without having made adequate plans for the future.

It is helpful if the practitioner is able to tune in not only to the particular child's circumstances, but also to the meaning and impact of the violence on the individual child. This careful assessment will inform the degree of support which needs to be offered, not only to the children but also to their mothers.

The NCH Action for Children's Study (1997) emphasises the importance of strategies for supporting women alongside the support of their children and see this as central to effective practice.

Protective factors?

O'Hara (1993 and 1994) has delineated areas for practice consideration in the context of domestic violence.

CONSULTATION WITH CHILDREN

It may be very important to raise the issue with children themselves as NCH Action for Children (1994) in their study discovered that fewer than one-fifth of mothers had discussed the violence with their children. The study demonstrated that this lack of consultation increased the children's feelings of both confusion and isolation.

The research shows that children have varied responses to domestic violence and it is important for practitioners to recognise that each child's experience will be unique. The fact that the violence is subjective underlines the importance of practitioners' awareness of the meaning of the violence to each child. It will then be possible to harness more effective supports for the most vulnerable child/children and devise intervention more appropriately. Whilst there are some children who need relatively little support, others may need not only intensive help, but also availability of this support over a longer period.

It is important to understand that the individual child's particular coping and survival strategies may be critical in helping them to elicit appropriate support from other adults as well as clarifying the underlying cause of what may be perceived as difficult behaviour.

Children need opportunities to communicate about a range of difficult issues in their lives but especially about domestic violence. For those children who attend day care centres or support projects, the provision of play materials, books or activities which raise the issue of violence in the family may allow the child a vehicle for communicating about their experiences. These may also provide opportunities for helping them to make sense of what has happened to them. Above all, it is vital that practitioners seek to understand the child's feelings and dilemmas and to take them seriously in their interventions.

More general work which raises issues about safety for children in a variety of settings, i.e. schools and other activities as well as within their family circle, are helpful in placing safety issues on the agenda for children.

Information about sources of help and protection for children and young people is vital in communicating an awareness that adults outside the family may be able to help them, as well as communicating information about some of the effects that living with violence may have upon them.

In particular, those children who face various forms of discrimination because of a number of factors, for example, race, disability or class, may need particular support in considering the impact of the violence in their lives.

DOMESTIC VIOLENCE AND RACISM

The NCH Action for Children publication (1997) emphasises the importance of the practitioner's awareness of the particular impact of domestic violence on children who already experience racism within their communities.

> Black children live in a society where the experience of racism outside the family is an everyday reality. Communities and families often provide safety and security from this violence and oppression, but when violence takes place within the home it further adds to the stress and vulnerability that black children experience. (pp.8–9)

Children also need personal help to make sense of their experiences and affirmation of their strengths and coping mechanisms in surviving the violence. Some children may need therapeutic aid in making sense of what may be encountered as overwhelming experiences.

THE FORMATION OF ALLIANCES WITH NON-ABUSING MOTHERS

It will be helpful initially to raise the issue of the prevalence of violence in families, as many women are reluctant to disclose that they are experiencing verbal and physical abuse from their partners. They also need reassurance that they are not going to be judged to be bad mothers if they have not been able to prevent the violence.

It is important for practitioners to be aware that many women have already developed a range of strategies for coping with the violence. Building on these strengths may well be a way of developing and strengthening a helpful alliance with an individual mother.

Given that so many mothers find it difficult to discuss the violence with their children, encouraging them to do so may well be of great help to the child.

Many women will also be experiencing racism or discrimination due to disability or class, which may have powerful effects on their ability to seek and make use of help.

They may well feel that they have very limited alternatives to continuing to tolerate the violence so the exploration of practical alternatives of seeking help for themselves and protection for their children may well be critical.

THE DIRECT CONFRONTATION AND CONTROL OF THE BEHAVIOUR OF VIOLENT MEN

Prior to engaging in work with violent men, it is crucial to make an assessment of the protection and safety needs of the women and children involved. An awareness of the effect the work with the man might have on the woman is vital in considering how to intervene.

THE DEVELOPMENT OF STRATEGIES FOR PROTECTING WORKERS AS WELL AS WOMEN AND CHILDREN FROM THE VIOLENCE

Contacts with the Police Domestic Violence Units in the local area, may well be useful in developing an alliance for workers which may help for developing strategies for safety and protection not only for the women and their children, but also for staff involved in direct work with violent men.

Emotional abuse

Whilst some children suffer emotional abuse from parents who do not deliberately intend to cause harm or distress, for example, parents who are mentally ill, abuse alcohol or drugs or who are themselves immature and do not understand the child's emotional needs, practitioners need to focus on the *effects* of the parenting interactions on the individual child.

It needs to be recognised that in a small number of situations we meet parents who deliberately target their children in an emotionally punitive manner. The following categorisation of various forms of emotional abuse has been used to examine parenting behaviour in relation to a specific child.

DEFINITIONS

O'Hagan (1993) suggests that emotional and psychological abuse may be differentiated from one another and offers the following definitions:

> Emotional abuse is sustained, repetitive, inappropriate emotional response to the child's expression of emotion and its accompanying expressive behaviour. (p.28)

> Psychological abuse is the sustained, repetitive inappropriate behaviour which damages or substantially reduces the creative and developmental potential of crucially important mental faculties and mental processes of a child; these include intelligence, memory, recognition, attention, language and moral development. (p.33)

Some parents, for example, fail to respond to a child's experiences of feeling, pleasure, distress or anxiety. Others ridicule or diminish the child's capacity to think for themselves, to develop links between cause and effect or to practise and enlarge their ability to memorise events and facts.

The author argues that, whilst the former primarily effects the child's ability to recognise and accept their own feelings, the latter interrupts the healthy development of broader cognitive skills, affecting the child's confidence in exploration and learning and their healthy moral development.

An alternative classification of types of emotional abuse is suggested by Garbarino and Garbarino (1986) and is described as follows:

REJECTING

The adult refuses to acknowledge the child's worth and the legitimacy of the child's needs.

ISOLATING

The adult cuts the child off from normal social experiences, prevents the child from forming friendships and makes the child believe that he or she is alone in the world.

TERRORISING

The adult verbally assaults the child, creates an atmosphere of fear, bullies and frightens the child and makes the child believe that the world is hostile and unpredictable.

IGNORING

The adult deprives the child of essential stimulation and responsiveness, stifling emotional growth and intellectual development.

CORRUPTING

The adult mis-socialises the child, stimulates the child to engage in destructive, antisocial behaviour, leading to problems in the child's social development. The authors caution practitioners to recognise the characteristics of emotionally abusive parents, suggesting that behavioural extremes are the most significant features to note.

They suggest that practitioners should be especially aware of the parent who is so over-controlled that there is no opportunity for the normal healthy ventilation of negative feelings on a day-to-day basis, and equally of the parent who is so under-controlled that the slightest distress that they experience will be projected on to the child. They note:

> children are resilient and they can handle parents' normal emotional ebb and flow; what most children typically cannot handle is a pervasive pattern of destructed emotions or extreme outbursts that threaten their world. In most cases, isolated trauma is not nearly so threatening as repeated emotional assault. (p.12)

When further defining emotional maltreatment Garbarino and Garbarino describe four ways in which parents may penalise the child for particular behaviours:

1. By punishing smiling, mobility, exploration, vocalisation and manipulation of objects. They emphasise that children have a natural drive to explore their environment and to achieve mastery. The punishing of this drive and the behaviour which accompanies it threatens the child's development of competence.

2. By the discouraging of care giver and infant attachment. Because the development of healthy attachment relationships is central to other aspects of development, persistent efforts on the part of parents to discourage this attachment imply a direct threat to healthy development.

3. By penalising a child for showing signs of positive self-esteem. The authors argue that discouraging self-esteem is undermining of a fundamental component of healthy development.

4. By penalising the child's use of inter personal skills which are necessary for adequate performance outside the home, for example, at school and in peer groups. Not only do abusive parents commonly discourage their children from social interaction, but they addition-

ally do not provide the positive reinforcement necessary for the development of important key interpersonal skills. (pp.19–20)

Physical neglect and emotional abuse

In examining practice frameworks which may be useful in making assessments and in working in this very difficult area it may be helpful to stress two main points: first, the value of a developmental perspective on all aspects of the child's growth and maturation; second, the importance of partnership and cooperation, both with families and with colleagues in other professions, when making critical assessments of 'significant harm' in this area.

We shall explore one framework for consideration when working with those situations where partnership with the family is problematic and there are long-standing concerns about the children.

Legislation requires that children's service plans will be made by local authorities for meeting children's needs. These plans are expected to include strategies for close cooperation, in particular with health and education staff. The reasons for this are clear, arising from detailed research into the often-neglected health and education needs of vulnerable children, both those living in the community and those in local authority accommodation.

Practitioners rely on health visitors, school nurses, general practitioners, paediatricians and other medical specialists to help in understanding the child's physical development.

We will also be dependent on cooperation with educational psychologists, clinical psychologists and psychiatrists (experienced in work with adults and with children) in our assessment of complex family situations.

We rely heavily on the detailed observations of education staff in nurseries and primary schools. Teachers are often a source of detailed information about the child and about parent–child interaction. Educational psychologists often play a key role in identifying and interpreting the specific intellectual problems of an individual child combined with any emotional and social difficulties. Education and health staff working in the area of special needs often hold crucial expertise in helping us to define precisely the nature of the child's problems and to identify strategies for managing the child in different settings.

Children with disabilities, whatever the nature of the special needs, may be especially vulnerable to experiencing various forms of neglect as well as abuse.

Our police colleagues involved in domestic disputes and other matters can often offer an insight into family functioning.

It will be most helpful to consult with social workers with special expertise in the areas of child abuse or those with particular interest and expertise in child development within their own departments.

In summary, we need to consult with one another as often as possible in cases of chronic physical neglect and emotional abuse if we are to meet the needs of vulnerable children and young people. Identifying the core group of professionals working with the child and family, and making sure that we meet regularly to monitor the effects of parenting style on the child's development, may well be critical in identifying interruptions and delays in the child's development which may merit further action.

In bringing together issues of attachment, progress in development and parental capacity and willingness to cooperate, some key areas of relevance emerge in considering cases of physical neglect and emotional abuse:

1. the family and relationship context in which the concerns arise

2. the process of development of the child in this context

3. the nature of any significant harm and its effect on the child's development

4. the changes which are required in order to meet the child's needs

5. parental willingness and/or capacity to do this and any conditions which would be fundamental in order to achieve change

6. an exploration of whether or not these changes can be achieved without compulsory measures of care

7. consideration of the least detrimental alternative if these measures are necessary.

Taking these issues one by one and exploring some of these questions may be helpful when considering individual cases.

This framework is developed in Appendix 1.

Emotional neglect

A very useful overview of what is known about child neglect can be found in a summary by Erickson and Egeland (1996). The authors emphasise the impact of psychological abuse on development.

Whether or not the child sustains physical injury, at the core of maltreatment is lasting damage to the child's sense of self and the resulting impairment of social, emotional and cognitive functioning. (p.5)

The authors argue additionally that a definition of neglect which requires that there are observable effects of an immediate nature presents problems for the practitioner as it becomes apparent from the research that the true impact of neglect may only emerge at later stages of development.

When commenting upon the theoretical debate centring upon the intentionality of the act of neglect, the authors echo Stevenson (1996) in stressing:

Although intentionality can be a critical variable in determining legal culpability, the end result for the child may be the same whether the parent is wilfully neglectful or neglectful due to factors such as ignorance, depression, or overwhelming stress and inadequate support. (p.6)

They emphasise in the findings of their own research the use of the term *psychologically unavailable* in describing parents who overlook, for whatever reason, a child's requests for comfort and support. They found that this more subtle form of neglect has serious long-term consequences for young children. The authors distinguish between the effects of abuse and neglect, suggesting that abused children are likely to be more aggressive than their non-neglected or maltreated peers, whereas neglected children demonstrate less social interaction. Abused children are often described as having difficult temperaments, demonstrating anger when under pressure, whereas neglected children in the study were more passive, tended towards helplessness when under stress and exhibited significant delays in their development.

In terms of language disorder or delay, in particular, although abused children experience these problems, those experienced by neglected children were found to be more severe.

Erickson and Egeland (1996) explore the use of the attachment theory as a helpful framework for considering some of the most powerful effects of neglect on children's development. They note that several studies of maltreated children, including those who are neglected, show a high incidence of attachment problems. Both abused and neglected children often demonstrate a pattern of anxious attachment.

The Minnesota Mother–child Project Study, (Erickson, Egeland and Pianta 1989), a prospective longitudinal study designed to follow the development of more than 250 children identified as being at risk from parenting problems, separates the children into four specific groups:

1. physically abused

2. mentally abused

3. neglected

4. those with emotionally neglectful or 'psychologically unavailable' parents.

In the study, the families were identified as being at risk of parenting problems due to a combination of adversities, poverty, youth of the parent, poor educational attainment, lack of support and unstable life circumstances.

In the group of children with psychologically unavailable parents, the mothers appeared detached and unresponsive to their children's bids for nurturing. Their interactions were described as 'mechanical and perfunctory' and they exhibited no pleasure in the relationship with the child.

Focusing in particular on the neglected children, mothers in the neglectful group did not provide appropriate health, physical care or protection for their children and, although they expressed concern and interest in their children, their care of them was seen to be inadequate to meet their needs.

The study showed a pattern of anxious attachment in two-thirds of the neglected children at one year of age. When seen again at two years of age, additional characteristics of low enthusiasm, low levels of frustration, considerable anger and non-compliance were also noted.

When seen later at 54 months of age, these same children demonstrated poor impulse control, extreme dependence on their teachers and other generalised behavioural problems in the classroom. This is underlined by the finding that there was a dramatic decline in the performance of these children on developmental tasks between the ages of 9 months and 24 months.

Practice points

The difficulty for the practitioner is that, despite the maltreatment appearing as very subtle, nevertheless, the consequences for the children are most severe.

Those children with psychologically unavailable parents during their infant years continue to have problems throughout their primary school years. When they were tested on the Child Behaviour Check List, they were found to be more socially withdrawn, less popular with peers, and in general demonstrating more of a tendency to internalise responsibility for negative life events. This links strongly with comments about attribution theory in Chapter 4.

The impact of neglect on children's development is at least as damaging as the more overt types of abuse. Emotional neglect, especially during the first two years of life, has a striking and long-lasting impact on the child's relationships with other children, with teachers, with family members and also with respect to learning and problem solving capacities. Overall, the effects of neglect are stronger than the negative impact of poverty in relation to their impact on development.

Protective factors

Three main factors are effective in breaking the cycle of maltreatment:

1. the presence of a loving, supportive adult relationship for the parent

2. the support of a partner at the time of becoming a parent.

3. the availability of therapeutic help in resolving early loss and trauma for the parent, resulting in increased emotional stability and maturity.

This latter finding parallels the work of Mary Main (1991) who considers the relevance of parents' own attachment experience as an influence upon the degree of nurturing, via a stable attachment relationship, which they are then able to offer to their children.

Linking this research with our own practice, we may meet neglected children who fail to develop the confidence, concentration and social skills that enable them to make secure relationships with adults and with peers and make progress in cognitive tasks. Unfortunately, we may see patterns of behaviour in the classroom which predispose them to a cycle of failure and disappointment unless effective intervention is planned.

Implications for agency policy

Crittenden (1996) identifies issues which have major implications for agency policy.

- It is unlikely that neglectful parents can respond to interventions which require rapid change.

- Involvement of multiple helpers engaged in a number of concurrent strategies is likely to overwhelm parents because their social competency is likely to be more limited.

- The children of neglectful families require compensatory services from all agencies to safeguard their overall well-being e.g. extra support with school, day care services.

- Only a few helpers should be involved and their relationship to the family should be long term and intensive.

- The parents failure to link cause and effect should be central to the work and treatment should focus on the 'meaning of behaviour' and to concentrate on generating positive and rewarding outcomes to interaction for the parents and the children. (p.164)

Practice points

Understanding the nature of the child's attachment relationships provides a useful framework, not only for understanding the impact of neglect, but also for effective intervention. Working to strengthen the child's secure base within the context of their family relationships may help them, not only at home, but also in the school setting. Emotionally neglected children may not ask for the kind of support they need from adults because they have ceased to expect a response and therefore do not even try to elicit nurturing.

Work with parents focused on helping them to understand the child's needs and on locating the precise nature of any attachment difficulties is likely to be most effective.

The interventions which bring about changes in parenting have been found to be multi-faceted and relatively long term.

Careful assessment of the nature of supports needed by each family, depending upon the particular constellation of issues they face, is the key to success. Approaches to supporting the family will need to vary depending on various family factors.

Thompson (1995) and Erickson and Egeland (1996) note that effective support programmes need to be carefully designed and evaluated within a clear, theoretical framework. They suggest that attachment theory provides a good place to begin to clarify the problems and to progress effective interventions.

Physical abuse

Effects of physical abuse on development in early childhood

Researchers Gibbons *et al.* (1995) reported on a 9–10 year follow-up study of pre-school children placed on child protection registers. Most of these children had been physically harmed. The aims of the study were to assess the physical growth, cognitive ability and school achievement, emotional and behaviour problems and relationships with peers in children who were placed on child protection registers when they were under five years as a result of physical ill-treatment. In this study 'normal' development, far from being a measure of 'ideal' development, was defined by the performance of children of the same age and sex who lived nearby and attended the same schools. In other words these children resembled the children in this study except that they had not been notified to the child protection system. The development of the ill-treated children was compared with the control sample.

Outcomes

Having evaluated the outcomes for the abused children compared with the control group, comparing their progress on various measures of development, significant differences were found between the physically abused and comparison children after adjusting for the effects for social class and disadvantage.

1. There were significant differences in behaviour as rated not only by parents but also by teachers. The abused children, both boys and girls, were more likely to display behavioural problems. These were:

    a) restlessness and fidgetiness

    b) looking miserable

    c) appearing to be both solitary and unpopular

    d) being more prone to lying, fighting, stealing and destroying property.

2. The boys who had been formerly abused were additionally identified as having more emotional problems than the non-abused comparison group.

3. The girls who had been formerly abused were rated by teachers as demonstrating fewer desirable behaviours and in particular pro-social behaviours than the comparison group.

The 'formerly abused' children had reported significantly more problems with friendships than children in the comparison group, additionally noting more bullying or lack of peer friendships and peer play.

There were some differences in intelligence and educational attainment. The 'formerly abused' children rated lower on a standard test of abstract reasoning.

In terms of physical development there were no differences in physical growth between the formerly abused and the comparison children.

An outcome profile was developed for each child. This was carried out by a statistician with no previous knowledge of the children. Three outcome clusters were identified.

GOOD

This group were identified by parent and teacher ratings as demonstrating few behavioural problems, good educational performance and an absence of fears and self-reported depression in the children.

POOR

These children were defined as having many behavioural problems, low educational achievement, above-average fears and higher scores on depression.

LOW PERFORMANCE

This was an intermediate group who demonstrated relatively poor educational achievement but both fewer behavioural problems and self-reported symptoms of fears and depression.

Whereas only 22 per cent of the formerly abused children had a good outcome, 48 per cent of the comparison children were in this grouping.

Whereas 42 per cent of the children in the formerly abused group had a poor outcome, only 19 per cent of the comparison group were found in this category.

Overall there was no evidence that children who had suffered physical abuse necessarily experienced developmental problems in the longer term. However, there were some real differences between behaviour and intellectual performance of children who suffered early abuse and those who had not, even after social status had been allowed for.

It was noticeable that child protection registration and subsequent actions, both by professionals and parents, often led to increased instability in the children's lives and loss of significant relationships. Subsequent life experiences, including the quality of relationships available to the child in the post-abuse environment influenced longer-term outcomes.

An important minority of school aged children were identified who were often in stressed and socially disadvantaged families. They were unhappy, low achievers and displayed troublesome behaviour, both in the home and in the school setting. These children also received more physical punishment at home, and were exposed to more punitive parenting styles but they were also less warmly involved with their parents.

Conclusion

The evidence from the study points to the likelihood that physical abuse in early life is, in some cases, a 'marker' for the continuation of adverse circumstances for those children who experience parenting which is not only punitive, but also characterised by less warmth and less predictability and reliability of care.

Practice points

The results of the study would, therefore, tend to indicate that more attention needs to be paid in assessment of children who have experienced physical abuse to the prevalence of these factors within a particular child's relationships and circumstances. The study suggests that a physical assault in a family where there are no serious problems and warm, rather than punitive parenting styles, is less likely to have long-term consequences for the individual child.

The authors would suggest that current policy and practice emphasises perhaps too strongly the protection of the child from physical danger and rather less firmly the need to find methods of intervention which act to promote children's longer-term healthy development. Social workers in the study responded in particular to the fears of serious or fatal injury to the child and consequently focused on surveillance and monitoring to ensure physical safety. Much less attention appeared to be paid to signs of interruptions or distortions in the child's socio-emotional development and to low achievement.

Even amongst those children who have been physically abused, those children with experiences of more punitive and less warm parenting who were living in families with significant other problems, were more likely to be more vulnerable to continuing effects following early abusive incidents.

Practitioners may too readily assume that by removing physically abused children from their parents, and in particular placing them for adoption, we are automatically ensuring their well-being. As there are so many behavioural problems experienced by physically abused children consequent upon the abuse, particular strategies may need to be rehearsed and developed in the preparation and support of adoptive parents if they are not to resort to punitive methods of behaviour management.

This observation would tend to affirm that over and above the experience of the abuse, what may be more significant is the behaviour that the child learns to adopt as a consequence of living with actual violence, or the fear of it, from adults.

An additional concern for practitioners must be that poorer outcomes in the 'abused' group in terms of demonstrated problems would render the children more vulnerable to all the other consequences of established behaviour problems during early to mid-primary school years. These children, we know, may be much more likely to be excluded from school and, if placed in substitute families, may experience more moves of placement and therefore fewer opportunities to receive stability of care over time, and hence more interrupted experiences of reparative care.

Crittenden comments that whether or not the child sustains physical injury, the most powerful effect of the ill-treatment is the negative impact on a healthy sense of self and the ripple effects on social, emotional and cognitive development. Crittenden and Ainsworth (1989) found that abused children were described as having difficult temperaments, becoming angry under stress and exhibiting developmental delays.

Summary

Much of the research would postulate some significant differences in the behavioural and developmental consequences for children who have been physically abused as compared with those children who have been emotionally abused or neglected.

Although these effects may partly be due to the disruptive effects of protective action following the physical abuse, there is no doubt that there is a need for practitioners to identify those children who suffer physical abuse in the context of already poor relationships with attachment figures within an atmosphere of punitive parenting styles. These children are likely to be more vulnerable and to need skilful therapeutic support in parallel with effective parenting strategies.

It is perhaps helpful to clarify first of all that, whatever the form of physical abuse, it always incorporates elements of emotional abuse. This may be experienced very differently by individual children, depending on the relationship context in which the abuse occurs. The work of McFadden (unpublished lecture) is helpful here in inviting us to explore the nature of the relationship, for example, it may be relevant to consider:

1. Is this child basically loved but over-chastised on a one-off basis? This could suggest that the child is likely to have a good enough attachment relationship with the carer but other stresses occasionally accumulate to the point where the child is over-chastised.

2. Or is the child frequently physically slapped or hit because they are seen as temperamentally difficult and persistently beyond control? The relationship here may be in much more difficulty. The child's behaviour may indeed by this time be very challenging. The parent may be struggling or depressed and the relationship deteriorating to the point where the parent no longer feels willing or able to reach out to the child.

3. Is physical abuse the only kind of physical contact a particular child receives in an otherwise profoundly neglectful emotional environment?

Some important factors here may be:

1. That the child may be singled out from their siblings and become the focus of parents' criticism, disapproval or rejection. When parents are feeling miserable it is very common for one child, often a daughter, to be used as a source of solace and comfort, and equally common for one child, often a son, to be the target and focus of anger and irritation.

2. It is not just differential treatment among siblings that matters but also the specifics of interactions with an individual child in one-child families.

Practice point

The lesson here is that attention needs to be paid both to the presence of family-wide qualities and to ways in which they impinge differently on individual children.

First, in terms of intervention, the assessment made of the *particular emotional environment* in which the abuse is happening is vital in considering the depth of the child's needs and his or her vulnerability. In the latter example, we have a number of factors operating together which will be potentially much more harmful to an individual child, i.e. not only physical abuse, but the absence of a warm nurturing relationship would be of additional significance if this child were the scapegoated child in a group of siblings.

A second consideration is the observation of the *pattern* of abuse. How does the abuse occur? It may be extremely helpful to understand what kind of circumstances provoke the abusive incidents. Is there a particular trigger? Is this combined with alcohol abuse, or perhaps even depression in a parent? Or does it coincide with a particularly persistent pattern of difficult behaviour in a child? Identifying the triggers will help to isolate a useful focus for intervention.

Understanding the pattern of abuse may be useful in two ways. It helps to clarify where the focus of intervention might be most necessary and effective, e.g. with the child, the parent, support from the community, etc. It also offers a clue as to what the child may be learning from the pattern of the abuse which they then may continue in their own home or transfer to a substitute care setting. For example, if a child, when behaving in a challenging way, knows that occasionally they will be slapped and that their parent will then feel guilty and buy them a treat, what has this child learned? Perhaps he/she has learned that if you're prepared to tolerate some minimal discomfort, you'll later be significantly rewarded! Therefore, the treat that follows the slap is perhaps acting to reinforce the difficult behaviour. The issue here may be how can parents be supported in developing a range of management techniques for the child's behaviour which avoid physical punishment but nevertheless are effective.

The child who is completely emotionally neglected and yet somehow discovers that a certain piece of behaviour may result in at least some attention, albeit negative, has learned something very different from their experience. Perhaps it is only through the abuse that they have been touched at all, and so it is only through being hit that their existence is confirmed. This case is a much more critical scenario for intervention in that the degree of reparative care which is necessary to support this child's recovery and healthy development is much more profound than in the earlier example. This child may well suffer severely from being returned home prematurely from periods of respite in foster care. It would be important here to work very fundamentally on:

- assessing the parent's capacity to meet the child's emotional needs and
- to learn other disciplinary techniques and to cease punitive measures.

The third major consideration is the identification of whether or not the child has transferred this learning to the degree that they have adopted a particular *role* in the family as a direct response to living in an environment of actual or threatened physical abuse. McFadden explores the particular roles which children may adopt when living in an abusive environment which they then either sustain where an abuser is removed, or take with them to substitute care environments. In either setting, the patterns of behaviour can threaten their interests, either by attracting further abuse or by perpetuating the neglect of their emotional nurturing. McFadden describes the following patterns of behaviour

THE SCAPEGOAT

This child has learned that he/she will probably be the focus of punishment and so come to expect that this will happen, whatever setting they're living in. For them, there may be no point in keeping out of trouble if you know that you will be blamed by adults anyway.

THE PROVOKER

This child has probably suffered so much from being completely powerless in the circumstances of abuse that they begin to take control in an unhealthy way by provoking situations which result in physical ill-treatment.

THE HIDER

This child has probably learned that the safest way of making sure you are not a target in a dispute is to hide. The child may hide by removing himself physically from a situation or he or she may 'hide' emotionally by withdrawing.

THE CARETAKER

This child has learned to propitiate adults by caring for them and subjugating their own needs. This child may be a significant caretaker for younger or even older siblings as well as adults in the family.

Activity 5.3

Either consider a case and answer the following questions or read the case study and answer the questions.

1. When thinking of the child you know who has been physically abused, describe the emotional relationship within which the abuse occurred. How nurturing is this to the child?

2. Can you identify a clear pattern to the abuse? How might this inform your intervention

3. Can you identify any learned patterns of behaviour or particular role in the family that the child has taken on in these circumstances?

4. What are the essential features of reparative care for this particular child?

    •   How might his/her behaviour be managed effectively?

    •   How might their particular emotional needs be met?

Case study

Julie is an immature 11-year-old girl who recently was accommodated into care after experiencing physical neglect and physical abuse by her step-father. Her step-father had hit her causing bruising and admits to finding her a 'real minx'. She has a history of poor quality care, with a number of changes and disruptions. These include an episode lasting a year when she was six and left with her grandmother while her mother moved away to start a new relationship. Recently her mother has been in and out of hospital and the main care for Julie and her younger brothers has been provided by her step-father.

Julie has difficulty with school work, relating to her peer group and managing self-care. She is unable to concentrate at school and irritates other children because of her over-intrusive behaviour. She tends to dominate the other girls and to challenge and taunt the boys.

The foster family with whom Julie has recently been placed report her to be very clinging and to be still wetting the bed. She postpones going to bed until as late as possible and frequently comes downstairs with a variety of excuses, much like a younger child. Julie does not appear to notice when the bed is wet and does not wash herself the next morning. Consequently she has a hygiene problem. Recently it emerged that Julie had been sexually abused by her step-father but Julie appeared unaware that this was inappropriate. Julie singles her foster father out for special attention and frequently attempts to tickle, play fight with him and sit on his lap. Because of her age and because of the known sexual abuse, both foster carers are uncomfortable about allowing this, but have never cared for a sexually abused child before and don't feel confident about how to manage this behaviour. At times she prefers to be physically cared for by her foster mother than to do things for herself, but at other times she rejects her approaches and shows anger by swearing and storming out of the house.

Julie takes no interest in her appearance and she eats voraciously, regardless of whether she likes the food. She is very naive about the facts of life and she does not seem to understand that her step-father was at fault and that is why she is in care. She often asks if she can go home and once asked if her step-father can come and live with them. She has said little about her mother.

1. In what respects is Julie's development delayed?

2. What kinds of problems is Julie likely to encounter as she faces the developmental tasks of adolescence, given her experience of abuse and neglect?

3. What are Julie's current developmental and parenting needs and who should attempt to meet them?

4. What advice and support are the foster carers likely to need and how should this be provided?

Hints for answers

1.

- Julie is still struggling with testing out whether she can rely on her carers to provide her with a 'secure base'.

- There are signs of a real imbalance in her ability to depend on adults and she is displaying her ambivalence in swinging between showing intense needs and demands for nurturing and resistance to adults' offers of support.

- There are indications of poor self-care but also a lack of awareness of her physical needs consistent not only with a history of neglect but also with insecure attachments.

- Her social development is significantly delayed and she appears to have no understanding of how to pick up social graces from peers or to appreciate the reciprocality involved in making and keeping friends.

- Her inability to concentrate at school will be masking her natural cognitive potential.

- At this stage of her development she should be consolidating her friendships and her intellectual competence in advance of the less settled time of puberty and adolescence.

2.

- In order to move with confidence into this usually more turbulent stage, Julie will need the security of trusting relationships with her female and male carers. Her ambivalent feelings about trust and healthy dependency are likely to complicate her separation from the family, even to activities with her peer group.

- Her step-father appears to have been her attachment figure as well as her abuser, which is likely to produce complications in her ability to address the complex issues around both the physical and sexual abuse.

- With the onset of puberty, even if she has shown no apparent distress about the sexual abuse, confusions and uncertainties are likely to be triggered by physical changes. There are signs of this confusion in her approaches to her male carer with a clear lack of generalised boundaries.

- Feelings of anger which are emerging may intensify with the emotional lability of adolescence and are likely to confuse or even frighten her.

- Having no friendship links will complicate her gradual separation from the family base to the identification with her peer group.

- Even although she is not identifying the sexual abuse as 'wrong' she will be becoming aware that she has had experiences different from her peers and this is likely to set her further apart.

- She is faced with a number of complex strands of her life predicament to unravel which are likely to be preoccupying.

- Because of the neglect, complicated by the abuse, she does not have a secure sense of self or healthy identity.

- It may be useful to consider questions such as: who am I? (fuelled by the tenuous relationship with her mother and no direct link with her birth father); why am I here? (confusions about the abuse and reasons for the separation); what happens next? (an uncertain future is preoccupying and may well consume emotional energy needed for catching up in her healthy development).

- She has learned unhelpful lessons about male abuse of power (physical and sexual abuse) and has been used for an adult's sexual gratification. These experiences are potentially damaging to moral development, self-esteem and self-efficacy, all of which are tested in the rigours of the adolescent stage.

3.

- Secure base and reparenting.
- Non-abusive care.
- Help with boundaries with adults and peers.
- Confrontation about her sexual activities in the context of supportive nurturing.
- Help with self-care.
- Activities and a living environment which builds her self-esteem.
- Help in expressing a range of feelings.
- Chances to rehearse social and friendship skills.
- Support with her learning.
- Direct support in expressing feelings about the abuse.
- Help to make sense of her experience of abuse, neglect and separation from the basis of a sound awareness of her current patterns of *thinking* and attributional style.

Sexual abuse

Berliner (1997) notes that it is only in recent years that mental health professionals have begun to develop a recognition that sexual abuse may have deeper and longer-lasting effects and be more strongly correlated with a variety of mental health conditions in children and adults than was previously appreciated.

When looking at the effects on children, many researchers point out that there is a significant variability in the type and severity of children's disturbances. However, abused children are consistently found to be more distressed in their behaviour than children who have not been abused. Within groups of abused children there is a considerable range of levels of disturbance.

Some children do not appear to be behaviourally distressed. For example, Conte and Berliner (1988) found that up to 20 per cent of children could be asymptomatic whilst up to 60 per cent of children showed signs of acute distress requiring immediate clinical help. Berliner notes that some variables in the circumstances of abuse are related to a worse outcome:

- a closer relationship to the offender

- more intrusive sexual behaviour, for example, intercourse

- longer duration, or more frequent abusive contact

- the use of violence

- where there are other negative factors in family relationships or where this is greater conflict and less cohesion, children are likely to show more long-lasting effects.

The type of effects which are most consistent are as follows.

Sexualised responses

Differences between victims of sexual abuse and other children in terms of sexual behaviour have been found consistently in assessments using standardised behaviour checklists. These sexualised responses appear to be most pronounced in younger children. A similar emphasis on sexual responses to abuse have been found in studies into adolescent victims

Symptoms of Anxiety

Many clinical studies describe reactions to the abuse which may be subsumed under the heading of fear and anxiety. These include various kinds of sleep disturbances, flashbacks, hypervigilance, regression, nervousness, clingy behaviour and withdrawal from usual activities.

While many children seen shortly after the disclosure of the abuse do not exhibit severe symptoms, nevertheless, a history of abuse is highly correlated with several serious disturbances. Berliner emphasises that the full impact of the abuse on an individual child cannot really be known until adulthood (see also Berliner 1990).

She explores some of the reasons why children may appear to be without symptoms of distress at the time of the abuse and considers the following possibilities:

1. Some children are particularly resilient to unpleasant experiences and the experience of the abuse may not be experienced as sufficiently negative to appear dramatic to the child. The child may have coping skills which are unusually well developed and come from environments which are supportive, helping them to deal with the experience of abuse without extreme distress.

2. Coping strategies developed in response to these experiences may, however, involve the avoidance or the shutting out of memories or feelings about the experience. These may be seen as psychological defences which allow a child to reduce or avoid the anxiety associated with remembering the abuse which include repression of the experience, denial, splitting, dissociation and the development of physical ailments.

Practice point

We must guard against assuming that children who lack an emotional response to the abuse at the time of disclosure are necessarily unaffected by what they have experienced. They may merely be using personal strategies which are focused on allowing the child to escape from unpleasant memories.

The experience of abuse alters beliefs or assumptions about oneself and shapes the attributional style of the child's thinking. For example, the child may take on all the blame of what has happened or may, alternatively, place the blame elsewhere. The way in which the child makes sense of what has happened to them may, therefore, have effects on many other aspects of functioning as it touches on the central areas of self-belief and self-concept. For example, victims of abuse who have an internal, stable and global attributional style are found to be less well adjusted.

Some effects of the abuse may not become apparent until particular stages of development or the occurrence of critical life events. For example, it may not be possible to ascertain the longer-term effects on a particular child until they have reached adolescence when sexual development and the development of the psychosexual identity are central to their maturational tasks.

Practitioners may therefore see certain children demonstrating very distressed behaviour shortly after the abuse and others who show little signs of distress. Some children appear to have no symptoms or only early or late symptoms.

Particular stages of development herald the need for additional support for children and young people, whether or not they have displayed overt signs of distress.

Children and adolescents may be sexually abused in many ways. What do we know about what helps children in individual situations?

- Belief in the child.

- Removal of self-blame.

- Placing of the blame clearly with the abuser.

- Intervention which does not further traumatise the child or young person.

- Non-abusive future care where the child can feel protected and secure.

- An environment which nurtures the whole child/young person.

- Therapeutic help as needed at the different developmental stages (recognising that issues of sexual abuse need to be readdressed as children grow and change).

- Links with other children or young people who have had similar experiences; particularly the availability of group support within a therapeutic setting for primary school age children or adolescents.

- The identification of trigger situations which may frighten the child.

- The identification of coping strategies which may have been effective in the abusive situation but later do not help the child to seek and use the support they need.

- Help in managing complex contact issues if the family is split, particularly if the child or young person is scapegoated for disclosing the abuse, or was the favourite child.

- Strategies for self-protection from further victimisation, or the securing of the protective net around the young child.

- Help with communication skills.
- Support in catching up on developmental interruptions.

Finkelhor (1986) identified particular factors which may influence the child's reaction to the abuse and the effects in the future on their well-being.

- *Betrayal*: The degree to which the child feels betrayed – in particular often by a close and trusted adult.
- *Powerlessness*: The degree to which the child experiences a feeling of being trapped within the cycle of the abuse with no opportunity for seeking help or escaping from the situation.
- *Stigmatisation*: The degree to which the child is marked out within the family and even within the local community. This tends to increase self-blame and poor self-esteem.
- *Traumatic sexualisation*: The degree to which the child has been sexualised in traumatic circumstances by the experience of the abuse.

Factors which mediate effect

THE CHILD'S AGE AT THE ONSET OF THE ABUSE

In general terms, the younger the child, the more likely it is that the experience of extensive abuse may distort the child's development.

THE CHILD'S RELATIONSHIP TO THE ABUSER

The nature of the relationship may determine particular sorts of effects on the child; for example, the child may be attached to the abuser and therefore very confused by other adults' reactions to the abuse. Alternatively, the child might have been terrified and this may also have necessitated the child taking on a very unhealthy degree of self-blame.

THE DEGREE OF INTRUSIVENESS OF THE ABUSE

The more invasive the abuse, the greater the impact.

THE DURATION OF THE ABUSE

The longer the abuse has lasted, the more pervasive and long lasting the likely developmental effects.

THE RELATIONSHIP WITH NON-ABUSING MEMBERS OF THE FAMILY

It is helpful to consider what level of emotional support might be available to the child and what role the child takes in the family system.

THE NURTURING ENVIRONMENT

The degree of nurturing available to the child within the family before the abuse and also the characteristics (especially in terms of nurturing) of the post-abuse environment are of major importance in reducing negative effects.

A key theoretical influence on practice wisdom in terms of understanding children's adaptation to sexually abusive experiences can be found in Summit (1983) which describes the Child Sexual Abuse Accommodation Syndrome. The article explores the stages an abuser will move through in obtaining the child's compliance to sexually abusive treatment. This process has a significant influence on the child's reaction to the abuse at the time, and also important implications for the way the child feels about the abuser, the abuse and themselves. (For more detailed discussion see Chapter 8.)

Some additional effects of sexual abuse on development

Smith (1992) has written from extensive practice experience of working with children and young people who have experienced sexual abuse, and notes key effects on areas of development.

Activity 5.4

1. What elements of support might be helpful to a particular child or young person on your caseload whom you know to have been sexually abused

   • from family members

   • from support services, including groupwork support?

2. How might a child with a further vulnerability, for example, a boy or girl with a disability or communication problems, or a child who is the victim of racial abuse and discrimination be additionally vulnerable?

SENSE OF SELF

This is often poor, fragmented or non-existent in an individual child. If the child was first abused at an early stage in their development, it is more likely that they will not have any sense of personal boundary or personal space. They are more likely then to encroach upon the personal body space of other people. They need particular help with healthy boundaries of intimacy. Alternatively, the child who was abused at a stage of development when they already had a sense of their own body integrity and sense of self would be more likely to feel a sense of outrage and may be highly sensitive even to minor perceived encroachments on their privacy and personal space. Support in these circumstances needs to be respectful of this sensitivity, otherwise the child may be re-traumatised.

SELF-ESTEEM

Self-esteem may be very low in children and young people who have experienced sexual abuse. This is particularly relevant as their sense of worth may be linked inextricably with their sexuality. They have been used as objects of adult sexual gratification and in any intervention will need reassurance about their sexuality but also significant active work on building self-esteem.

AFFECTIVE RANGE AND EXPRESSION

This is often very limited in children who have been abused over a significant period of time. It is common to find the existence of sadness or even depression, emotional flatness, or angry, aggressive outbursts. The child's range of awareness and expression of feelings may be very limited and indeed many children and young people who have experienced long-standing abuse at times, have no clear language for their feelings.

CAPACITY TO JUDGE PEOPLE AND SITUATIONS

The betrayal of adult trust implied by sexual abuse within the extended family setting may impair the development of this capacity. The child may trust anyone equally or may trust no one at all. Healthy survivors of sexually abusive experiences have often developed a healthy scepticism and wariness which alerts them to the need to monitor the behaviour of the other person in order to make a healthy judgement as to their trustworthiness.

SENSE OF RESPONSIBILITY

This may well be significantly under or over developed. We need to be alert for signs of self-blame in the child or, alternatively, for a complete abdication of any responsibility for their own actions. It is common also to note the 'learned helplessness' explored in the section on childhood depression (see Chapter 4).

The introduction of healthy choices to the child and active support with making sense of cause and effect in a more realistic way may also be useful. This should help them establish, over time, a healthier sense of appropriate responsibility for their own actions.

MORALITY

Young people who have been sexually abused have a distorted experience of adult morality. They may come to believe that as long as you are strong enough it is legitimate to abuse younger, weaker people, as this is their own experience. However, in healthy survivors we find a particular sensitivity to the feelings of others and this is what we would wish to model and promote in the direct care and nurturing of the child or young person.

MAKING AND SUSTAINING RELATIONSHIPS

Pseudo-maturity is common, allied with a failure to accomplish developmental tasks. This pseudo-maturity can lead to relationships developing prematurely to the stage of sexual intimacy for which the child is not emotionally equipped. The child or young person needs help in developing other ways of relating, in evolving an awareness of their own feelings, alongside a capacity to communicate feelings and to negotiate within relationships.

COMMUNICATION SKILLS

Many children or young people who have been sexually abused have learned that the real meaning of adult communications is hidden and/or contradictory. Commonly, they misread social cues and are not in touch with the signals they give out to other people.

SEXUAL DEVELOPMENT

Many children and young people have been sexualised by the abusive experiences. This may make them feel different, isolated, marked out. Their emotional needs have been met in exchange for sexual activity. It is also common for the child or young person to have a distorted body image, or to fear that they have been physically damaged.

AUTHORITY ISSUES

Frequently, they have not seen adults who exercise authority in a responsible way, therefore it is not only unknown to them but also unrecognisable. They have experienced the misuse of power and may have learned the very unhelpful lesson that this is acceptable behaviour or even necessary for survival in an adult world.

These aspects of development are complex and interrelated, but it may be helpful in planning work with an individual child or young person to focus on a particular area and to clarify plans for how they may be nurtured in their current living environment in a way which challenges the messages they have received from the abuser.

Protective factors?

Berliner (1997) emphasis two therapeutic aims in helping children to recover from sexually abusive experiences. These are the *emotional* and *cognitive* processing of the experience.

She underlines the importance of assessment of the child because, as she makes clear in her exploration of the impact of abuse, children may internalise their reactions, either by way of avoidant responses or distorted beliefs about themselves or of the abusive experience. She suggests that it is important to assess the level of intrusiveness of thoughts about the abuse and also the level of psychological effort the child is spending on avoidance.

Secondly, the importance of assessing the family's capacity to offer support to the child needs to be evaluated, in particular, the degree of belief of the child.

Third, because disclosures of abuse generate crises within families, attention can be taken away from the child's distress about the abuse itself and their reactions to it. Practitioners are urged to take seriously carers' responses to the meaning of the child's victimisation in terms of feelings of guilt and blame, and to be ready to protect the child, but urge that focus on the support for the child needs to be that of victimisation therapy.

EMOTIONAL PROCESSING

This involves repeated exposure of the child to the memories of the abuse within the context of a therapeutic environment and is designed to reduce some of the fears and distress. Teaching the child some strategies for managing fear and anxiety are helpful in increasing the child's sense of self-efficacy.

COGNITIVE PROCESSING

This focuses on the way in which the particular child *understands* the experience of abuse. The child may be very confused about the experience but the greatest concern is the tendency of children to attribute blame falsely, either to themselves or other adults, rather than to the abuser. Feelings of attachment towards the abuser are significant here as some children may prefer to believe that there is something about them which caused the abuse rather than to accept that their attachment figure was responsible for taking advantage of them.

It is emphasised here that it is important for the worker to ascertain what the individual child believes, how they come to have this belief and to understand the purpose the belief serves in the child's rationalisation of the abuse. Rushing to reassure the child that they are not to blame may be counterproductive in obscuring the particular child's adaptation to the abuse; in other words, the way they have explained and made sense of it themselves. It is this process of thinking and adaptation which is invaluable in helping to articulate the therapeutic task with a particular child.

Berliner summarises:

> Eventually, the child should be able to give, at an age appropriate level of comprehension, an explanation for both the offender and the child's behaviour which is accurate and meaningful. In addition, the victim should be able to identify what is different now in terms of knowledge and resources which would enable them to avoid victimisation in the future. (p.220)

Summary points

In our work with individual children and young people it is important that we make no assumptions about which stresses or negative life events will have had the most powerful effect. Individual children and young people vary in a number of respects. The more that is known about the circumstances of the abuse, the child's relationship to the abuser and other key unique features of the experience for an individual child, the more readily the worker can tune in to the central dilemmas or messages the child is left to manage and live with.

It is the combination of circumstances which affect the impact of the abuse. McFadden (1986) has produced a child's information sheet which suggests key areas of the child's life, relationships and experience of abuse which need to be explored if they are to be offered a protective, nurturing environment by foster carers.

Caution is needed in tuning into what may have been the most significant events and circumstances as far as the child is concerned. For example, we may be appalled at the nature and degree of abuse experienced by a child but they may be more preoccupied with threatened or actual separation.

Sibling abuse

There appears to be a need for an increased awareness of sibling abuse and the particular ways in which it can occur. It could be argued that high levels of parental tolerance of sibling rivalry has helped to legitimise children's negative behaviours towards their siblings. Negative sibling interactions are considered to be so commonplace that they have become accepted by parents and other adults. Much of the abuse is hidden from parents. Consequently, the impact of negative sibling behaviour on children is easily dismissed and ignored. Yet similar behaviours are considered as bullying in the context of the peer group.

Kosonen (1997) argues that the issues for parents and carers is one of determining strategies for encouraging and building positive sibling interaction and fostering a longer-term aim of building supportive relationships between siblings. She considers that sibling abuse can have a lifelong consequence on the child's development and well-being.

1. Inadequate supervision of children is likely to allow sibling abuse to occur more readily. This implies that the professionals need to be alert to situations where children are left together for long periods of time with inadequate supervision. The usual warning signs applying to the detection of child abuse should also be responded to when considering potential abuse by siblings.

2. A further suggestion is that children who may be at risk of abuse by their siblings may explicitly be offered the opportunity to alert adults to their predicament in various ways. Parents, professionals and carers working with children in families should be aware of the general power relationships within the family in terms of gender relationships and relationships between generations and

how these are negotiated in the course of family life. Children take their cues from the adults around them by observing power negotiations between adults in the family. If such negotiations are hostile and aggressive as opposed to being cooperative, children are presented with an unhelpful pattern to follow. (p.15)

This alerts us to the possibility that, particularly in families where abuse of power by the adults is an evident feature of the relationships, the possibility that sibling abuse is occurring needs to be considered in the assessment and also in focusing helpful interventions for vulnerable children, particularly younger siblings.

It may now be helpful to return to the framework offered at the beginning of Chapter four and to plot the predicament of an individual child or young person with whom you are working so as to reflect upon your view of the critical elements in the case. It may be, for example, that the child is so vulnerable and the adversity so severe that separation from the family becomes necessary. Alternatively, it may well be that some protective factors could be harnessed or introduced into the child's environment which may build their resilience and act as a buffer against the effects of stress.

Summary of main issues and considerations for practice

Key themes

1. Although some children appear to be resilient to living with parental depression, there is an increased likelihood of behavioural problems.

2. Marital discord is a significant stressor for many children and is often linked with maternal depressions.

3. Domestic violence may have many negative effects, the precise nature of these depending, not only on the child's resilience and temperamental style, but also on the circumstances surrounding the child's involvement with/knowledge of violent incidents.

4. Women and children who are subjected to racism and experiencing domestic violence are especially vulnerable as they may be particularly isolated from sources of help.

5. For children and families from different racial and cultural backgrounds, the sensitivity of the helping systems to the experience of

racism is vital in structuring effective, accessible support systems and in informing the active work with individual children.

6. The experience of racism for children and their families adds a dimension to the impact of other adversities such as marital violence, abuse and neglect and disability. A keen awareness of the ethnic, cultural and linguistic background of families will be vital to sensitive anti-racist practice.

7. Psychological unavailability in parents is a key factor in interrupted development.

8. Neglect is a complex area for assessment and requires effective multi-disciplinary cooperation on a continuing basis with regular developmental monitoring.

9. Physical abuse is more likely to lead to behavioural problems.

10. Family members or existing social supports are not always beneficial to children of abusing families as they may criticise parents or confirm them in abusive and punitive management methods.

11. It is necessary to consider a child's adjustment into adulthood to determine impact, as effects often emerge at key developmental stages or around critical life events.

12. Children who have been physically abused have learned unhelpful lessons about the abuse of physical power and may seek to identify with the abuser and even replicate their behaviour or hide and subjugate their own needs.

13. The availability of a secure base of at least one warm attachment relationship is protective against stress.

14. Predictability of care is an important component of recovery for abused and neglected children and young people.

Messages for practice

- Professionals involved in making both assessments and arrangements for child contact after divorce are generally not considering domestic violence as a primary concern.

- Contact, generally regarded as beneficial to the child may not be in the best interests of some children and/or may place the mother at renewed risk.

- Contact with an abuser after abuse, if the child remains with the family, is a matter which requires careful consideration and should be judged according, not only to any trauma triggered by the contact, but also to risks of further abuse.

- One of the most powerful factors which influences the likely negative effects of life stresses is a lack of warmth in close relationships available to the child.

- When considering the effects of physical abuse beyond any injury, other helpful factors may be:
  - an assessment of the warmth and nurturing in the attachment relationship
  - the pattern of abuse and the messages it conveys to the child
  - learned patterns of behaviour as a consequence of the abuse and
  - consideration of the role the child held within the family.

- An assessment of emotional nurturing and attachment and bonding are important components of any work on parenting skills with parents who have learning difficulties.

- The most effective work with neglectful families is long term and based on a small number of helpers who can develop relationships and trust with parents and children over time.

- Children who experience sexual abuse may exhibit early and/or late symptoms of distress, or show no apparent immediate signs of trauma.

- What helps is an appreciation of the messages the individual child has taken from the abusive treatment so as to tune in to their particular dilemmas: e.g. I'm to blame.

- Work on the child's feelings about abuse/neglect and on their patterns of thinking about themselves in order to support them in developing a coherent story is the key element of therapeutic work.

- Challenging negative, internal, global and stable attributional styles of thinking, through the provision of good experiences which challenge these set patterns is of value in developing a more positive self-concept.

- Strategies of care and work with these children which focus on the building of resilience send messages about the adults belief in the child, in their potential and their future.

- A focus on whether or not a parent is abusing a child intentionally or unintentionally may cloud a clear assessment of the potential or actual harm caused by the abuse.

CHAPTER 6

Early Years

This chapter focuses on the maturational tasks of the early years and reflects on the contribution of recent research to our understanding of key aspects of healthy development.

Core developmental problems will be explored and, as with the ensuing chapters which concentrate on particular stages of development, a summary will be offered at the end emphasising key factors which may be particularly relevant for workers to hold in their minds when assessing and working with individual children.

An assessment framework is provided in Appendix 2 which may add to the range of tools available to help with the complex process of the assessment of individual children. The aim here is to facilitate the clarification of key features of a young child's development, focusing on the careful interpretation of the impact of key relationships and of significant life events, for example, separation.

This is based on the hypothesis that it is the impact of relationship support available to a young child as well as the effects of life events which shapes the practitioners' understanding of an individual child's needs.

The core theme of the central importance of the availability of at least one 'good enough' attachment relationship for promoting healthy maturation is continued from earlier chapters and the contribution of the child's own initiatives, responses and temperamental style is emphasised. Fahlberg (1994) observes that: 'a child's developmental progress is the result of the individual's unique intermix of genetic endowment, temperament, and life experiences' (p.61).

Although it is clear that not every child demonstrates the same behaviours or reactions to different challenges of development, there are however some universal themes attributable to different stages of development. The sequencing of developmental milestones is much more consistent than is the actual age at which they are attained. We see great variation between different children at the same age.

As stated in Chapter 2, relationships with family and others are the primary forces in shaping an environment that encourages the child to achieve their full potential in terms of different domains of development, that is, physical, intellectual, social, moral and emotional growth. Successful mastery of the different developmental tasks is completed only within the context of relationships. Ideally, if all is going well, families help children to accomplish these developmental tasks. Children learn much earlier than was supposed about the emotions of others, and through establishing a 'secure base', learn to trust others and to value themselves. They also learn to use language and how to think. Because children need emotional support and structure if they are to meet these maturational tasks with confidence, we are well reminded of the importance of safety and security, stimulation, encouragement, reasonable expectations and safe limits.

In our work with families with young children, it is crucial that we are able to distinguish between normal, healthy behaviour for a particular stage of development and those aspects of behaviour which might indicate unmet developmental needs.

Maturational tasks of the first year of life

The primary developmental task of the first year of life is that of building feelings of safety, trust and security in other human beings. This trust is established as a result of day-to-day experiences and it is the quality of the frequent interactions between the parent and the young child which promotes all aspects of development. These exchanges not only help the child to feel safe and secure in an otherwise bewildering world, but also facilitate the organisation of the child's nervous system and set the stage for the establishment of patterns of learning, another primary task for the first year. When very small, infants do not differentiate between different kinds of discomfort. They often react in a similar way, whether or not their discomfort is physical or emotional. They are entirely reliant upon the adult's capacity to 'tune in' to their discomfort, discover the source and alleviate the distress. The parent's attunement to the child's discomfort, when in a state of high arousal, is critical for the development of a secure attachment.

The ability of a parent to keep 'in mind' the needs of a very young child is an important consideration as the child's dependency needs are at their height at this stage of development. For example, does the parent anticipate what will cause confusion or distress to their infant or toddler? Do they have a sufficiently clear picture of what might constitute a hazard for a mobile toddler in the home or community, e.g. fires, open windows? Do they show signs of being able to read their child's cues for support and comfort? Do they offer the child pleasurable experiences, e.g. playful activity? Do they show an awareness of the child's need for age appropriate stimulation, e.g. activities which promote safe physical exploration? If there are few positive signs, it may additionally be important to assess whether or not some education in the detail of young children's needs may be helpful.

Alternatively, there may be a lack of acceptance that both a particular level of *responsiveness* and *frequent initiation* of contact with a young child is vital to healthy development.

For example, Mr and Mrs Jones, with two small children, came to the attention of the social services department because of a health visitors' concern as to severe nappy rash and generally poor physical care of their 18-month-old and 30-month-old sons. In the children's centre, they were able to demonstrate, not only ability to cope with their physical care but also ability to stimulate the children. However, in discussion they acknowledged that they did know what to do but did not accept that these caring actions were necessary to promote healthy physical and emotional development.

The attachment relationship may be poor and the focus of work may need to be on building more secure attachments rather than merely on teaching parents about their children's needs. Parents may need help in reflecting upon their own early attachment relationships in parallel with the work on the parent–child relationship (Main 1991).

Making a careful analysis of the child's pattern of attachment (see Chapter 2) will not only clarify the child's current level of security in trusting key adults, but also inform the focus of work with the adults, the child and/or the relationship between them. Appendix 2 includes a framework of questions about a young child's attachment behaviour, in the context of their overall developmental progress.

Dunn (1993) explores other elements of attachment relationships apart from the security dimension. She observes that humour and warmth are equally important in creating a bond between the child and another human being. Perhaps this could be said to parallel Vera Fahlberg's second circular interaction which describes the importance of the adult's persistence in reaching out to the child, anticipating what will bring him or her pleasure and enjoyment. Of clear importance here is the adult's enjoyment of contact with the child.

Young children's capacity for early interaction

There has been much recent research into very early development, notably by such researchers as Trevarthen (1991), who makes observations of his own and other recent studies. He notes:

- From three months of age, babies show clear signs of pleasure in response to games which their mothers initiate. He asserts that mothers intuitively structure simple interactions to promote the 'synchronisation of actions, experiences and expressions of feeling'.

- Infants of five months old can take part in the familiar pattern of a nursery rhyme.

- From six months onwards, however, the infant plays an increasingly active part, often taking the initiative in repeating an action designed to elicit play or laughter from the mother.

Between 6 and 12 months Reddy (1989) notes that infants show 'an increasing awareness of their capacity to link and reciprocate their feelings and actions with a partner' (pp.143–158). Trevarthen believes infants to be innate companions and cooperators 'who show us that emotions and the communication of emotions are central in the development of cognitive capacities in the very young child'. This underlines:

- the importance of these early interactions for the development of language and the beginnings of social understanding

- their importance in introducing humour and shared pleasure and connectedness in the parent–child relationship

- the contribution of the child's *initiatives* as well as *responses* to the development of the relationship.

The importance of particular features of attachment relationships

Ainsworth and Bowlby (1991) focus on the crucial features of attachment for healthy development. Bowlby explores three key themes:

1. An emphasis on the security dimension, as differentiated from other aspects of the relationship: the idea that the feeling of safety is of paramount importance and by implication more crucial than other features of attachment relationships.

2. A stress on selective attachments as key to security and later opti-
    mal socio-emotional development; the child's capacity to recognise
    particular attachment figures and to prefer their company is of crit-
    ical importance here. This implies a recognition of strangers and
    noticeable experience of distress or discomfort in their company,
    that is, what is commonly called 'stranger anxiety'.

3. The idea that later close relationships are built on the basis of the
    first attachment relationship.

Shared feelings and experiences

Dunn (1991) argues, however, that within Bowlby's framework of attachment, several important elements concerning the significance of these central
relationships remain unexplored. She outlines these as follows:

THE CHILD'S CAPACITY TO SHARE FEELINGS AND EXPERIENCES WITH ANOTHER

This is an aspect of intimacy that is thought to be important in adolescence
and adult relationships. However, she asserts that even when very young,
some children show considerable curiosity about their parents' feelings,
intentions, and worries, although in such curiosity there are marked individual differences.

SHARED HUMOUR

Humour is important in the relationships of young children as well as those
of adults. She asserts 'its significance lies both in the shared warm emotions
enjoyed together and in the intimacy that is reflected when two individuals
each know what the other will find funny' (Dunn *et al.* 1991, p.23).

Dunn argues that this dimension of relationships has been almost
completely ignored in studies of parent–child relationships. She goes on to
say

> these shared jokes begin extremely early: during the first year of life
> when babies begin to find the antics of their parents and siblings
> uproariously funny. In the early months of the second year, it is not just
> simple clowning and slapstick by parents that is the source of shared
> laughter, but the children themselves are often the clowns. (p.24)

Dunn sees very marked differences between mother–child pairs in the frequency with which they joke and share humour together.

CONNECTEDNESS

Dunn defines this dimension of relationships as: 'the degree to which two individuals sustain a connected thread of communication when they interact' (p.24).

She argues that this dimension has not been explored as a significant feature of young children's relationships with their parents, even though there are marked differences in the degree and nature of connectedness in the communication between different mother–child pairs. Dunn (1991) found in some of her own research that the frequency of mother–child conversations about feelings, for example, was related to differences in children's understanding of emotions. She argues that we need to broaden the framework within which we reflect upon children's relationships with their attachment figures.

Pro-social development

Since Piaget's assertions that children could not be aware of other people's feelings and perspective until they reach the age of six, much has been learned about the far earlier development of empathy and pro-social awareness and behaviour in even very young children. Schaffer (1996) reviews the recent literature and notes that pro-social behaviour can be noted in children as young as two years of age.

The term 'pro-social' has come to represent all aspects of helping, cooperation, caring and sympathetic behaviour toward another person (see also Chapter 7). In particular where this behaviour does not involve any personal gain it has been defined as empathy. When children are confronted with distress in another person, these behaviours are most dominantly apparent. This has been found to increase markedly in the second year of life. Notably, this behaviour occurs and persists even in the absence of explicit parental reinforcement. However, some types of parental behaviour are more closely linked with the development of pro-social tendencies. These are as follows

THE PROVISION OF CLEAR RULES AND PRINCIPLES

Where the parent makes their expectations clear 'Don't hit your brother' and links this with consequences 'You will hurt him' this is most effective.

EMOTIONAL CONVICTION ON THE PART OF THE PARENT

The more forceful the parental message, the more likely the young child is to take it seriously and the more it will affect behaviour.

ATTRIBUTING PRO-SOCIAL QUALITIES TO THE CHILD

Labelling the behaviour as 'kind' or 'generous' is more likely to reinforce it.

MODELLING BY THE PARENT

If the parent themselves acts in an empathic manner this is likely to have positive effect in reinforcing pro-social acts.

EMPATHIC CARE GIVING TO THE CHILD

Warmth in the relationship with parent figures is highly influential, secure attachments in the early years are related to the development of empathy and pro-social skills.

Practice points

This underlines the more general positive developmental consequences of healthy attachment relationships. They contribute to the growth of social skills and so can add not only to more harmonious sibling relationships, but also to the development of friendship links, which are so important for resilience in later child and adulthood.

The key variables noted here (Schaffer 1996) also offer helpful pointers to focused work with parents in helping their young children to develop pro-social skills, contributing to the foundations of moral development.

Exploring not only the aspects of security within the child's attachment relationships, but also providing opportunities for shared humour and feelings of connectedness in the interaction can be helpful for practitioners to bear in mind. For example, as described in Chapter 2, Binney *et al.* (1994) explore practice methods for using shared games in playful contact to promote healthier attachment relationships between parents and their young children.

Gender development in pre-school children

Golombock and Fivush (1994) emphasise the importance of the early years for the development of an awareness of gender differences in children. During the pre-school years children learn about gender and their knowledge through the primary school years becomes more complex. They suggest that gender stereotyping may reach its peak during pre-school years and diminish later, somewhere during middle childhood. They emphasise that an awareness of gender is not merely imposed on children but that they actively seek to make sense of the significance and meaning of being male or female.

Unger and Crawford (1992) observe that by the time children have reached three years of age they will have developed preferences, not only for toys, but also the play involved with the use of those toys, based on their earlier experience. If we see play as to some degree a rehearsal for adult roles, it is clear that these very early influences reinforced by parents, by advertising in the media and later by peers, are likely to have a significant affect on later life choices.

Apparently parental beliefs combine with biological differences to produce differences in the interaction between parents and their sons and daughters. An interesting influence at three years of age is that peers become important agents of gender socialisation. They too are gender typed in their beliefs and strongly reinforce gender type behaviours of other children. Golombock and Fivush observe that parents talk more about anger with their boy children than with their daughters and more about emotions in general with girls than with boys.

SUMMARY

The pre-school years are a critical period in gender development. Children's concept of gender becomes increasingly important and increasingly stereotyped between the ages of two and five.

Hence we see that by the time children are three years old, numerous pressures, some more subtle than others, have combined to establish clear ideas about gender difference. Feelings, activities, and personal attributes have become associated with gender. We may meet children in our practice who do not conform to their parents' stereotyped gender role expectations. These children are likely to be under particular emotional pressure and it can be seen that there are numerous additional, powerful sources of influence outside the immediate family environment, for example, peers and the media. These influences are so powerful that by the time a child reaches the pre-school years, some vulnerable children may be particularly inhibited, may require particular encouragement to express feelings which are defined as unacceptable because of adults' expectations of gender appropriate expression of feeling.

This may be especially relevant in circumstances where a child is separated and experiences powerful feelings which are prohibited by adults close to them.

Cognitive development in young children

Piaget

Although there have been criticisms of Piaget (1932 and 1952) the contribution that he has made to our understanding of children's intellectual development is still highly significant. He suggested that children progress through a series of stages in their thinking, each of which corresponds to broad changes in the structure or logic of their intelligence. He suggested, moreover, that these stages occur in a fixed order, those stages being sensory-motor, pre-operational, concrete operational and formal operational.

SENSORY-MOTOR STAGE: BIRTH TO TWO YEARS

During this stage the baby knows about the world through actions and sensory information. The baby learns to differentiate him or her self from the environment and begins to understand causality in time and space. Through imaginative play and symbolic thought the child demonstrates its earliest internal mental representations of the outside world.

THE PRE-OPERATIONAL STAGE: TWO TO SEVEN YEARS

During this stage, for example, through the use of language and intuitive problem solving, the child is beginning to understand how to classify objects, but is still characterised by egocentricism, that is, a view of him or herself as central. However, by the end of this stage social perspective-taking skills are emerging and the child is beginning to grasp conservation and number.

Piaget considered intellectual development as a continuing process of the assimilation and accommodation of information. During the sensory-motor stage the child changes from a newborn, focusing almost entirely on sensory and motor experiences, to the toddler stage, characterised by a rudimentary capacity for symbolic thought.

OBJECT PERMANENCE

Piaget argued that the child in the earlier stages of sensory-motor development does not understand that an object continues to exist when it is no longer in sight. It is as if when something disappears, for example, a person leaves the room, they automatically cease to exist. He postulated that the baby only gradually acquires what he calls 'the object concept'. Piaget thought that the beginning of object permanence occurs when a child actively looks for an object which has been removed from view. The active searching for objects out of sight is viewed as a significant intellectual milestone since it provides evidence that the child has developed an internal representation of objects even when they are not present. Piaget's experiments suggested that a baby is not totally confident that an object which has been removed still exists until he or she is about 18 months old.

REINTERPRETATION OF PIAGET'S IDEAS ABOUT DEVELOPMENT

Piaget's observations of development at this stage have been largely confirmed by more recent research, but in some areas it would appear that he has significantly underestimated the young child's mental capacity to organise the sensory and motor information he or she takes in. For example, Trevarthen (1975) demonstrated that young babies show an ability to imitate much earlier than Piaget would suggest.

The clearest criticism however has come from the work of Bower (1977). He describes experiments involving infants aged five to six months old who are presented with an object which is then made to vanish by dropping a screen over it. When the screen is removed the object has gone. If the babies think that the object has disappeared when shielded by the screen then they should logically show no surprise at seeing nothing when the screen is removed. If, however, they think that the object still exists behind the screen, they should be surprised if it does not reappear when the screen is removed. In Bower's experiments babies showed much more surprise at the non-reappearance of the object than by its reappearance.

THE PRE-OPERATIONAL STAGE

Piaget divided this stage into the preconceptual period: two to four years; and the intuitive period four to seven years. For the purposes of this section we will focus on the preconceptual period. At the end of the sensory-motor stage we observed the emergence of the capacity for symbolic thought.

One example is the rapid increase in language which in Piaget's view results from the growth of symbolic thought. Two central ideas here in Piaget's thinking are animism and egocentrism.

Animism

Children at this early stage of development between two and four years show a tendency to attribute feelings and intentions to inanimate objects, e.g. a doll has a sore arm. Piaget called this animistic thinking. Also at times the child finds it hard to distinguish between fantasy and reality at this stage and nightmares may be responded to as if they were real events.

Egocentrism

At the pre-operational stage, according to Piaget, thinking is still very centred on the child's own perspective and he or she finds it difficult to understand that other people can see things differently. Piaget called this self-centred stance egocentrism, i.e. the inability to understand that another person's thoughts, feelings or perceptions are different from one's own. He argued that egocentric thinking relies upon the child's view that the universe is centred on him/her. The child therefore finds it hard to 'de-centre', that is to take the perspective of another person.

Several researchers, principally Donaldson (1978) concluded from more recent studies that the nature of the task set can greatly affect the nature of the child's ability to demonstrate their capacity to adopt the perspective of another person. Recent findings also indicate that there are different kinds of skills in perspective taking, some which involve empathy with other people's feelings and some which involve the ability to know what other people are thinking.

Children as young as three and four years are aware of other people's feelings and can take the perspective of others. Using a series of short stories children were asked to indicate how the child in each story felt by selecting a picture of sad, happy, angry or afraid faces. Even the youngest children (three years old) showed that they could empathise with the feelings of another child in some situations. These results significantly challenge Piaget's argument that children between the ages of two and seven years are primarily egocentric.

In summary, more recent research suggests that given appropriate tasks with sensitive use of language in the explanation, the child seems capable of demonstrating at least some of the abilities which Piaget thought would not appear until later stages of development. Within, therefore, an appropriate social context, the young child can demonstrate more capacities than Piaget's work suggested. Donaldson (1978) points out from her own work that we normally interact within a context and that the child negotiates meaning through social interaction with significant others.

Vygotsky

Lev Vygotsky, a Russian psychologist, recognised that children's cognitive development does occur in a particular social context. His early theories are increasingly receiving attention. One of his most important ideas was that of the 'zone of proximal development' (Vygotsky 1933c/1935; cited by van der Veer and Valsiner 1991; see also Chapter Seven).

Toddlers have to be motivated and must be involved in activities requiring skill at a reasonably high level of difficulty that is towards the upper end of their ability. The teacher and the child also must adapt to each others' requirements. The adult structures a task beyond the child's current level of achievement and offers support. This has been found to be effective in extending skills even in young children.

This has clear implications for the kind of skilled support which may be offered in day care or nursery settings to develop and significantly extend very young children's cognitive development.

PERSPECTIVES ON PARENTING AND EDUCATION: APPRENTICESHIP TRAINING

Rogoff (1990) argues that children's cognitive development is an apprenticeship that occurs through participation and social activity, guided by companions who stretch and support children's understanding of, and skill in, using the tools of the culture. She draws heavily on Vygotsy's theory in arguing that guided participation is widely used round the world, that is, the support of caregivers in arranging children's activities and revising their responsibilities as they gain skill or knowledge. The idea is that, with guidance, children participate in cultural activities that socialise them into skilled activities.

This suggests that we need to be sensitive to those different cultures represented within our own community, to systems of guided participation traditional to these cultures and their likely significance in building even young children's competence and skill in learning and problem solving.

The development of memory in young children

There are several reasons why practitioners may be interested in the memory capacity of young children. Two of the commonest reasons are:

1. To facilitate the recall of events and circumstances in order to help a young child to clarify the past so as to contribute to the 'coherent story' over time. Additionally, the child's capacity to make use of

an ability to remember external features of their environment helps them to prepare themselves for new situations. For example, we may use many tools like photographs, videos or drawings in order to familiarise a child with a new setting when preparing them for a significant move.

2. When young children are involved in forensic interviews we may be dependent on a young child's memory of events in order to explore the detail of circumstances surrounding possible abuse.

What is known about young children's memories suggests that they may be able to remember a great deal and that it is possible to trigger these memories by the use of visual clues, for example, pictures and objects. Indeed, depending on the type of event, a very young child may have a visual and sensual memory of places and events before they have the capacity of speech. For example, Paul who is now eight years old and greatly preoccupied with making sense of his parents' separation when he was two years old says, 'I remember sitting in my high chair and hearing my mum and dad shouting at one another above me. I was scared and remember my mum picking up her bag, leaving and not coming back for a long time. I remember the shouting and have a picture in my head but I had no words and couldn't do anything.'

Many adults assume that young children remember very little of what happens to them, but often the reverse is true, particularly if the events have salience and meaning for the child, for example, events surrounding a separation or other trauma.

It is common for separated children to be able to recall the visual details of their removal from home, especially if this was sudden and accompanied by strong reactions from the important figures in the young child's life. For example, Tammy now aged six recalled recently, 'I was very little and you came in a red car and it was very cold outside and you wrapped me in a blue blanket. Mummy was crying and Daddy was very angry and shouting.' Tammy was three years old when taken from home late at night.

Hence the memories are very often a combination of visual pictures and other sensory memories connected with the child's direct experience of the event through their other senses for example, smell, sense of hot and cold. When practitioners are working with young children they can use these visual clues to remind the child and hence to tune in to and support him/her with the remembered feelings surrounding the event. These memories can then be incorporated into a visual record of events which is built upon the child's own particular strands of memory and then used:

- to build a bridge between the child and the helping adult
- to help to avoid misperceptions of the past and any unhealthy self-blame in the very young child
- to begin to build the basis of a coherent story of the past, which can be worked and reworked during the subsequent developmental stages.

For example, Tommy is now four years old and has significant language delay, he is thought to have other learning difficulties. He was very confused about his past life with his mother. His social worker noticed that he did recognise his old house and began to encourage Tommy to remember details through taking photographs and encouraging him to draw the house.

Together he compiled with his carer a large folder of pictures. Using play people Tommy was able to re-enact memories of events at home and to elicit comfort and basic explanations from his carer and worker about the events that confused him. The play people are kept with the folder and consistently represent particular familiar adults and children. Using this medium, Tommy can express his understanding of the course of events and his feelings about them.

For example, he has used this to communicate to his mother the fear and anger he feels towards her violent partner and also to ask questions about the future. Tommy will, unfortunately, not be returning home and it is now possible to use the same medium to continue the story by introducing pictures and figures of his new family alongside photographs etc. so as to help facilitate the move.

This is a useful reminder that we should always assume that a child with particular problems with language and other learning difficulties is as much, if not more, in need of support in making sense of life events and may need help to record them through a different medium. Tommy surprised his worker and carer by having a much greater capacity than might have been supposed to make active use of an alternative method of communication.

FORENSIC EXAMINATION AND YOUNG CHILDREN'S MEMORY

Whereas one can be more relaxed in exploring young children's memories of events in direct work with them which has a therapeutic focus, the forensic interview imposes more restrictions. Saywitz and Goodman (1996) offer a very useful summary on what is known from current studies of children's memory and suggestibility at different stages of development.

MEMORY AND SUGGESTIBILITY

The ability to provide accurate testimony depends upon being able to remember and communicate memories to others. Therefore the amount of information a witness reports about an event generally increases with age.

It is often assumed that young children, for example pre-schoolers, are more suggestible than older children and adults. Nevertheless even young children do not necessarily have poor memories and they are not necessarily highly suggestible, they may merely be more compliant. Memory abilities and the ability to resist suggestion vary at any age, be it child or adulthood, depending on the situation and on personality factors. Variables include:

- the type of event experience
- the type of information to be recounted
- the conditions surrounding an interview
- the strength of the memory
- the language used
- post-event influences.

Researchers consistently emphasise the importance of the context in which the child is questioned, e.g. a context can provide physical reminders of an incident, it can also provide a socio-emotional atmosphere which can support or interfere with accurate and complete reporting of the child's memories. Much of the research suggests that other factors apart from age can play a large role in influencing eye witness accuracy.

FREE RECALL AND OPEN ENDED QUESTIONS

The research literature (Dent and Stephenson 1979) suggests that free recall is typically the most accurate form of memory record, for example, a response to an open ended question like 'what happened?' One problem however, is that such reports predictably are the more limited in detail when young children are questioned. Young children when asked more specifically about the details of an event, commonly demonstrate that they can provide more detailed recall than when offered an open ended question.

A problem for the interviewer is that it can be hard to determine, based on a young child's free recall, whether or not something major happened to them. The atmosphere of the questioning is very important, for example, if the interviewer implies accusation in their questions about the adult, this may lead to false reports about events especially from the accounts of pre-school children. Equally, if negative expectations about the person are suggested in the child's mind by the interviewer, the young child may seek to meet this expectation by providing a report of a negative experience with the adult which has not occurred.

SPECIFIC LEADING QUESTIONS AND SUGGESTIBILITY

Despite the fact that young children's free recall can be inaccurate at times, young children's responses to open ended questions provide accurate but abbreviated information rather than false information.

The amount of information one can obtain is increased if children are asked specifically about information of interest or when their memory is triggered by physical cues, for example a picture of the child's home or pre-school.

The cost of a more detailed questioning and cueing however is that inaccuracies in the account may then increase. A balance here needs to be found between free recall and specific questions. It may well be very helpful for joint interviewers to have some discussion prior to an interview about their own definition of what constitutes a specific question as opposed to a leading question in a particular set of circumstances. A supportive context is especially important in bolstering young children's resilience to suggestive misinformation about abuse.

Practice points

There needs to be interviewing protocol for children at different stages of development. These must be sensitive to:

- developmental differences in free recall
- suggestibility
- communicative competence
- socio-emotional concerns, i.e. the variability in children's emotional state depending upon their circumstances when they are interviewed.

Practitioners are often involved in working with young children who have experienced severe negative life events and multiple separations. One of the most contentious issues for those working directly with these young children concerns the debate as to whether or not young children between the ages of three and five have a capacity to move beyond egocentric thinking and involve themselves in perspective taking, i.e. the ability to connect imaginatively with another person's point of view or experience. Some of the challenges to Piaget's ideas of egocentrism might imply that, because even young children are aware of the perspectives of others, they are less likely to assume self-blame as a result of traumatic experiences within their family setting. However, it is far from unusual to work with a young child who has taken all the responsibility upon themselves for family events which, to an adult, appear to have no connection whatsoever with the child's behaviour or intention.

It may be that, as practitioners, we see in our work a particularly painful combination in traumatised young children, of a tendency to take too much responsibility on themselves (believing that they must be central in the causation of a negative event) combined with more sensitivity to other people's feelings, reactions, especially pain and distress, than was earlier thought by Piaget. This underlines the possibility that young children may be more significantly burdened and troubled by life traumas.

The effects of loss on young children

We work with many young children who experience traumatic losses, for example, the loss of a parent through divorce, abandonment, death or the child's compulsory removal from home. If we think of the impact of the death of a parent, the very young child is extremely vulnerable.

The loss of a parent when the young child is at the stage of self-centredness (approximately two to five years) and believes that everything that happens has a direct connection with his/her actions and/or wishes, can bring problems for those who care for such young children. Very young children have limited comprehension and their thinking is both concrete and full of magical ideas. They cannot grasp the idea of death being final and not infrequently they expect their lost parent to return some day.

Whether a parent dies or leaves home, then, a young child is likely to believe that Dad or Mum has left because the child has driven them away by their naughtiness or badness. All too often the parent who remains either explicitly or implicitly discourages questions about what has happened. The child may react by being particularly demanding towards the remaining parent or regress to an earlier stage of development, perhaps by bed wetting or having temper tantrums. This may be partly due to a fear that this parent will leave them too if they are difficult, which sometimes leads them to test this out.

We see how, all too easily, the very young children experiencing separations from significant adults may well, not only have their sense of trust severely shaken, but also take from the experiences an idea that they alone are responsible for what happens in their world (see also Chapters 4 and 5). This not only threatens the child's sense of a 'secure base' but also distorts the child's perception of the 'coherent story' of their life course. Therefore, they need at this stage and later, not only additional reassurance, but also help from supportive adults to make sense of family experiences, loss and change.

It is important to work to minimise the trauma of separation for toddlers, in particular, because of the profound impact of loss at a stage of development when the child is unable to 'think through' the experience. This understanding emphasises the importance of adequate pre-placement preparation for children of this age. If the child is unprepared, long-term worries and fears are likely, as well as a lack of trust in parental figures on whom the child needs to depend to keep them safe and secure.

Activity 6.1

Think of a child known to you between the ages of two and five who has experienced at least one significant separation.

1. Consider the negative messages the child may have taken from such events.

2. What might be said and done to reassure this child as to the continuity of their secure base?

3. How, in particular, might significant adults contribute to the child's understanding of the 'coherent story' of their life to date?

Practice point

Taking care to note the detail of events and circumstances surrounding an experience of loss for a young child can be helpful in:

- anticipating future triggers for painful memories and anxieties and

- making links with the young child's sensory memories when, as an older child, they are to put together their 'coherent story' of past events.

It pays great dividends if workers and carers take care to collect detailed information at the time, recording the facts of the events, the child's reaction and details of comfort offered. The availability of such information at a later stage, all the more valuable if recorded by an attachment figure, helps to provide a sense of continuity of the child's experience.

Separations at this stage of development often tend to interfere with the development of healthy autonomy in the very young child. For example, some children who have separations or loss experiences will tend to become particularly dependent or clingy. They may be more timid in expressing any age appropriate autonomy. As they have lost their trust in adults, they continue to need to keep them constantly within view. This may contribute to a pattern of 'anxious attachment' (see Chapter 2).

Other children, however, who have had similar experiences may reflect the opposite extreme in becoming too autonomous. These children can be recognised as they make considerable attempts to parent themselves. They may also withhold affection and seem stubborn and resistant. This type of reaction, if it persists over time, may promote a pattern of 'avoidant attachment'. It is important that we are aware that such developmental reactions to separation and loss may persist if not recognised and remedied. Because the conflict between dependency and independence characterises this stage very particularly, it is most important that the child experiences considerable reassurance, contact with key people after separation if at all possible, and many opportunities for increasing trust and age appropriate autonomy.

Because of the prominence of magical thinking and continued egocentricity, children between the ages of two and five are particularly vulnerable to misperceiving reasons for any move. The pre-school child tends to act out worries through play and significant adults need to pay close attention to the child's pattern of play as often what they say and what they do may give clues as to these misperceptions. Additionally, many pre-school children who have been abused or neglected frequently show delays in their language development.

Three key themes linked to this stage of development are:

- assertion and anger
- dependency and autonomy
- magical thinking.

These are key issues to consider when supporting a child at this stage of development and avoiding developmental delay.

The use of play with under-fives in promoting social and cognitive development

Observation of young children's play is often of great importance, not only because it provides clues as to the child's development progress, but also because it may offer an indication of the child's thinking about events. Play is also a key medium through which it is possible to support the child in giving them an opportunity to play out, and begin to make sense of their life experiences. It is therefore a potentially powerful therapeutic tool in direct work with very young children. As Santrock (1994) observes

> play therapy allows children to work off frustrations and is a medium through which the therapist can analyse children's conflicts and ways of coping with them. Children may feel less threatened and be more likely to express their true feelings in the context of play. (p.480)

The use of play as a medium for reparative work with young children

OPPORTUNITIES TO EXPLORE THEIR SENSES

The young child who is allowed to explore their senses of hearing, touch, sight and smell is more securely based in the world and this is a sound building block for later healthy development.

PLAY CAN HELP A CHILD TO MAKE SENSE OF THE WORLD AROUND THEM

Opportunities for young children, not only to explore in a physical sense and develop physical coordination, but also to investigate how things work, helps significantly in the learning about cause and effect. In play children can explore their own potential, their skills and limitations and, with support, can gain enjoyment in extending themselves.

THE OPPORTUNITY TO EXPRESS A RANGE OF FEELINGS

This is clearly particularly helpful in any direct or reparative work with children in distress. Play, especially social play, enhances the making and sustaining of relationships. In a setting where creative play is encouraged, the child's capacity for imagination can be developed. The play experience can help the child to handle fear and worry. In a general sense anxious children may be helped literally to enjoy themselves and thus be released from some of the anxiety they carry about their life circumstances. Children can re-enact in play particularly worrying or frightening experiences.

THE ROLE OF PLAY IN THE MANAGEMENT OF SPECIFIC LIFE STRESSES

Examples of these are hospital visits or planned separations. In reflecting on how we can incorporate the child's own experiences and their feelings about them, it is common to incorporate children's drawings, stories, photographs into a life story book. Fahlberg (1988) suggests that a life story book, when it is a record of the child's view of events can:

- provide a chronology of the child's life
- enhance self-esteem and identity formation
- help a child share his or her history with others
- assist in resolving separation issues
- identify connections between past, present and future
- facilitate attachments
- increase trust for adults
- help the child recognise and resolve strong emotions relating to past events
- separate reality from fantasy or magical thinking
- identify positives as well as negatives about their family of origin.

As young children in particular often express their feelings and perceptions through play, frequently concrete play, the harnessing of their chosen mode of communication in our own direct work with the child can be a powerful reparative tool.

Physical development

Determinants of early physical development

Bee (1995) explores three key factors which act as determinants to growth and early physical development. These are:

1. maturation
2. heredity

3. environmental factors, including diet and practice.

MATURATION

Maturational sequences are critical in the early physical development of young children. These apply in particular to changes in bones and muscles and neuronal development. Whereas the *rate* of development varies between children, the sequence is virtually the same for all children, even those children who have marked disabilities. Therefore we have the idea of developmental milestones which children with developmental difficulties take longer to reach than healthily developing infants. Esther Thelen (1989) a leading expert on motor development, points out, however, that many of us hold a simplistic view of the whole idea of the maturation process. Thelen challenges the idea that somehow all physical development unfolds in a sequence. She argues that a particular new movement or motor skill is what she calls 'a final common pathway' which results from a complex system of factors operating together which include cognition, perception and motivation as well as underlying physical changes.

HEREDITY

Because of our genetic heritage, Bee (1995) argues that each of us receives instructions for unique growth tendencies. She argues that both size and body shape seem to be heavily influenced by specific inheritance. For example, if parents are tall, then they will tend to have tall children. She argues additionally that the rate or tempo of growth, in addition to the final size, also seems to unfold in an inherited pattern. Therefore, for example, parents who are early developers would tend to have early developing children.

When working with children living in disadvantaged circumstances, it is very important that we do not make too many assumptions about their restricted potential for physical growth. Parents themselves may have never reached their own growth potential because of adverse environmental factors in their developing years, for example poor nutrition. This is where we see the significance of different environmental effects which are often revealed when a young child goes to a substitute family placement, and we see rapid 'catch-up' growth.

ENVIRONMENTAL EFFECTS, DIET AND PRACTICE

There are two obvious explanatory features of environmental effects which are of significance – diet and practice. Serious malnutrition during pregnancy can have a permanently negative effect on the developing foetus, retarding growth. This is very difficult to determine because most malnourished babies also grow up in environments that are deficient in other aspects. What is known is that poorly nourished children grow more slowly. If their diet later improves, such children may well show some increase in the rate of growth, but they are often still typically shorter and grow more slowly than their peers.

One particular significant effect may be that malnourished or undernourished infants and children often have less energy which can then affect the nature of interaction the child has, both with people and objects around him/her. Espinosa *et al.* (1992), when observing a group of Kenyan children in the playground, found that children who were undernourished were more solitary and less active than their well-nourished peers.

The practice of various physical activities also has some significance for the child's physical development. For example, the opportunities the individual child has for practice in walking, climbing stairs, and other basic physical activities, has an effect on the rate at which they acquire these skills. The results of most studies suggest that, for the development of such universal basic skills as crawling or walking, babies do need some amount of practice just to keep their physical system working. Therefore, whilst maturation can help to determine when a child is able to learn a particular skill, practice is clearly necessary for effective performance.

INDIVIDUAL DIFFERENCES IN EARLY PHYSICAL DEVELOPMENT

As well as the factors already mentioned, there are two further considerations

- whether or not pre-term babies develop more slowly and
- whether gender has some influence on early physical development.

PRE-TERM BABIES

Pre-term or low birth-weight babies move at a delayed rate through all the developmental sequences of the early years. This is what we might expect, as the pre-term baby is in fact maturationally younger than the full-term baby. Parents of pre-term babies need help to keep this difference in mind as they may become overly concerned when they compare their baby's progress with that of a full-term baby. A significant cause for optimism is that by the age of two or three years, the physically normal pre-term baby will catch up with his/her peers but in the early months, the baby's physical development is likely to be delayed and may cause parents significant anxiety.

BOYS AND GIRLS

Bee (1995) asserts that there are remarkably few sex differences in the physical development of young infants. Ethnic differences, however, do exist. Black African infants develop somewhat more rapidly than their white peers and Asian infants rather more slowly. The key point to remember is that our own cultural patterns and assumptions may strongly influence what we consider 'normal' growth for an infant. We must therefore be cautious in our interpretation of patterns of physical growth in babies from different cultures.

A general guide for the practitioner is that babies triple their body weight in the first year of life, and add between 12 and 15 inches to their length before they are aged 2.

Some particular problems

Children's difficulties

LANGUAGE DELAY

Language development is a critical component of learning because it promotes the development of cognitive processes and allows the child to attain self-control and to delay the gratification of urges. It gives the child a way of expressing their feelings other than acting them out behaviourally. It also makes it possible for the child to memorise events as the child's memories of a time before he can speak are scanty and are usually stored either in visual images or feelings. Many studies identify an association between language delay and behavioural problems in young children (Stevenson, Richman and Graham 1985).

Early identification of any particular reason for the language delay, including medical difficulties with intermittent hearing loss, is important in clarifying an appropriate focus for intervention. Douglas (1989) notes that:

> the frustration in communication that these children experience is evident in their behaviour. Toys are frequently thrown when children cannot make themselves understood, social skills develop slowly as they snatch instead of asking for what they want. Poor social relationships with other children as well as adults are common. (p.7)

The early identification of language delay and the careful exploration of the possible causes may be of vital importance in promoting the child's healthy emotional, cognitive and social development. There may be, for example, a hidden learning difficulty, a problem with the development of speech or the child may not be speaking because of very limited social interaction with adults and low levels of stimulation.

DEVELOPMENTAL DELAY OR DISABILITY

We meet many children in the course of our work who exhibit mild developmental difficulties and we often hear of them when their parents complain of behavioural problems. The child may be struggling with their developmental milestones and the parents may interpret the behaviour as a problem rather than seeing it as appropriate behaviour for the child's actual developmental stage. Helping parents to tune into appropriate expectations at one with the child's ability is clearly helpful here. Early counselling may well help parents recognise more appropriate ways of playing with their child and helping them to maximise their potential.

OVERACTIVITY

This is a frequent complaint from parents and is a crucial feature of a child's behaviour as it frequently disrupts the development of confident parenting patterns. These children need much more supervision and have difficulty entertaining themselves. This is exhausting for parents. Even babies can show a significant tendency in this regard, and as Douglas (1989) notes 'matching the level of stimulation to the needs of the baby is a very fine art and takes skill, patience, and good observation' (p.8). The support of a well-attuned health visitor and sensitive day-care services is clearly of great benefit here.

Parental and Social Problems

MATERNAL DEPRESSION

Researchers in recent years have found a disturbingly high numbers of mothers with young children who show marked symptoms of depression. (For a useful summary see Goodyer 1990.) There is a very strong association between maternal depression and behavioural difficulties in young children. Mothers who are particularly vulnerable are those who have had difficult relationships with their own parents and poor marriages, and whose husbands or partners have had long histories of personality problems, aggressiveness and anti-social attitudes. Commonly in these circumstances, a vicious circle of poor communication and low levels of cooperation exists so that both partners feel unsupported. The availability of marriage counselling is clearly indicated here and the more recent focus on family therapy and parenting skills training methods in helping parents in the joint management of their children focuses appropriate attention on the importance of the adult relationship.

Mary Main (1991) in her description of her framework for assessing parents' own attachment relationships, the Adult Attachment Interview, explores the ways in which a parent's perception of their early attachment history can have a very significant effect on the attachment pattern they establish with their own child. For example, the parent who experienced abuse and neglect in their own early years, providing they can reflect maturely on this experience and see the gaps and inadequacies as well as the good experiences from their own childhood can, nevertheless, provide a secure attachment relationship for their child.

Alternatively, parents who are out of touch with these abusive and neglectful experiences in their own account of their childhood may be more at risk of promoting a pattern of anxious or ambivalent attachment in their own children. This demonstrates the value of helping parents to reflect upon their parenting and to tune into their own early experience in order to sensitise them to the qualities and interactions in their parenting of their own children. This may well be a critical area for preventing the cycle of unhelpful attachment patterns within particular families and mirrors the focus on support for children in developing a coherent story of life events.

Environmental stresses

The stresses of poor housing and poverty are specific factors which add to the problems for parents in caring for young children. As Douglas (1989) comments:

> the large proportion of homeless families with young children and unsupported mothers living with pre-school children in single bedsits is an immense area of deprivation and distress. (p.9)

The existence of a local self-help group, community support or an individual professional, focusing on developing parents' self-reliance and working collaboratively with them, rather than imposing solutions, would appear to be most successful. The existence of a 'warm, confiding relationship' for isolated parents has been found by Richman (1977) to mediate to some degree this type of stress. Clearly, the broadest political perspective is of core relevance here in terms of ensuring that people have access to a job, a sufficient income and appropriate adequate housing in well-resourced neighbour- hoods.

Thompson (1995) encourages practitioners to consider the careful assessment of parents' needs for social support to identify the area of greatest difficulty with which they need help. For example, the parent may be isolated and need help to connect with effective local supports. They might need specific education to learn about realistic developmental expectations of their young children. Health, nutrition and hygiene may be a particular problem and focusing support as accurately as possible is likely to be most successful in outcomes for the children. We need to be cautious in assuming that informal supports to parents in their management of young children are helpful, as some informal supports merely confirm parents in unhelpful, punitive or damaging practices.

Moreover, parents are not necessarily supported by extended family as depending on the nature of the relationship, parents may be undermined by their own parents' criticism. Therefore, a careful assessment of the child, parent–child relationship, parents' circumstances and relationship with partners and extended family, alongside an awareness of the links with community supports is especially valuable in the effective planning of key resources for helping parents of very young children.

Sometimes it is possible to help parents with the direct information they require about how to cope with a particular problem, but at times, especially when parents are depressed, a wider approach of providing emotional support to the parents before even considering intervening in management techniques is required.

Rutter and Rutter (1993) highlight protective factors in children's responses to stress and disadvantage. These risk-reducers are:

- a positive temperament in the child
- gender (girls are less vulnerable than boys)
- the presence of an adult who has a warm, supportive and affection-ate relationship with the child and who does not show severe criti-cism
- the socialising influence of a positive school atmosphere.

They add that four possible mediating mechanisms stand out as likely to be most significant in protecting children from stress. These are:

1. reduction of risk impact

2. reduction of negative chain reactions

3. establishment and maintenance of self-esteem and self efficacy

4. an opening up of opportunities.

Activity 6.2

Reflect on the circumstances of a young child whom you know to have early behavioural difficulties.

1. Identify key factors from those already explored here, adding additional ones which appear to you to be of significance.

2. What mediating factors exist:

- within the child, for example, an outgoing temperament
- within the broader family setting, for example, a healthy attachment to someone within the family or a supportive adult relationship for the parent
- and within community and professional resources, for example resources of the local family centre, which may be harnessed for potentially effective intervention.

The importance of sibling relationships for development in the early years

Dunn (1993) is engaged in much fruitful research into the significance of sibling relationships in the early years. She explores the ways in which sibling relationships affect development.

Practice points

The nature of the sibling relationship, in particular pairings, should not be assumed. Therefore practitioners need to pay careful attention to the particular interactions between an identified sibling pair. The sibling relationship checklist (DoH 1991) is a useful tool for exploring the particular dynamics of an individual relationship.

Dunn and Kendrick (1982) have noted that infants under one year of age can demonstrate attachment behaviour towards their older siblings. This has real significance for separation effects when placing siblings in local authority accommodation. When placed together, siblings can provide comfort in an unfamiliar setting. Older siblings have been observed to calm younger children in strange situations and may be seen as the 'secure base' from which the younger child can obtain security.

Of significant concern is the fact that sibling behaviour is of prime importance in the promotion and maintenance of aggressive behaviour in some sibling pairs and has been shown to remain consistent over time. However, in sibling relationships where high levels of rivalry are observed, warmth and playfulness is often also seen. The conflict between the children is likely to have particular salience, especially when parents are under stress, and it would be easy to undervalue the connectedness and warmth which may also exist. There is no substitute, therefore, for the careful observation of the details of interaction and the particular dynamic which exists between an individual sibling pair.

Promoting a sense of healthy racial identity

Derman-Sparks (1991) explores the research evidence into the development of a young child's racial identity and notes the following key points.

- Very young children begin to notice the differences between them and their peers and to put together classificatory and evaluative ideas which they apply to these groupings.
- There are distinguishable developmental stages in the construction of racial identity and attitudes towards difference, whether this be to do with race, disability or other distinguishable differences.
- Even very young children are influenced in their self-view and in their attitudes towards other children by wider social stereotyping.

Young children's sense of identity and attitudes formulate through the interaction of three factors:

1. their own bodily experience and sensory information

2. their contact with their social environments

3. their developmental stage in cognitive terms.

Katz (1982) examined the development of racial awareness in young children from the age of two to six years. There appears to be no doubt that young children make early observations of racial difference and these evaluative judgements begin to influence this growing awareness at an early stage. The stages described are:

1. the early observations of racial cues

2. the formation of rudimentary concepts of racial difference

3. moving towards conceptual differentiation

4. recognition that these cues, for example skin colour, remain constant

5. the development of group concepts

6. the elaboration of these group concepts.

Alejandro-Wright (1985) confirms the observation that racial awareness begins at the pre-school stage but elaborates upon this to suggest that a full understanding emerges at a later stage of development at around 10 or 11 years. She delineates the process from:

> a vague, and undifferentiated awareness of skin colour differences to knowledge of the cluster of physical-biological attributes associated with racial membership and eventually to a social understanding of racial categorisation. (p.186)

By the age of two years, children are learning about gender difference and linked with their learning about colour, begin to apply these to skin colour. By three years of age, children demonstrate signs of being influenced by the broader societal biases and prejudices and may exhibit an early prejudicial attitude towards others on the basis of race. Between the ages of three and five years of age, children are struggling to make sense of the permanence of their personal attributes and are curious as to which of these attributes will remain constant. It is helpful at this stage to support children in sorting out the many experiences and variables of identity both in relation to themselves and in relation to peers who may exhibit particular differences. By the age of five, a child may begin to use racial reasons for avoiding other children who are different from themselves.

Derman-Sparks (1991) emphasises the need for what she calls anti-bias education with young children in relation to racial difference as well as gender and other differences.

As a child grows he/she needs a care environment which reverses any negative picture associated with the child's colour. The child needs encouragement in developing a positive view of him/herself in relation to the difference signalled by their skin colour.

The growing black child will need active support in developing strategies for combating racism in daily life, at school and in the community.

As McDonald (1991) notes, many black adults:

> have developed great strengths in the face of this adversity, and consequently teaching their children the skills for surviving and feeling proud in a white racist society.

Describing racist attacks, she continues:

> To convey such horrors to children in order to prepare them to defend themselves and to grow into integrated, positive adults is a major task of all black adults. (p.6)

This stresses the need for careful consideration of the attitudes of those adults caring for, and working with, young children and an awareness of the images and play materials which are made available to them at this stage. Maxime (1986) suggests some particular ideas for encouraging a healthy self-concept in a young child:

TECHNIQUES FOR WORK WITH CHILDREN UNDER FIVE

- When bathing a young child, even though the child may be at the pre-verbal stage of development, it is helpful to make comment about the child's skin colour, linking this with positive attributes.

- The photographs and posters, and so on which may be in the home or family centre need to contain black images.

- It is important to refrain, in a deliberate way, from any comment which may link the child's skin colour with lack of cleanliness, or any negative connotation.

- There has to be a preparedness to acknowledge the reality of the child's skin colour difference and to link this wherever possible with black adults in the child's life.

Maxime goes further in emphasising the role of the family:

> Black families, of course, have the task of heightening their level of racial awareness so as to provide positive ammunition for their children's self-esteem. The black family face the major task of enhancing and maintaining the positive self concept of their young in a world that

constantly negates their performance. Workers should draw on this information, and other useful strategies from the black community at large. (p.114)

Derman-Sparks and the ABC Task Force emphasise the importance of help-ful guidelines in direct work with young children. These include:

- The importance of connecting cultural activities to individual children and their families. Developing an awareness of other cultures builds on each individual child's understanding of their family context as culture is initially experienced in relation to family living.

- Remembering that whilst broad cultural patterns may affect all members of a specific ethnic group, each individual family expresses this culture in their own particular way.

- Connecting cultural activities to concrete daily life. This may be expressed through particular use of language, family stories, family values and spiritual beliefs and also in household customs.

There is very helpful guidance in *Looking After Children: Good Parenting, Good Outcomes* (DoH 1995). In particular, the Assessment and Action Record materials contains a section on identity which encourages the consideration of important questions. These can be used by the sensitive practitioner in part-nership with parents and with the child themselves, in order to clarify the child's needs and ensure the provision of services which are sensitive to all those needs.

As noted in Chapter 2, there has been considerable criticism of attachment theory because of a perceived over-emphasis on the exclusivity of importance of the mother–child bond. We need to be open in all substitute care settings to the range of patterns of family composition and a range of child rearing practices. It is helpful to remind ourselves of the importance of the 'hierarchy of attachment relationships' so that we can be open to accepting that a particular child may be cared for by a number of adults without their security being compromised.

This is not to imply that, if the child is disturbed by the lack of predictability in any aspects of their care, it is not an issue of concern. However, it appears important to guard against assumptions that role allocation in terms of caring for children will fit a eurocentric pattern.

Equally, in our assessments of attachment relationships, we must take care to take into account the fact that the *signs* practitioners may look for as indicators of positive bonds may have different significance in other cultures. For example, Rashid (1996) cites the eurocentric emphasis on the positive considerations of direct eye contact when assessing parent–child inter- actions. He sees this as merely one culturally specific notion of the strength of a relationship and adds:

> This becomes particularly important when the professionals' own cultural norms are markedly different from those of the children and care givers. Practitioners need to be aware of their own cultural norms, and those that underpin their professional judgements, as well as the cultural norms of their clients. (p.61)

We need to be curious as to the particular ways in which different cultural ideas and beliefs shape the operation of the attachment dynamics in different cultures. Maitra (1995) offers some useful pointers for practitioners in explaining unhelpful stereotyped assumptions and offers useful suggestions in providing more effective partnerships with families from other cultures.

Activity 6.2

Considering any child under five in a day care or nursery setting who is black or of mixed parentage, how far do you think the issues explored are being ad- dressed within the care setting?

Disability and self-image

The Disability, Discrimination.Act (1995) offers a definition of disability as follows: 'A physical or mental impairment which has a substantial and long term effect on the ability to carry out normal day-to-day activities' (Argent and Kerrane 1997, p.12).

Additionally, there is a definition of disability often called the 'social model' definition which stresses the combination of the effects of impairment and social oppression. This definition emphasises the role that society plays in adding to the disability of a person with impairments, acting to prevent their fullest participation in society and forming cultural, physical and social barriers to this full participation.

We often meet children in our work whose pace of development is causing concern to parents. Some of these children have underlying health problems, for example, significant hearing loss which can affect global development. We can support parents in identifying these at an early stage. However, other children have recognised developmental problems of a more severe nature and it is vital that families are supported by a network of self-help and professional services to boost the coping strategies of the individual family.

Argent and Kerrane (1997) emphasise the traumatic nature for most families of the birth of a disabled child. They stress the shock, grief and anger and the ensuing need for adjustments and readjustments for the parents. All parents with a disabled child run the risk of experiencing a crisis at some time during the child's development with which they will need help.

Argent and Kerrane stress the need to hold to principles enshrined in the Children Act (1989) and the Children (Scotland) Act 1995 which stress the importance of considering children with disabilities as 'children in need' with the accompanying right to request an assessment of the child's needs and of the parent's continuing capacity to offer care.

Stopford (1993) emphasises a number of factors that affect children with disabilities and their families, and offers practice suggestions. The stage at which the child is diagnosed as having a disability is a critical point at which to offer follow up and necessary support to families. Lack of such support may affect the development of healthy parent–child bonding. Lack of information about the disability at birth seen by many parents to be very frustrating as they may recognise for themselves at a very early stage, often before the diagnosis is reached, that all is not well.

Feelings which are very similar to those involved in bereavement, whether in relation to a child's physical or intellectual impairment, may result in additional stress on the family, increasing the trauma of adjustment to the disability, and at times resulting in only partial acceptance. This process of adjustment for parents may affect the child's view of him- or herself as a family member.

Families may have an understandable desire to protect the child and may be reluctant to allow the child with the disability the degree of independence offered to other children of the same age. This may lead to difficult behaviour at a later stage or to the child not reaching their full potential.

It is common for children with disabilities to have less opportunity for social and interpersonal interaction. They may well be expected to take less responsibility and they may have lower self-esteem than their non-disabled contemporaries. This may actually encourage increased dependency, loss of autonomy and reinforce poor self-esteem.

Young children's identity within society alongside the psychological and emotional progress in developmental tasks are related to the degree of physical autonomy and independence they are able to experience.

The involvement of medical professionals and others concerned with physical or cognitive problems arising from the disability, may reduce the possibility of an emphasis on the emotional needs of the child or young person with a disability.

What helps

Stopford makes a number of suggestions. An awareness in the professional support systems of critical points in the life cycle of the child or young person with disabilities may be vital in ensuring that support is available to the child and to the family at times when future difficulties may be mediated or even prevented. For example, birth/diagnosis, entry into schooling, adolescence and entering employment, may be particularly difficult stages.

Good information offered to the family is extremely important. Support at all stages for parents who are coming to terms with the reality of the disability and its meaning for the child and for themselves may be extremely helpful in preventing family difficulties as well as encouraging the independence and fulfilment of potential in the child themselves. Clear information about the availability of services, including social and emotional supports for the children and parents as well as medical advice may be extremely important in building the family's understanding of the child's needs and dispelling myths and misunderstandings about the disability.

Working with children in a way which encompasses an awareness of the whole child is likely to facilitate a focus on the development of a positive self-image and is likely to promote a more resourceful approach to life.

Stopford emphasises the value of a comprehensive care team being available to the whole family and offering support to any family member in relation to medical, social, educational and emotional issues. It is argued that the availability of such services, far from increasing dependency, may act to reduce the frustrations and anxiety for the child and the family.

Summary of developmental issues and considerations for practice

During the early years, development is specific to the individual, but occurs within a context of sequential developmental stages. The presence of at least one *attachment* relationship is of central importance as a mediating factor in circumstances of stress, and as a vehicle for practising social learning, the practice of physical skills and the support to cognitive development. Key elements which appear vital are *warmth* in relationships offered to the child and the experience of attaching to at least one adult who can be relied upon as a *secure base* from which healthy exploration and learning can be ventured in confidence.

- Early identification of significant difficulties in primary attachment relationships can be a focus for preventative and supportive work with parents and their young children.

Loss in the early years when young children do not have the cognitive abilities to make sense of these experiences has a profound impact.

- Unavoidable separations need to be carefully planned wherever possible for children at this stage and care must be taken to be sensitive to details of the circumstances which may both trigger later distress and/or facilitate the ensuing work on the child's 'coherent story.

Even very young children are *active participants* in interactions. Different temperamental styles can render individual infants or toddlers more or less easy for parents to manage and nurture.

- Individual workers need an awareness of the maturational process within the different developmental domains so that children who are struggling to negotiate key milestones can be identified and offered support.

- Practitioners need to be aware of the responses of the individual young child to stress. Rather than making assumptions, practitioners need to be aware of temperamental style, and personal history in the context of current circumstances.

- This overall assessment will sensitise practitioners to the particular vulnerabilities and resilient features within a particular child, their circumstances and existing attachment relationships.

This stage of development is significant for the beginnings of *social* understanding. Allied to this, there is an emergence of a sensitivity to differences principally in the areas of *gender, race* and *disability*.

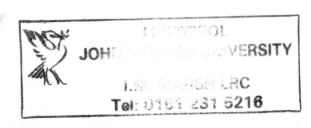

- It is helpful to take account of the importance of the nurturing environments offered within families and day care services for the provision of sensitive care for children from all ethnic groups.

- Strong multi-disciplinary links are valuable in the early identification of various forms of disability and strategies for supporting parents.

- It is of vital importance to listen to parents and to develop support which is sensitive to their religious, cultural and linguistic traditions.

Sibling relationships are highly salient and even very young children have the capacity to empathise and seek to support their younger siblings, implying an earlier growth of the capacity to take another person's perspective than was previously understood.

- Sibling relationships have to be respected as complex and important, with potential for both positive and less positive aspects.

CHAPTER 7

School Years

Introduction

This chapter will describe the major developmental changes that usually occur during school age years. First, the main intellectual changes in language, memory and cognition will be described. Social workers cannot be expected to carry out detailed intellectual assessments, as these should be done through the education system. However, an understanding of what is generally expected when development is progressing well can be helpful when assessing children in difficulties. Second, the socio-emotional developments of self-concept, relationships with others and morality will be described.

It is important to bear in mind that this division is, to some extent, artificial because of the way different strands of development interact. For example, growth in moral understanding may depend to a large extent on a child's level of cognition. Or peer relationships may be affected by the level of language competence.

Early and middle school years are times of tremendous developmental changes. Some of these changes, such as the development of literacy, are a direct result of formal education. Schools also provide the opportunity for significant changes in children's social lives and experiences. At the same time during this period there are surges in physical, cognitive, social and emotional maturation. Children's lives outside the home usually become increasingly important, they have friends, join clubs, are involved in sports and so on. During this period it can become painfully obvious if a child's potential is not being supported. It can also become clear if one child's potential is different from another's. Because of the number of changes to which the child is subject, adversity or abuse can have further dramatic effects on the child's life. At the same time there are aspects of school life in particular that can protect vulnerable children, as will be described below.

In keeping with the themes introduced in the earlier chapters this chapter will draw heavily on psychological literature with the aim of describing individual development within the human environment. Any actual ages given are drawn from the literature, but should be taken only as a guide. Each individual child develops at their own pace and, as indicated in previous chapters, trauma and adversity can affect children's development in different ways. \ .

The challenges in child protection are:

- to identify whether what would have been a child's normal pattern of development has been interrupted or disrupted in some way
- to establish whether the environment in which a child is living is likely to adversely affect their developmental path
- to find ways to maximise the possibility of them attaining their developmental potential.

Intellectual development

In this section we will describe the major intellectual developmental tasks in relation to language, reading, memory and cognitive development. The psychological literature on each of these subjects is vast and some issues are hotly contested, for example the nature of reading difficulties. Therefore, this book can only give an introduction to the concepts and further reading would be necessary to follow up any particular interest in more detail.

Language and literacy
LANGUAGE

By the time children start school they can usually understand and use language efficiently and effectively. This includes both the understanding of language and the use of language to express themselves. They already have experience of using language in fun for games and songs. Once in school they start to develop an understanding of ambiguity, verbal jokes and metaphor. By the age of six children can see that language can have multiple meanings and can therefore understand puns, and by eight love riddles and word games. They also understand about narrative and that language can be used to tell stories, not just about events, but also about motives and feelings.

However it is not until about 11 that they can really grasp abstract language (Smith and Cowie 1991).

During this time children change in the way they think about language. For example if pre-school children are asked to give the first word they think of when they hear the word 'dog' they will respond with characteristics of a *particular* dog, e.g. 'black' or 'big'. School-age children tend to respond in terms of categories, for example with 'animal' or another example of the category, e.g. 'cat'. They also begin to understand common characteristics between words such as 'emerald' and 'diamond' and can distinguish between similar words like 'cousin' and 'nephew'. They develop an understanding of comparatives, e.g. 'shorter' and ' deeper'. These may seem subtle differences but indicate that children's language moves away from relating simply to their own experiences in the here and now. They also start to have an understanding of the different uses of language (Santrok 1994).

In practice, this means that children may well be able to use language not only to talk about events that have happened to them, but also to relate some of the subtleties of events. When interviewing children about distressing or abusive events it will be important to assess their level of language comprehension and expression. People who already know the child well should be consulted wherever possible.

The relationship between thought and language is complex and not fully understand as yet and the extent to which a child can understand a concept for which they do not have the language is not clear. Children may experience more emotions than they have the vocabulary to describe. For example, Fahlberg (1994) notes that seven-year-old children find it much easier to act out feelings than to talk about them.

Language appears to develop independently of intelligence as measured by IQ tests and therefore cannot be used as the only guide to a child's intellectual development. Some environmental circumstances can delay development of language, specifically situations which limit the opportunities for responsive, sensitive communication with an adult (see Chapter 4 for more about adult–infant communication) such as occurs in some large families or institutions. In some cases children catch up once they are in school but if the delay persists through the first few years of school, children affected are also likely to show problems with literacy skills. Severe language delay in childhood can also be associated with social problems that persist into adulthood, including difficulties with intimate relationships and job and leisure prospects (Rutter and Rutter 1993).

Research with bilingual children has shown that having two languages may lead to slightly slower acquisition of both, but does not interfere with performance in either language. In fact, it can be associated with a better grasp of some concepts and flexibility of thought (Diaz 1983; Hakuta and Garcia 1989). However, this research has been done with children where neither of the two languages is stigmatised. The effects on children who enter an education system that does not understand their first language may be less positive.

Most profoundly deaf children have major deficits in spoken and written language and have difficulty speaking and reading at a basic level. However, children who have deaf parents do better on language and literacy skills. The indications are that this is because they have learnt to sign and therefore have a language that parallels spoken language (Schlesinger and Meadow 1972). This early language appears to help with later literacy. These findings are important as about 90 per cent of deaf children are born to hearing parents and therefore grow up in a world dominated by spoken language with which they cannot participate (Bee 1995).

In summary, therefore, the importance of language cannot be over-emphasised. It forms the foundation for the continuing development of early attachment and develops into the primary way for children to interact with the human environment. The main aspects of language development to remember during this stage are the move to a greater understanding of abstract concepts, an increased understanding and use of more subtle forms of language and the effect that language delay can have on other areas of

---

Activity 7.1

Ignoring other cues of communication such as body language, gestures etc., listen carefully to the verbal language of children ranging from the ages of five to ten. If possible, get a recording of the language of these children.

Listen to the way children use language to express themselves. Note the extent to which the children appear to be aware of their use of language to convey certain messages.

1. Are there obvious differences in the way they use language to themselves, adults and peers?

2. Do the older children demonstrate more sophisticated language forms?

development. Language problems can give rise to considerable adversity in childhood. Conversely, adversity such as abuse may be associated with delays in language development. Therefore, social workers must be alert to the level of language use of the children they are working with and take steps to address delays as appropriate. Some children will need specialised speech therapy, while others can benefit from the kind of language stimulation that results from attending a day centre or nursery, for example.

LITERACY

Learning to read and write also affects the way children think about language. Reading systematises language and allows the child access to many new forms of language and variations in its use. Increasing literacy also helps children with logical and scientific reasoning.

Children generally start learning to read and write by six or seven. In order to do this effectively it helps greatly if they come to school with an understanding of the reading conventions. In other words, they need to have some understanding that stories can be written down and that letters make up words that represent sounds etc. They also need to have the perceptual skills gained from drawing, doing jigsaws, pretend writing and so on (Meadows 1986). A child who has missed out on these experiences for any reason is in danger of falling behind right at the beginning of school, therefore, everything possible should be done to maximise their chances of gaining these skills before school age.

Figure 7.1 (adapted from Meadows 1986) shows the main stages of reading that can be expected through school years. Again reading skill is not an indication of overall intelligence as measured by IQ tests. There are many children who have specific problems with learning to read and spell whose overall intelligence is unimpaired. There is evidence that this may be due to a specific problem with rhyming skills, although the underlying cause is not yet completely understood (Rutter and Rutter 1993).

Problems with reading therefore can be extremely disabling to a child and can greatly interfere with school adjustment. Early intervention with reading difficulties is, therefore, very important. However, the number of different specific learning problems, the number of different theories about the causes and the number of different remedial programmes can lead to difficulty in gaining the appropriate help for an individual child. In practice, social workers would need to liaise closely with parents and education staff to ensure that a child receives prompt and effective help.

Stage 0 Up to 6	Prereading, 'pseudo-reading'	Understand thousands of words, but can read few if any. Understand stories read to them.
Stage 1 Ages 6–7	Initial reading and decoding	Level of difficulty of language read by the child is much below that understood when heard. By the end of stage 1 most understand up to 4000 words and can read about 600.
Stage 2 Ages 7–8	Confirmation and fluency	Listening is still more effective than reading. At end stage understand 9000, read 3000.
Stage 3 Ages 9–13/14	Reading for learning the new	Reading and listening about equal for comprehension, for some, reading may be more efficient for understanding.
Stage 4 Ages 14/15–17	Multiple viewpoints	Reading comprehension is better than listening comprehension for material of difficult content. For poorer readers, listening and reading comprehension may be equal.
Stage 5 Ages 18+	Construction and reconstruction	Reading is more efficient than listening.

Figure 7.1 Showing the stages of reading at different ages (adapted from Meadows (1986))

Memory

The study of memory is extremely complex because of its many components. Accurate memory depends on first attending to the important features to be remembered, then having the capacity to process and store that information and finally being able to retrieve and reconstruct the information. Memory is used in so many contexts, socially and educationally; there is a great difference between learning information by rote for exams and remembering who your best friend is. There is much research on each of these topics, but for the purposes of practice it is important only to know how children's memory can generally be expected to perform. When considering children's memory it is useful to remember that

- any person's memory will be affected by their thinking and language capacity
- people's memories are better for information that makes sense to them

- people do not store information like computers; memory is an active function that involves processing.

In experiments of *recognition* of previously seen pictures four-year-old children perform as well as adults. However, they are not as good at free *recall* from a list of items. This kind of ability gradually improves in young childhood. By twelve years, short-term memory (that is, quick recall of information) is at about the same level as that of most adults (Flavell 1985). At this age children have more knowledge of memory as a concept and begin to understand that techniques can be used to improve memory; for example, by nine or ten they know that it is easier to tell back a story in their own words rather than word for word as heard. They also become more accurate and realistic in predicting how good their memory will be, while younger children tend to be over-confident about what they will remember (Bee 1995; Meadows 1986).

Long-term memory also improves during middle and late school years. The effectiveness of long-term memory depends, in part, upon the strategies used when processing it in the first place and when retrieving it later on. Children's use of memory strategies increases with age. To some extent strategies can be learnt and formal and informal learning in school will impact upon the development of memory. Flavell (1985) describes four common memory strategies that develop during school-age years:

1. *Rehearsal*: Verbal rehearsal of information to be remembered significantly improves recall and its spontaneous use increases between the ages of five and ten. So, for example, school-age children can be seen muttering to themselves in order to remember. Children who do not spontaneously rehearse can be taught the techniques and their recall subsequently improves significantly.

2. *Organisation:* When having to remember a number of items it helps to cluster by types; for example, if remembering a shopping list it is easier to cluster the items into categories such as fruit, tins and so on. As children's understanding of categorisation increases so they are able to use this information to improve memory. Again, this is a strategy that can be taught.

3. *Elaboration*: Similar to, but developing later than organisation, elaboration involves more extensive processing of the information to be remembered, maybe by finding a way to associate items, or of linking a word to a personal experience.

4. *Retrieval strategies:* As they get older children learn that it may be worth persisting in trying to remember something. They also learn to be more systematic in their memory searches, so for example, if they have to recall three items from each of a number of categories they will try to get three from one category before turning their attention to the next.

Of course, it is easier to use techniques if one knows in advance that material must be recalled. In everyday life it is rarely important to remember lists of words or to repeat information word for word. However, memory is important within education and if children miss a lot of school because of other problems they may not learn and practise the above techniques. The fact that memory can be improved with help suggests a potential for practitioners, teachers and parents or carers to support a child who is exhibiting difficulties. Another important factor in memory is that very young children can exhibit powerful memory for information that they have interest and expertise in. So, for example, young children who develop an interest in dinosaurs can remember a lot of complex names, can incorporate new information quickly and put the information into categories. They are also extremely likely to have a much better memory for information about dinosaurs than many adults. The same is true for children with expertise in particular games or sports, for example chess: 'expertise makes any of us look very smart, very cognitively advanced; lack of expertise makes us look very dumb' (Bee 1995, p.212). When helping children who have difficulty with remembering information learnt at school, it may be worth exploring any particular interests and expertise they have, for example, knowledge about football, or a favourite pop group, both to *reassure* them that their memory can work well and to *encourage* them to consider the strategies they use. The kind of techniques that help memory at any age are the use of imagery, remembering the context of events, thinking about different modalities, e.g. smells and sounds, changing the order of events in the telling, trying to tell events from another perspective and using mnemonics.

MEMORY UNDER INTERVIEW CONDITIONS

In a comprehensive review of the recent research into children's recall under interview conditions, Saywitz and Goodman (1996) set out the main developments from pre-school to school years and describe practice implications. The following summarises some of their conclusions. It should be considered to be a guide only because of the huge individual differences between children and the number of factors that impinge on the recall of traumatic events.

Five- to eleven-year-old children often notice details that adults do not notice and therefore can produce a lot of information under free-recall conditions. Free-recall can then be followed up with open-ended specific questions and then increasingly specific questions and finally yes/no questions, if necessary. School-age children show more resistance to leading questions. When interviewing this age-group the issues above should be borne in mind as well as the following:

- This age group can benefit from information about the process and the legal implications.

- It is helpful to warn school-age children that they might not understand all the questions and help them with strategies for saying if they do not understand a question.

- Children may think they know what legal terms mean, but their knowledge should not be assumed and should always be explored.

Bee (1995) sums up general characteristics of child memory:

- Children can be very accurate in free-recall of events if given the chance to use their own words.

- Children can accurately pick out a picture of a 'culprit' in staged events which they have witnessed.

- In some circumstances children's memories may be better than adults for information that is very familiar or distinctive to them.

- Younger children provide less detail and less information about events, and it is only by about 13 or 14 that their accounts reliably become similar to adult levels of free-recall.

- Children rarely report something that did not happen.

- Younger, especially pre-school children, can be led into reporting inaccurately about physical events such as having been kissed while bathed.

Saywitz and Goodman describe two techniques for enhancing children's recall. One is the use of *cognitive* interviewing in which the child is asked to:

1. mentally reconstruct the *context* at the time of the crime

2. report even *partial* information regardless of its perceived importance

3. recount events in a variety of orders, for example, describing events in reverse order

4. report events from a variety of perspectives, for example, by asking what a toy on the shelf would have seen (to be used only from seven years old on, as younger children find it hard to describe from another's perspective).

A second technique is *narrative elaboration* in which children are taught to give a high level of detail about the following, and prompt cards are used to remind them of:

1. participants

2. settings

3. actions

4. conversation/affective states.

TRAUMA AND MEMORY

Children who have undergone traumatic experiences may be unlikely to want to recall them, and indeed may well have used techniques to help forget events.

There is some evidence that supports the possibility of the repression of traumatic memories (although see also Chapter 6). Saywitz and Goodman cite three such studies. Briere and Conte (1993) interviewed 450 men and women with alleged histories of childhood sexual abuse and more than 50 per cent said that for at least part of their childhood they had had periods of partial or total amnesia. Feldman-Summers and Pope (1994) surveyed 500 people about memories of abuse: 40 per cent of those who reported having experienced some form of abuse also had a period of total or partial amnesia. Williams (1994) interviewed women who as children were taken to hospital because of sexual abuse. Some 38 per cent of them had no memory of the assault or the hospital visit.

In Britain, 1121 survivors of sexual abuse wrote accounts of their experiences for the NSPCC National Commission of Inquiry into the Prevention of Child Abuse (Wattam and Woodward 1996). Of these, nearly a

Activity 7.2

Consider a child you are familiar with who has undergone traumatic events in the past. What techniques have you found or could you imagine finding useful in helping them to recall any good parts of their childhood.

Hints for answers

For example, you may ask them to recall a particular person that they felt safe with (who may not have been a member of the family). You could then ask them to remember colours, smells, places, sounds etc. that they associate with that person.

The same could be done with places, pets or events such as school trips etc.

A child could also be asked to tell the story of their childhood from the perspective of another person, e.g. a sibling.

quarter described total or partial memory block for a time. Half of them recovered their memory during therapy (Rickford 1997).

COGNITIVE DEVELOPMENT

This section elaborates on some of the theories of the development of thought processes or cognitive development described in Chapter 4 and relates them specifically to this age group. Underlying the growth in intellectual capacity are:

- the capacity to learn from experience
- the ability to adapt to one's environment. (Rutter and Rutter 1993)

PIAGET

It is now widely accepted, largely because of the work of Piaget (see, for example, Piaget 1952 and 1954), that children's cognitive development is an active and motivated process involving constant learning, unlearning and relearning. Again, it is accepted that children's thought processes are different in some ways from those of adults. Adults, therefore, need to be sensitive to the child's level of understanding in order to relate directly to them. Finally, Piaget saw that the main developmental feature was changes in styles of cognitive performance, not levels of achievement. As described in Chapter

4, Piaget's rather rigid stage theory of development has been challenged by experimental findings, but the outline of his theories about this age group will be presented as the concepts are still used widely.

As recounted in Chapter 4, pre-schoolers are described as moving through the *sensory-motor* stage where they have no mental representation of events, and the *pre-operational* stage when internal representations are beginning and can be seen in the use of language and make-believe. So they use some symbolism, but have difficulty with ordering too many objects, ordering by more than one dimension, and with reversibility of operations. Piaget described children at these stages as being essentially *egocentric* and unable to appreciate another person's point of view.

From the ages of about seven up to eleven children move through the *concrete operational* stage. Now children become less egocentric. Their mental functions involve the use of logic and they can think ideas through in order to work out the properties of objects in the world and to make deductive inferences.

Thus, by five or six they are able to understand, for example, that six objects placed in a small heap represent the same number of objects as six spread out in a long row; in other words they develop number *conservation* skills. At around seven or eight they develop mass conservation. This can be tested by rolling a piece of clay into the shape of a ball, then rolling it into a sausage shape. The child is asked whether the sausage contains the same amount of clay as the ball had. Younger children will say that the sausage contains more clay. A similar test can be done for the conservation of volume. A low, wide glass is filled with water which is then poured into a taller, thinner glass. It is usually not until around eleven that children fully grasp that the taller glass contains the *same* amount of liquid and not more.

Using more ecological and naturalistic methods researchers have found that children can, in fact, demonstrate many of these operations earlier than Piaget described (Donaldson 1978). However the experiments do seem to demonstrate some fascinating shifts in cognitive processes during school-age years. First, the change seems to be a development of the ability to *infer* about underlying reality, rather than simply responding to the surface appearance; in other words, the child can distinguish between what *seems* to be and what really is. Second, they demonstrate the ability to attend to, and take account of, *all* the features of the situation, not just the obvious change in shape. So, for example, in the liquid test, they observe that the second glass may be taller, but also that it is thinner. Third, the older child is more able to take account of the *transformation*; for example, the act of pouring the liquid from one glass to another. That is, instead of responding to each *state* as a snapshot of the situation as younger children do, school-age children see the dynamics of the *process*. Finally, they grasp that the process can be *reversed*, that the liquid stays the same amount despite the container, and can be poured back into the first glass (Flavell 1985).

As well as being important for academic work in school, all of these developments in cognitions will also have an influence on children's social cognitions. So, for example, there will be an improvement in children's ability to look below the surface of another person's action and make inferences about the underlying state of mind and reasons for actions. They should also have a greater understanding of cause and effect and the relationship between their actions and possible outcomes.

After this stage young people are described as moving into the stage of *formal operations* when abstract thought is possible, hypothetical reasoning becomes possible and logic is more sophisticated (see Chapter 8).

At all these stages children are described as adapting and organising their thought processes by both assimilation and accommodation. Assimilation requires the taking in of a new idea and fitting it into an existing way of thinking and accommodation requires adjusting the existing thought process to fit the new information.

Some ideas from Piaget that are useful for practice are:

- We should expect to see children actively trying to work out how the world they live in works and it is a cause for concern if they are not doing so.

- Initially in the school years, children's ability to grasp abstract concepts is limited, therefore explanations for what is happening to them need to be couched in concrete terms.

- If children are not able to assimilate new ideas and concepts their thought processes may be disorganised and unpredictable. Similarly, if they are unable to accommodate their thought patterns to new ideas and concepts their thinking could be rigid and unchanging.

- If a child's thought processes seem bizarre or unusual it may be helpful to try and see the world from their own viewpoint and work out what their logic is.

For example, some children whose cognitive skills are limited have great difficulty with understanding concepts of family relationships. Many of the young people encountered in practice are part of reconstituted families and may have half and step-siblings. Understanding these relationships may be even harder for children if they are not living at home. To help children understand where they fit in a family network it could be helpful to draw simple family diagrams, or use dolls. They could also be encouraged to play with the concepts by making up other families and working out the relationships. Such practice with logical skills could help a child who is cognitively delayed.

VYGOTSKY

Piaget deliberately ignored individual differences and also underplayed the role of the social environment of development. As described in the earlier chapters, all development occurs within an immediate and wider environment. Theories deriving from Vygotsky's work placed much more stress on the social aspects of cognitive development (see also Chapter 4). The use of language is central to Vygotsky's theory, especially the transition from external to internal speech. When children first start using language, Vygotksy argues, it is largely external, and is used to communicate with others. Then between the ages of three and seven years, children develop the ability to talk to themselves, to reflect on their own mental processes and to engage in a form of inner speech. Vygotsky linked the use of inner speech with social competence (Smith and Cowie 1991).

Vygotsky criticised Piaget for concentrating on the *content* of children's thought at the expense of considering the *functional* aspects. He also criticised the fact that Piaget was not interested in the way in which thinking is shaped by education. He claimed that Piaget assumed cognitive development to be a natural process. However, Vygotsky considered there to be a complex interaction between the maturation of cognitive processes and teaching so that 'teaching is only effective when it points to the road for development.... The school child has to learn to transform an ability "in itself" into an ability "for himself".' (van der Veer and Valsiner 1991, p.331). Teaching can therefore help a child's cognitive development along. Further, learning a specific task will help the child with learning a structural principle that can be applied to other situations. The key is that teaching can precede cognitive development: 'the teacher may faithfully explain a task or concept for six or seven lessons until, suddenly, the child grasps the idea' (van der Veer

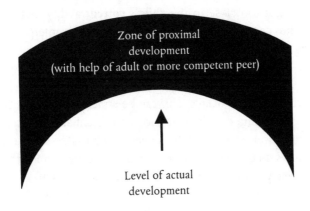

Figure 7.2 Vygotsky's 'Zone of Proximal Development' (Smith and Cowie 1991)

and Valsiner, p.335). This was an important idea because previously it had been widely considered that teaching should be pitched at the child's *current* level, not beyond it.

The central concept of his theory is the *zone of proximal development* (see Figure 7.2):

> The zone of proximal development of the child is the distance between his [*sic*] actual development, determined with the help of independently solved tasks, and the level of the potential development of the child, determined with the help of tasks solved by the child under the guidance of adults and in cooperation with his more intelligent partners. (Vygotsky 1933c/1935, cited by van der Veer and Valsiner p.337)

Therefore, according to Vygotsky it is through social interactions that a child gains the tools for thinking and learning. Rather than seeing the child as independently working out how the world works, Vygotsky stressed the importance of the cooperative process of engaging in mutual activities with more expert others. Adults or older children at a more skilful level can help the child's cognitive development with appropriate instruction and demonstration, known as *scaffolding*. It is crucial that the level of help is pitched appropriately: not too close to the child's current ability, but not too far ahead of it. Thus cognitive development is an essentially interpersonal activity occurring within a wider societal context (Smith and Cowie 1991).

It is not difficult to consider the links between such a theory and attachment. As described in Chapter 2, problems with attachment are associated with cognitive delays. This can be understood if one accepts that Vygotsky is correct and cognitive development is enhanced by a process of sensitive stimulation of thinking by someone who takes an interest in the child and knows their level of functioning. Such are the characteristics of the kind of sensitive parenting that promotes secure attachment.

This kind of support need not be confined to parents. Grandparents, teachers, relatives and other interested adults and older siblings could all play a role in providing a child with such support, and this could be especially important for children whose primary attachment is not secure. If a child is looked after away from home the theory should remind practitioners of the importance of involving those who already know the child in sharing information about them. If an alternative carer is to provide appropriate support for cognitive development it is essential that they have an understanding of their current level of functioning. There is also a message for intervention with children with disabilities. There may be a temptation to pitch material at the current level of functioning of a child with a disability so that they can experience success. However, if it is considered that each child has a *potential* level of achievement, regardless of physical or mental disability, there is a need sensitively to present children with more challenging material.

Social workers often find that their intervention with children is concentrated on socio-emotional issues. However, it is important to remember the complexities of the interaction between the social, emotional and cognitive domains. Children who have undergone trauma or abuse often have difficulty in understanding what has happened to them and in making intellectual sense of the events that may follow, such as moving to foster carers or appearing in court or at children's panels (e.g. the Scottish child care and justice system). This can then have an impact on their emotional reaction to events. It is, therefore, essential to be aware of the importance of cognitive factors and that cognitive deficits can act as a real vulnerability factor for children.

Activity 7.3

Using the theory of the zone of proximal development consider ways in which the social worker can either act as the skilled helper or support carers or parents in acting as skilled helpers in 'building the scaffolding' to help the child move to a better level of understanding of events. This would require finding out what the child's level of understanding is and starting from there.

Hints for answers

Any intervention would have to be tailored to the child's level of current functioning. For example, a young child may have difficulty with understanding cause and effect. An adult could spend time with the child playing games such as snooker, while pointing out that hitting one ball into another causes it to move. They could also look for computer games that involve cause and effect and keep pointing out the links. They could also take advantage of real life situations, such as the link between pressing the button on pedestrian crossing lights, the lights changing colour and the cars stopping.

Another example would be a 'looked after' child with a limited understanding of the notion of long term-care. The worker would need to build on the child's current understanding of timescales, for example, using the passing of birthdays or Christmas. These measures of time could then be used to mark out a 'long time' in more concrete terms.

In summary this section has described cognitive development using the frameworks of Piaget's and Vygotsky's theories. Vygotsky's emphasis on the social aspects of cognitive development make his theory particularly applicable to social work because of its basis in attachment theory. It also takes account of the context or environment in which the child's thought processes are developing.

Socio-emotional development

This section will describe the development of self-concept and relationships with others. We will then look at the world of school and, finally, moral development. Again, as stated at the beginning of the previous section, each one of these issues has a large literature of its own.

Self

Through social interaction children start to appreciate that others have a view of them, and from this start to build up a view of themselves. The evidence shows that during school years children shift from defining themselves only by external characteristics such as 'tall' or 'fair haired' and start to use internal characteristics such as 'easily upset' or 'having a good sense of humour'. They increasingly use terms of social characteristics and social comparison. By seven they have usually internalised those reactions that depend on the expectations of others, for example shame or pride, and can describe situations that bring these about. By this age they can also describe mixed feelings. From about eight to ten years they become increasingly able to put themselves in another's place and view things from their perspective (Bee 1994; Santrok 1994; Smith and Cowie 1991).

ATTRIBUTION

In Chapter 4 the concept of attribution was introduced. This describes the kind of explanations people give about success or failure on tasks. At any age success on a task can be attributed to one's own efforts or to outside factors such as the intrinsic difficulty of the task or to luck. Soon after starting school, probably because success or failure is very clear cut in school, children develop an idea of their own relative ability. They become aware of the need for effort and start to distinguish between the relative contributions to success or otherwise of ability, effort and external factors. If they are not accurate in judging these relative contributions then attributions can be confused. Consider, for example, children who always attribute failure to their own inability, even on tasks that no child of their age could be expected to achieve; or children who take personal credit for success on tasks that have been joint endeavours.

SELF-EFFICACY

The way a child views the outcome on tasks will then affect their sense of self-efficacy; in other words whether they believe that they have the ability to achieve on future tasks (Bandura 1981). Adult reactions are crucial in the development of self-efficacy. If important adults appear to expect them to fail on a task there is little motivation for them to try. Moreover, the arousal caused from fear of failure can cause failure and further contribute to a lowered sense of self-efficacy. These feelings of having poor ability and of low efficacy can in turn lead to poor development of self-esteem. Children who have undergone trauma that has reduced their sense of efficacy and control may well demonstrate such problems.

SELF-ESTEEM

'One of the most basic postulates in an individual's self-theory concerns self-esteem' (Ricks 1985, p.213). Self-esteem and the related concept of self-efficacy recur again and again in the literature of resilience (Brooks 1994; Gilligan 1997; Ricks 1985; Werner 1990). The roots of self-esteem lie firmly in early attachment experiences as can be seen in the positive-interaction cycle described in Chapter 2 (Falhberg 1994). Ricks suggests that someone with high self-esteem carries with them a 'loving parent' who approves of them. It is related to the experience of at least one close relationship and can be improved by the experience of success in relationships or on valued tasks (Gilligan 1997). It continues to be of importance throughout development. For example, a recent study of outcomes for teenagers subject to social service intervention showed an association between good outcomes and pre-intervention high self-esteem and good school progress (Triseliotis*et al.* 1995).

A useful definition of self-esteem is: 'Appreciating my own worth and importance and having the character to be accountable for myself and to act responsibly toward others' (California State Dept of Education, cited in Brooks 1994, p.547).

This definition incorporates the goal of much long-term work with children, which aims not only to help them to feel better about themselves, but also to recognise the importance of interrelationships and of empathy with others. Many of the school-age children encountered in practice, including those with attachment difficulties, have very poor self-esteem, very little sense of personal efficacy and feelings of being out of control of events. Intervention aimed to reverse some of this process should boost resilience and help prevent the escalation of problems.

Brooks gives pointers for identifying children with low self-esteem. Some young people show signs of low self-esteem only in some areas of their life, for example, school work, but not in others, for example, sport. Others show it in all aspects of their life. With some it is easy to identify, especially those who verbalise it, for example, by saying 'I'm useless'. With others it can be inferred from the coping strategies that they use, for example, counterproductive behaviour, giving up on tasks, avoiding tasks, messing about, making excuses and so on. Children with high self-esteem see successes as due to their own efforts, resources and abilities, but are realistic, and have a sense of personal control over successes and failures. Those with a low self-esteem see their successes as due to chance or lack of control. They view failures as caused by unchangeable factors, for example, a lack of ability or intelligence. They demonstrate a sense of helplessness and hopelessness, expect to fail and show self-defeating behaviour.

'The importance of personal control and empowerment as the basic scaffolding for self-esteem, motivation, and resilience has been emphasised by a number of clinicians and researchers' (Brooks 1994, p.548).

It is during school years that problems with self-esteem can become very evident, it is also during these years that there is great potential for positive intervention, particularly as improvements in one area of life can have spin-off effects:

> experience of success in one arena of life led to enhanced self-esteem and a feeling of self-efficacy enabling them to cope more successfully with the subsequent life challenges and adaptations. (Rutter 1985, p.604, cited in Brooks 1994)

Brooks (1991; 1994) describes ways in which self-esteem can be enhanced:

1. Create an environment at home and school that reinforces the probability that a child will be successful and will experience that success as due to their own abilities and efforts. That is, attempt to empower children and reinforce their sense of personal control with the aim of increasing their sense of ownership and responsibility for their own life.

2. Create an environment that reinforces the child's belief that mistakes and failure are acceptable and to be expected and are ways of learning. Convince them that failures can eventually lead to success.

3. Look for *islands of competence* for the child and work with them to help the child experience feelings of success and mastery. Do this by:

    a) encouraging contributions

    b) enhancing decision-making skills

    c) offering encouragement and positive feedback

    d) encouraging the development of self-discipline

e) enhancing ability to deal with mistakes and failure.

Harter (1982), suggested that self-esteem is based in the balance between what the child would like to be and what they think they actually are, particularly for areas that matter to them. The greater the difference the lower the self-esteem. For example, a child who would like to be good at art, but perceives their drawings to be poor will have a lower self-esteem than a child who does not value art and whose drawings are poor. Santrok (1994), drawing on Harter's work, identifies four ways to improve self-esteem:

1. Identify the causes of low self-esteem and the domains of competence *important* to the child from the following categories (for younger children):

   a) scholastic competence

   b) athletic competence

   c) social acceptance

   d) physical appearance

   e) behavioural conduct

   f) and general self-worth, (for adolescents add):

   g) close friendship

   h) romantic appeal

   i) job competence

2. Give emotional support and approval.

3. Help with achievement.

4. Encourage coping through attempting a task, not avoiding it.

GENDER IDENTITY

By the time children start school, gender identity and sex-role behaviour is strongly established (see Chapter 6). By about two years most children have a correct gender *identity*, that is, they can correctly label themselves and others. From three they play mainly with same-sex peers and begin developing sex-role knowledge. By four or five they understand gender *stability*, for example a boy knows he will grow up to be a man. Over the next few years they develop gender *constancy*, in which they understand that gender does not change with change of clothes, hair or activity (Schaffer 1996).

There have been numerous studies into the complex processes involved in the development of gender identity. Many of these have been reviewed in detail by Golombok and Fivush (1994) and some of their conclusions will be summarised here.

The reinforcement of different sex-role behaviour begins very early. By school age most children will have been encouraged to engage in sex-typed activities and to play with sex-typed toys. There will be individual differences between children, but the boys are likely to have played with toys that encourage invention, manipulation and understanding of the *physical* world, while girls' toys encourage initiation, proximity to the caretaker and understanding of the *interpersonal* world. Children will also have engaged in an active process of observing others and working out appropriate sex-role behaviour. The boys are likely to have received the strongest messages about 'appropriate' sex-role behaviour and to have been discouraged from or even punished for engaging in 'girl'-type activity.

Once they start school children develop more complex notions of gender which are less rigid and stereotypical. They realise that individuals can vary in their personal preferences. However, the gender divide in activity and experience continues throughout the school years. During middle childhood girls' friendships tend to be one-to-one, close and intimate, while boys play rule-governed games in large groups. One study showed that by the age of six and a half, children are eleven times more likely to play with a same-sex peer than an opposite sex peer (Maccoby and Jacklin 1987). By the age of seven children will actively avoid playing with opposite sex peers. Boys are particularly rigid in this and control *each other's* behaviour by using labels such as 'sissy'.

There tend to be differences in the ways in which girls and boys behave in school. Unless controlled by the teacher, boys dominate in class, especially with the use of computers. They tend to use more direct demands with peers and generally are allowed to express more aggression than girls. There is also some evidence that teachers treat girls and boys differently, praising boys for getting the right answers and girls for being obedient and working neatly.

In a feminist analysis of the gender development of boys and girls, Unger and Crawford (1992) conclude that by the middle school years girls are in some ways limited by their gender roles. For example, they are subject to greater adult supervision and are given much less freedom to travel alone outside the home. As they progress through school girls are more likely to opt out of mathematics and science subjects.

Those who avoid taking on rigid sex roles fare better, that is, girls who could be described as 'tomboys' are more likely to be popular, creative and to carry on sports into teenage years:

> girls who resist becoming gendered continue to take math and science courses and to compete in sports. Such activities help to maintain the high self-esteem needed by girls to fight pressures toward conformity that become stronger as adolescence approaches. (Unger and Crawford 1992, p.262)

In order to avoid the limitations of rigid sex-role behaviour girls need:

- positive female role models
- positive images of women in books and on television
- parental support and encouragement
- school support and encouragement.

Overall, it seems that gender stereotyping can lead to limitations for both genders: 'While girls are socialised for over-independence and passivity, boys are socialised for over-independence and a lack of close ties' (Unger and Crawford 1992, p.264).

Boys may have the advantages of more freedom, more activity-oriented toys and more power. However, the pressure on boys to be 'boys' is very great: it is far more socially unacceptable for a boy to be labelled a 'sissy' than for a girl to be labelled a 'tomboy'. It is often not until adolescence that boys are able to develop close and intimate friendships, and these are usually with girlfriends.

The implications of these issues for practice are many. As described in Chapter 4, resilience is associated with a lack of rigid gender stereotyped traits, thus resilience in boys is associated with the ability to express emotions, social perception and nurturance while in girls resilience is associated with autonomy and independence.

Both male and female social workers can act as role models themselves: women as role models of working women, men as males demonstrating care and concern. They can encourage children to take part in a wide range of activities, including some they may not normally consider to be gender appropriate. Boys can be given the opportunity to care for younger children while girls can be given the opportunity for autonomy and independence.

Staff in children's centres, nurseries, residential homes, residential schools and foster carers should all be aware of the ease with which gender stereotyping can occur and the power of self-policing by groups of children. For example, any child who demonstrates interest in non-stereotypical activity will need active support. Groupwork can be a fruitful arena for the exploration of gender roles with children and has been used to particularly good effect with girls (Carpenter and Young 1986).

ETHNIC IDENTITY

Ethnic awareness may change and develop during school years. Schaffer (1996) points out that there are majority and minority groups in most societies and that on a number of quality of life indicators minority groups will be at a disadvantage. The effects of such disadvantage filters down to the children so that 'how society is stratified will affect the behaviour of all its members, whether they belong to the majority or to a minority' (p.348). Something that all minority groups experience is a high likelihood of encountering prejudice. There is evidence of developmental stages in the expression of prejudice. Aboud (1988) found that up to about three or four years of age there is a lack of ethnic awareness and of prejudice but that from four to seven children become more aware of ethnic difference and have negative attitudes to those who are 'different' from them. From eight this effect begins to decline again as their thinking becomes less rigid. There is evidence that *all* children in a society are affected by societal prejudices. In studies carried out in white dominated societies when four-year-old children are shown pictures of white and black children and asked who they would prefer to play with white children choose white children and black children also mainly choose the picture of the white child. This effect strengthens up to about seven when black children start to choose the picture of the black child (e.g. Vaughn 1964). More recently the extent to which children of minority groups choose pictures of their own group has increased (Davey 1983). Children also tend to segregate by race in their actual play, although the segregation by sex is greater (see Smith and Cowie 1991).

This suggests that there is potential for positive work with children on issues of racial prejudice at around seven to eight years and schools can play a major part in this (Smith and Cowie 1991). However, it is within school that children from ethnic minorities may also experience subtle forms of racism from adults. Schaffer (1996) cites two British studies that found evidence of teachers treating children differently on the basis of race. One, with pre-school children, carried out in Scotland, showed nursery teachers' interactions with Asian children to be more controlling, directive and less responsive than those with white children (Ogilvy *et al.* 1992). Another, carried out in England showed that teachers over-estimated the level of activity of six- to seven-year-old Asian boys. They were more likely to rate Asian boys as hyperactive than white boys, even when objective measures of actual activity showed them to have equal levels of activity (Sonuga-Barke *et al.* 1993).

What, then, are the implications of these findings for the development of ethnic identity within individual children? By the age of four children can usually recognise their own ethnicity, but on a superficial level. Their understanding of ethnicity as a constant attribute does not fully develop until about eight or nine years (Aboud 1988). However, the sense that is made of ethnic identity depends on a number of factors and the complexities of how children develop both *group* identity and *individual* identity are great:

> Belonging to a particular social group, and being able to define oneself in terms of that group, may have many advantages for a child, but when that group is subject to adverse discrimination and is looked down upon by the rest of society there may be unfortunate consequences for the way in which children define and evaluate themselves. (Schaffer 1996, p.350)

Schaffer further describes how before the early 1960s it was taken for granted that black children grew up feeling inferior because they internalised the dominant views of their society. However, more recently there is increasing recognition of the role of the immediate family in mediating the effects of living in a racist society. Thus children may be aware of being a member of a group that is discriminated against, but may have a positive sense of self because their family has fostered a sense of pride in and acceptance of their racial identity. This again demonstrates how a positive family relationship can provide the black child with protection in the face of the adversity of living in a racist society.

Maxime (1986) suggests that black identity is an active developmental process influenced by various internal and external factors. While the majority of children do develop a positive racial identity, some may pick up negative images which are internalised. She describes school years as being the time when children are most vulnerable to the problems of 'identity confusion' as a result.

The over-representation of black and mixed race children in the care system, and the fact that the care system itself is still predominantly white may render such children vulnerable to low self-esteem and negative self-images (Parker *et al.* 1991). Maxime sets out suggestions for supporting children aged twelve and under in the development of positive ethnic identity which include using natural opportunities to discuss race, taking racially motivated incidents seriously and providing children with positive role models.

Dwivedi (1996) emphasises the extent to which black children are disempowered by social work services that negate their cultural, racial and linguistic needs. Modi and others provide a checklist for workers in assessing the needs of black children and state that:

> A black perspective empowers black children by promoting a positive black identity... All practitioners involved in working with black children and young people have a positive contribution to make in enhancing and nurturing a positive racial identity. (Modi, Marks and Wattley 1995, p.95)

In summary, then, it is during school years that important aspects of self-concept are developing, and adversity during this time can have a devastating effect upon a child's sense of self. Therefore practitioners need to be alert to the potentially damaging impact of disruption and provide appropriate and prompt intervention aimed at promoting the healthy development of the child's core being.

Family

Although school-age children can cope with longer periods of separation from attachment figures, the attachment itself is just as strong as in pre-school children. Their experience and increased cognitive powers means that they appreciate that relationships endure over time and distance. However, the family or substitute family's role as the secure base is crucial, especially during the early years of school. Children need to feel that they are exploring the new world of school from a secure background.

SEPARATION AND LOSS

At these ages children can show prolonged grief reactions at the loss of such an attachment figure and may also find it harder to make new attachments to substitute parents than pre-school children.

Separation or loss can create anxiety, and cause a child to feel frightened, unwanted and unloved. They may show their upset by impulsive behaviour, or by becoming depressed and withdrawn. They appear to need adult models and seek approval, sometimes by making exaggerated claims. Trauma may lead to them regressing somewhat in their behaviour; for example, they may use more 'babyish' language, or ask for help with self-care tasks that they could previously manage. For children who are just adapting to early school years, such regression may be difficult to manage.

In practice, children undergoing loss or separation need to be given as much age-appropriate information as possible that takes account of their level of emotional and cognitive development. Because they are at a stage of considering issues of fairness they may be very concerned with the question of 'why me?' As described above, school age children should be able to understand that people can have mixed feelings and therefore should be able to explore such feelings with support. In addition they need the comfort and supportive structure of familiar routines (Fahlberg 1994).

Peers

Friendship in childhood has six functions (Gottman and Parker 1987, cited in Santrok 1994, p.472):

1. Companionship

2. Stimulation

3. Physical support

4. Ego support

5. Social comparison

6. Intimacy and affection

Just as children change in their descriptions of *themselves* during school years, so children start to describe their *friends* by increasingly referring to internal characteristics. This change parallels the developments in the way friends are chosen. Thus up to about 7 or 8 years friendships are often based on proximity and common activities. So younger children will play rather indiscriminately with other children in the neighbourhood. At about 9 or 10 children start to see their friends as people with whom they have shared values and things in common. From 11 to 12 friendships are increasingly based on understanding, self-disclosure and shared interests (Smith and Cowie 1991).

As described in the previous section, children's friendships are strongly grouped by gender and to an extent by ethnicity. Observations have shown that boys tend to play in larger groups, with more ethnic mix. Their games appear to focus on competition and team games. Girls play in smaller groups and their activities focus on intimacy and exclusiveness. When children move into adolescence the strict gender divide in activities starts to break down (Golombok and Fivush 1994).

Although good peer relationships can compensate to some extent for poor attachment experiences, there is evidence of an association between the quality of attachments and the quality of friendships. Children with secure attachments tend to relate to peers in a positive, fair and responsive way, whereas children with insecure avoidant attachments either exhibit aggression towards or detachment from peers (Howe 1995).

PEER RATINGS

A study exploring children's own ratings of their peers found that children are categorised in one of five ways which can be described as popular, controversial, rejected, neglected or average (Coie and Dodge 1983).

- *Popular* children lead in a cooperative way. In particular, they have better skills at joining in group activity because they participate in a way consistent with the group's activities and do so in a friendly manner that avoids conflict and is open to compromise.

- *Controversial* children may have some leadership skills, but also fight and are disruptive, so although they may be looked up to, they are also feared.

- *Rejected* children are both disruptive and lack cooperative or leadership skills. They tend to join group activities by 'barging in' and may disagree with the group activities and attempt to assert their own ideas and feelings aggressively. Essentially they appear to lack social skills when interacting with peers.

- *Neglected* children are not aggressive, and lack cooperative or leadership skills.

- *Average* children make good friendships and are neither overly aggressive nor shy.

When children were followed over four years 30 per cent of those being originally rated as 'rejected' were still in that category. Another 30 per cent had shifted to being 'neglected'.

Peer rejection in childhood is associated with psychiatric disorder at the time and also with school failure and a range of psychiatric and psychosocial problems in adulthood. These are correlational findings only, but there could be a number of reasons for poor outcomes (Rutter and Rutter 1993):

- Rejection in itself is a stressor.

- Lack of friends means having a lack of social support, which is a major buffer from psychiatric problems.

- Lack of friends can mean a lack of involvement in school activities and missing out on opportunities for personal development.

- Peer rejection can lead to low self-esteem and poor self-efficacy

- The behaviour that is associated with peer rejection, especially aggression, may in itself be associated with later problems.

AGGRESSION

In their work with children, social workers are often presented with children who have problems with aggression, a main characteristic associated with rejection. Most children show some aggression, although by seven this is mainly expressed verbally. Some consistently show a lot of aggression. This kind of persistent aggression is related to irritable and ineffective discipline at home, poor parental monitoring and lack of warmth.

Rutter and Rutter (1993) provide a detailed examination of child aggression drawn extensively from research material. They describe how, normally, anger outbursts are common in infancy, peaking in the second year, accompanied by physical manifestations. This anger can be of two kinds:

1. manifestation of *distress*

2. to gain something, i.e. *instrumental.*

Instrumental anger, in particular, should decline between the ages of three and seven, while aggressive behaviour normally drops during pre-school years. So that before starting school, tantrums, fighting and destructiveness usually decline. By the time children are in school their anger is usually expressed as:

1. person-directed *retaliatory* aggression

2. *hostile* outbursts.

Activity 7.4

What advice would you give carers, parents and teachers of a child who appears to be rejected by their peers? Compare your ideas with those described below.

Dodge (1980) has described a 'hostile' cycle that illustrates how aggressive behaviour can escalate. Pre-school children tend to see all acts as intentional, by school age, children should learn that some outcomes are unintentional. For example, they should be able to differentiate between a child accidentally bumping into them or deliberately pushing them. Dodge suggests that some children attribute hostile intent to peers who cause accidental hurt. Because they then retaliate with aggression they are likely to increase their chances of becoming unpopular and therefore of becoming victims of intentional hurt. This cycle can spiral so that the child becomes increasingly rejected.

Aggression can also become bullying. In one survey one in ten children stated that they were bullied sometimes, while one in fifteen said they were bullied several times a week (Yates and Smith 1989). The aggressors are usually boys while the victims are both boys and girls and especially children from an ethnic minority or with some form of disability.

HELP WITH PEER PROBLEMS

In their review of peer relations, Malik and Furman (1993) describe six approaches to helping with peer problems; which include the following.

Social skills training

This can be done with either individuals or groups and is based on the assumption that unpopular children have difficulties with interpersonal interactions. They describe two commercial programmes which aim to teach a number of social skills in a series of lessons. These programmes seem to work best with children aged ten or under. The skills include listening, handling 'saying no' to stay out of trouble etc. Each skill is broken down into components which are explained to the child and role play is used to practise skills. For example, one component may be advice on how to enter a group of children appropriately.

Social cognitive training

This approach focuses on underlying cognitive processes in the hope that changing them will alter overt behaviour. For example, they describe a programme called 'Think Aloud' that aims to teach children a more effective problem-solving style and to reduce impulsivity. Briefly, children are taught to ask themselves four questions in peer situations:

- What is my problem?
- How can I solve it?
- Am I using the best plan?
- How did I do it?

Another cognitive approach is to encourage children to think about situations from another's perspective.

Fostering successful peer experiences

This approach aims to help children with the unstructured world of unsupervised peer group activity. The programme takes children through a carefully graded series of activities:

- The children participate in a highly structured therapy group to learn social skills.
- They then participate in a highly structured naturalistic peer group, e.g. swimming lessons.
- Then they are encouraged to increase participation in a pairs interaction with adult monitoring.
- They then move to participate in a naturalistic peer group of 'intermediate difficulty', e.g. outdoor activities.
- Finally they join a naturally occurring semi-structured group, like scouts or sports groups.

Changing social contexts

The social milieu appears to affect peer interactions. Malik and Furman describe work in Norway which aimed to change the social context for peer relations (Olweus 1993). Information and guidelines were distributed to schools and parents aiming:

- to create an atmosphere of warmth in schools
- to communicate that certain behaviours would not be tolerated

- to ensure that adults were clear authorities; unacceptable behaviour would have clear, consistent, non-hostile, non-physical sanctions.

The results appeared to show a decrease in bullying and victimisation.

In summary therefore it is a cause for concern if a child is not forming close friendships during school years. Both the reasons causing the lack of friends (especially aggressive behaviour) and the lack of friends in itself may contribute to current and future psychosocial problems. Conversely, having healthy friendships can be a powerful protective factor for children under stress.

School

As described above, schools provide the formal environment for the development of literacy and cognitive skills. But they are very particular social worlds in their own right which therefore have a tremendous impact upon children's social development. Meadows (1986) describes the factors that define the school culture:

- Children need very quickly to learn the social world of school which requires understanding the, often conflicting, demands of peers and teachers. Clearly, a child can be more or less prepared for the transition to school, depending on the home environment.

- The kind of language between adult and child is different in school from that at home. For example, often the teacher asks questions the teacher already knows the answer to and the child knows that they know the answer. In other words, there is a ritual to checking learning that the child has to learn.

- There are many rules of behaviour that the child has to either learn or infer; for example, to put their hand up before speaking. Children who are not able to or choose not to adapt to school ways are liable to be categorised as 'bad'.

- Children can gain self-esteem and dignity from success at school. These positive self-images can come about from pleasing teachers or through achieving good peer relationships. For certain children these are not compatible goals and a choice has to be made. Some children belong to a group of peers who have a culture of rejecting these values and choose to mess about instead.

- The children who are most likely to be able to adapt to school culture come from a home background that understands and supports that culture. Good links between home and school are also supportive. Children's school performance is greatly dependent on learning to read. Children also need to have a sense of control over their own learning processes. Anxiety about inability to do the academic work is one of the main reasons behind school refusal.

LONG-TERM EFFECTS OF SCHOOL EXPERIENCES

Not only does school have an overall effect but specific positive school experiences can have a specific positive effect, for some children. Rutter (1991) has described the role of school in affecting developmental pathways. The comparison of different schools shows that they have an effect on intellectual performance and on behaviour improvements. The chances of effects lasting into adulthood depend on later circumstances. However, crucially, these later circumstances are themselves partly determined by current circumstances. The lasting effects on children of effective schooling are due to improvements in cognitive performance such as task orientation, persistence, and in attainment of skills such as literacy and positive effects on self-esteem and self-efficacy which improve competence in school and increase other people's expectations of performance.

Such increases in self-esteem and self-efficacy act as protective factors in the future after school by allowing young people to exert more control over their own lives and to engage in better planning, for example, in choice of partner. Such socio-emotional effects provide more protection than intellectual effects.

These positive effects are particularly noticeable in children under stress because of other circumstances (Gilligan 1998). Rutter summarises the research into the negative and positive effects diagrammatically (see Figures 7.3 and 7.4). Each experience can be seen to have an effect on subsequent and later events. A poor schooling experience means that poor school attendance is twice as likely, which in turn means that early school leaving is twice as likely and so on. Conversely, having positive school experiences means that someone is three times more likely to make plans for work and marriage, with the resulting greater chances of marrying for positive reasons and so on.

Education can therefore act as a protective factor in the face of adversity. However, ironically, those children who could most benefit from this, that is,

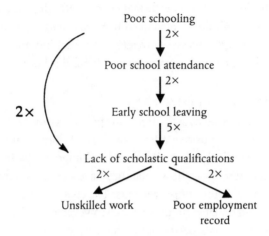

Figure 7.3 Simplified pathways from poor schooling to poor job success (from Gray, Smith and Rutter 1980)

Figure 7.4 Simplified chain of circumstances in institutionally reared women (from Quinton and Rutter 1988)

children whose lives have been disrupted by being looked after away from home, are those whose education is most likely to be problematic: 'there are many indications that at present children's education is given a low priority by child care social workers in Britain' (Parker *et al.* 1991, p.88). There are a number of reasons for this, including problems the child has brought with them, lower expectations of such children and the lack of a person taking the kind of interest in their education that a concerned parent would (Parker *et al.* 1991). As a recent report in England suggests, 75 per cent of young people leave care without any qualifications (Utting 1997). It may be that emotional issues can dominate the care planning for such children, however, as described in this section, neglecting a child's education can have disastrous consequences for their developmental pathway.

Activity 7.5

List ways in which parents or alternative carers could help children to reap the potential benefits of school.

How can practitioners encourage parents to hold a positive view of school?

Hints for answers

Many parents whose children have problems at school may themselves have had very negative experiences there. They may avoid going to the school building because of images of school from their childhood. If such parents can be encouraged to visit the school, to see the classroom, meet the headteacher and discuss their child's progress they may feel less intimidated by their child's school problems. Some parents may themselves decide to further their education.

Children can be encouraged if someone takes an interest in their school work on a day-to-day basis, asking what they have done at school and helping with homework.

Development of morality

Lying, stealing, cheating, disobedience and cruelty to younger siblings or peers are the kinds of behaviour that social workers are frequently presented with in children both living at home, or in alternative care. They all represent difficulties with some aspect of moral development. 'Some aspect' is the key expression here as morality encompasses a complex interaction of a number of different factors. It begins at a very young age, continues throughout school-age and adolescence and depends on cognitive, emotional and behavioural maturation.

COGNITIVE

Moral development depends in part upon children's increasing *understanding* of the difference between right and wrong within the context of societal conventions. They need to appreciate that there are rules for governing behaviour and that there are reasons for such rules. They also need an appreciation of the fact that other people have thoughts and feelings and that their own actions may have consequences for others.

As described in Chapter 6, by the time children reach school years they should have developed a 'theory of mind', that is they should know that others have independent inner worlds and are thinking and feeling beings. This is one vital part of the social knowledge required for moral development. However, considerable empirical work has also been carried out to explore the development of children's moral *reasoning*. It was again Piaget who first systematised the study of this aspect of cognitive development (Piaget 1932). He used a combination of methods, including observing children at play, asking them to explain the rules of their games and setting them moral problems in the form of stories. He concluded that children move through three stages of moral reasoning:

Premoral judgement

Up until about four years of age children have no systematic understanding of rules or the reasons for rules.

Moral realism

Between the ages of four and nine or ten, rules are seen as absolute and unchangeable and laid down by a higher authority such as god or parents. The seriousness of an action is judged by the amount of damage, rather than the intent behind the action. Punishment, similarly, is seen as related to the amount of damage and is inevitable. So, by this reasoning, a child will consider that it is worse to accidentally break three cups than to deliberately break one.

Moral subjectivism

From about nine or ten children begin to realise that rules are made by people and, in certain circumstances, can be changed. Thus, a group of this age children may decide to change the rules of a game, for example by agreeing to go down the ladders and up the snakes! They also exhibit a clearer understanding of the importance of intent rather than outcome for judging the seriousness of an action and realise that certain moral principles underlie rules.

As with other aspects of Piaget's work, some of the elements of the more advanced moral reasoning has been demonstrated at younger ages. Using similar methods, Kohlberg refined the stages of moral reasoning (Kohlberg 1969). He paid more attention to the reasoning people gave for their answers than the answers themselves (Schaffer 1996) and discerned six stages of moral reasoning which he placed into three levels:

Level one: preconventional morality

This level represents the thinking of most children up to the age of nine, and of some adults. Stage one (obedience and punishment orientation) is similar to Piaget's moral realism in that morality is based on obedience to those in authority. In stage two (individualism, instrumental purpose and exchange) children judge morality as that behaviour which meets one's own needs, but begin to recognise intention as important.

Level two: conventional morality

Stage three (mutual interpersonal expectations, relationships and interpersonal conformity) represents obedience in order to please and help others. Judgement by intention is further developed. Stage four (social system and conscience), similar to Piaget's moral subjectivism, represents the recognition of law and the need for maintaining social order. Most adolescents and adults respond at this level.

Level three: post-conventional morality

Stages five and especially six represent levels of moral reasoning that few attain. Stage five (social contract or utility and individual rights) allows for laws to be broken in order to preserve such basic values as life and liberty, although there is an acceptance that rules are needed to preserve order. By stage six (universal ethical principles) laws are seen as relative and as such can be broken if they conflict with basic ethical principles according to individual conscience.

Both Piaget and Kohlberg have been criticised for an apparent over-emphasis upon *justice* in what could be described as a male orientation to morality based on rights and rules (Gilligan 1993). As a result of the detailed study of women's approaches to various moral dilemmas, Gilligan suggested another important component of morality whereby decisions are based on principles of *responsibility* to others, taking account of feelings and interpersonal issues:

> In this conception, the moral problem arises from conflicting responsibilities rather than from competing rights and requires for its resolution a mode of thinking that is contextual and narrative rather than formal and abstract. This conception of morality as concerned with the activity of care centres moral development around the understanding of responsibility and relationships, just as the conception of morality as fairness ties moral development to the understanding of rights and rules. (p.19)

In practice, we should expect school-age children to be developing more sophisticated thinking about moral issues. They may believe that it is important to be good in order to live up to the expectation of family and important others and appreciate that morality is socially defined. They should also start beginning to appreciate that intention is a factor in making decisions about action.

As with other cognitive skills, one could expect there to be a zone of proximal development for moral reasoning. This would mean that there is scope for children's moral reasoning to be encouraged by appropriate scaffolding (Bee 1994). So, for example, as described in the section on peer relationships, some children may get into fights because they do not appreciate the difference between deliberate and accidental actions. It is unlikely that simple statements such as 'Don't hit John, he only accidentally bumped into you!' will change such cognitive processes. Instead, it would be necessary to explore their understanding of terms such as 'accident' and 'deliberate' and 'intent'. Support would then need to start from their point of understanding, perhaps by using simple scenarios in the form of cartoons or stories to help them disentangle issues of intention.

AFFECTIVE

In addition to the intellectual understanding of the need for moral behaviour, children also need to develop the facilitative *feelings* of empathy and concern for others and feelings of well-being and positive self-esteem for doing the right thing, as well as the inhibiting feelings of guilt and remorse after doing the wrong thing.

Empathy

In order to behave in a way that is 'pro-social', that is in a caring and helpful manner towards others, children need to feel empathy. Principally, children need to realise that, like themselves, others can feel pain, distress, happiness and so on. Empathy depends on developing a sense of self in relation to others and the ability to see things from another's perspective. Although much younger children demonstrate empathic feelings and behaviour, during school years empathic behaviour becomes increasingly based upon an understanding of other people's perspectives. In the early school years, up to about eight, children realise that other people have a social perspective and that it may not necessarily be the same as their own, but they find it difficult to coordinate different viewpoints and therefore tend to focus on one.

From eight to ten children not only know that each individual is aware of another's perspective, but also know that this awareness affects people's views. They, therefore, know that it is possible to judge another's intentions, purposes and actions by putting oneself in their place. Because they know that someone's reaction may be different from their own they are able to respond more appropriately to another's distress. For example, although they may like physical comfort when in distress, they can realise that another child in the same position may prefer to be left alone. They can use objective ideas about fairness, using more universal principles. During later school years they develop a greater appreciation of the effect of life circumstance and feel empathy for people in less fortunate circumstances than their own (Santrok 1994).

Schaffer (1996) summarises the main findings about the kind of parental factors that are associated with pro-social behaviour in children (citing Zahn-Waxler, Radke-Yarrow and King 1979; Robinson, Zahn-Waxler and Emde 1994). Like morality itself, these factors include cognitive, affective and behavioural components, suggesting that children need support with their development in each of these domains:

1. Pro-social behaviour in children is associated with the provision of clear rules and principles for *behaviour*, with an explanation of consequences.

2. The manner in which such messages are given also seems to have an impact, thus, contrary to what some might suppose, pro-social behaviour is associated with parental messages given not in a calm, cool way but with a strong *emotional* component.

3. Children who are attributed with good intentions, for example described as 'helpful', are more likely to incorporate such *attributions* into their self-definition and live up to them.

4. Caretakers who behave in a moral way towards others provide positive models for children.

5. Finally, what Schaffer describes as 'the most essential attribute, i.e. the existence of a warm and responsive relationship between parent and child. Those parents who behave in a loving, accepting manner towards their children are most likely to have children with high rates of pro-social behaviour'. (p.276)

Children who have difficulty in understanding their own feelings and emotions (as is the case with many children who have suffered abuse or neglect) are also likely to have difficulty in understanding other people's feelings and emotions. Experiences of abuse and neglect may therefore impede the development of empathy. If such children have to be looked after away from home, carers need to provide an environment as described above that will foster the development of empathy. For children living at home, practitioners need to consider all attachment figures as possible sources of support for the development of empathy. Other adults such as social workers themselves, teachers, home visitors and volunteer befrienders could also provide such input.

Conscience

As well as the positive feelings of empathy that encourage moral behaviour, children also need to experience feelings that will *inhibit* immoral actions. In other words, they need to develop a conscience. Fahlberg (1994) firmly locates the development of conscience in early attachment. Children, in trying to please attachment figures gradually internalise their values, standards and constraints. By the age of five children have an internal critical voice, but, because of their lack of self-control they still require adult supervision which prevents misbehaving. At this stage it is crucial that children receive consistent and appropriate messages of approval and disapproval, otherwise they have nothing on which to base their own conscience development. By nine or ten they have the cognitive ability to consider alternative possibilities and to imagine possible outcomes. By this age their sense of right or wrong is normally strong enough to prevent them from misbehaving without adult supervision. From then on conscience continues to be refined and modified as values develop.

Fahlberg also describes three main types of problems of conscience, all of which may be seen in children within the care system:

1. Some do not feel guilt because they do not believe they could survive the experience of guilt.

2. There are those, described as psychopathic, who appear to feel no guilt and show no restraint or remorse.

3. Most commonly seen, is the problem of those who feel guilt after the act, but whose conscience does not warn and/or restrain them in advance.

Fahlberg suggests that school-age children with conscience problems may need to be supported as a younger child would be. They can be helped by providing sufficient supervision to monitor behaviour and giving them the consistent messages of approval and disapproval they have missed. These messages are more effective if constructed in the 'I' form, for example, saying 'I don't like it when you do...' rather than 'you are naughty to do...'.

BEHAVIOUR

Knowing and feeling also need to be put into *action*. Some children may feel remorse after an action, but not be inhibited from doing wrong again. Others may know that their actions are wrong, but do them anyway. In younger children action is mainly monitored by adults; increasingly, children need to learn to exert control over their own actions.

It is therefore evident that the underlying reasons for immoral behaviour can be very complex and require detailed assessment. Ryan (1979) provides a specific discussion of lying and stealing in children being looked after by

---

Activity 7.6

Think about a child you have worked with who shows some behaviour problems related to delays in moral development and consider:

1. At what stage of moral reasoning they appear to be operating.

2. What level of empathy they demonstrate.

3. Whether they demonstrate one of the three problems with conscience described above.

4. How their continued moral development may best be supported.

foster carers. She points out that very few people are totally honest all of the time. She explores some of the reasons as to why children may lie and steal. For example, children may lie about their family to present a different picture than the unbearable reality, some children will have witnessed their parents lying, and may have been lied to themselves. Children may steal because they have not had their needs fulfilled or because of a lack of appropriate experiences at home.

Summary of developmental issues and considerations for practice

During school years *language* use should become increasingly sophisticated, and children increasingly incorporate abstract concepts. Language delay has to be appreciated as a factor that will render a child vulnerable to problems in school and in communication with friends and adults.

- Social workers must recognise the importance of language, and find help for the child who has problems in communication.

- Similarly, they need to be alert to the potential impact of adversity upon the development of language.

Reading provides the fundamental underpinning for nearly all school subjects, and, as such, is crucial. However, it also allows children to take part in other aspects of peer culture, for example reading books, comics and magazines. Many computer games and activities also require some literacy skills.

- Problems with reading must therefore be tackled as soon as possible.

- Joint planning with educational staff is essential.

- The development of reading skills can be greatly promoted by interest from home and parents or carers may need encouragement to be involved in the process of improving reading ability.

During school years children's ability to use *memory*-enhancing techniques improves. As children move into adolescence their memory performance may approach adult level. The main considerations for practice emerge from the impact of trauma on memory development and on recall of adverse experiences.

- The key message is that no assumptions should be made about a child's level of recall, because of the diversity of factors that can impact on memory.

- Finally, it is important for the practitioner to ensure that a child has emotional support if he or she is in a process of recalling disturbing events.

As has been stressed throughout the book, there is considerable interaction between cognitive and emotional development and all domains should be accorded equal attention.

Along with secure attachment experiences, *self-esteem* and *self-efficacy* form the foundations for resilience. During these years problems with self-esteem can become entrenched, especially if school experiences are difficult. At the same time there is scope for positive intervention.

- Imagination is needed to help find islands of competence for a young person. Clubs, hobbies, sport, arts and drama all provide fruitful avenues to explore.

Children develop their *gender* and *racial* identity within the context of family, peer, school and society. These layers of influence all exert powerful forces, which if restrictive, negative or undermining are significant adversities that may increase vulnerability.

- Assessment at any age and stage must explicitly explore these vital aspects of self-concept.

During school years a secure *attachment* base remains important. Because of the burgeoning of cognitive processes young people experiencing loss or separation are likely to try to make sense of events.

- Children undergoing loss or separation need information, and crucially, care has to be taken to make sure that they do not blame themselves for loss. As described in Chapters 2 and 3, children need a coherent story that explains life events and social workers can play a part in checking that children can account for changes in their lives.

- During any disruption practitioners need to ensure that as much continuity can be maintained as possible, for example, children should have the opportunity to keep contact with family, even if they move from home.

Friendships should play a large part of the school-age child's life. The implications for practice depend on whether children have friends or not.

- If children have friendships they must be taken seriously. The obvious first step is to ask children who their friends are and start from this point. Friends can be an important source of resilience during adverse life events and every effort should be made to support and nurture children's friendships.

- If children do not have friends then there must be careful assessment as to why. It may be due to different factors including lack of confidence, lack of self-esteem, overt aggression, an insecure inner working model of relationships and so on.

School features strongly during these years; for some it may act as a source of support. For others, school problems may be the reason for referral for social work intervention. The fact that school experiences have such long-term implications means that prompt intervention is essential when it has become a source of difficulty for a child.

- The intellectual, emotional and social aspects of school should all be taken into account when assessing a child's overall school experience. Good inter-disciplinary relationships are critical here.

Moral development depends on cognitive, emotional and behavioural maturation. It parallels development in these domains, so for example, as a child's cognitive skills evolve, they are able to engage in more sophisticated moral reasoning.

- The key message for practice is that moral development can be supported by the social environment, particularly through encouragement to feel empathy and to act pro-socially.

- Children's moral development is also influenced by observation. Adults and other children's behaviour will be copied. Residential staff and other carers need to work towards creating an atmosphere of mutual respect and responsibility.

CHAPTER 8

Adolescence

Introduction

This chapter will look at the concept of 'adolescence'. It examines the developmental tasks of adolescence in the light of common assumptions about adolescence. As there are so many myths about adolescence, the chapter sets out the research findings about the experiences of the majority of teenagers to help set the problems of troubled adolescents into context. It has to be borne in mind that the bulk of research findings are based on work with white European and American young people and, as such, are limited in scope.

After exploring these common myths, the chapter sets out an approach to conduct disorders and also looks at the challenges of fostering teenagers.

Adolescence

Place the label 'adolescent' on a young person and they are immediately subject to a number of myths. It is not unusual to hear parents, carers and even, on occasion, social workers describing adolescents in stereotypical terms.

Activity 8.1

Think about the adolescents you have on your caseload and have worked with in the past. Recall ways in which their behaviour was described and explained. List the kinds of stereotypes that you have heard (or used!)

Your examples may include terms such as 'identity crisis', 'generation gap', 'acting out', 'typical adolescent', 'raging hormones' etc. Though they may contain a grain of truth most of these stereotypes are frequently misleading or wrong. Usually they act as a shorthand way of 'explaining' a difficulty that a young person may have. However, to attribute behaviour solely to the fact of being 'adolescent' is not particularly helpful when trying to help young people and parents in distress.

Adolescence as a concept is relatively new and has its roots in the industrial revolution. With increasing affluence and longer periods of education the gap between childhood and independence has been prolonged and has been called adolescence. In fact, theorists whose ideas are called 'inventionist' believe that adolescence is purely a political and social construction (Steinberg 1993).

Nevertheless, there are important biological, cognitive and social changes to which all young people are subject (Steinberg 1993). Although individual responses to these changes may differ, social workers need to be aware of how development can usually be expected to progress along the path from childhood into early adulthood.

Five of the most commonly held assumptions about this period of development will be presented as a series of questions and the related evidence set out.

Generation gap?

Is it the case that during adolescence young people cannot communicate with their parents? Do they reject their parent's values and ideas and stick with a group of peers who have more influence over them than parents and teachers or indeed social workers?

Studies do not support this popular myth about teenagers. Three-quarters of young people interviewed in one study said they felt they could count on their parents and that if they had children in the future would hope their own families to be similar to the one they grew up in (Steinberg 1993). 75 per cent of teenagers do not experience major problems; of the 25 per cent that do, 80 per cent already had problems before their teenage years (Rutter *et al.* 1979). Teenagers also appear to hold very similar values and attitudes to their parents, with differences between young people being greater than those across the generations. When they occur, differences are normally about day-to-day issues of clothing, tidiness etc. They usually arise when parents define an issue as a matter of custom, for example, in relation to suitable clothes for school, whereas the young person sees it as a matter of personal choice (Smetana 1989).

The myth of the generation gap is closely associated with the notion that adolescence marks a transition phase from dependence on family to independence from family. However, as indicated in Chapter 2, the concept of 'independence', is artificial from the perspective of attachment theory. Adolescence normally marks a move to a maturer form of inter-dependence, not independence. It is a rare person who survives as an 'independent'; healthy adult functioning normally depends on having a network of support, including partners, friends, peers, colleagues etc.

Schaffer (1996) stresses that during adolescence parents are often the main source of support and that a good relationship with one or both parent 'moderates the negative effects of adverse life events'. Parents can buffer young people against some of the stresses of teenage years, especially if they are able to maintain a close relationship despite the inevitable changes. In other words, a good parental relationship can be a *protective* factor in the face of adversity.

There is evidence that the importance of peers increases during adolescence, but they do not usually become more important to the young people than parents. During early adolescence, studies show an increase in intimacy with friends. This intimacy is based on equality, whereas intimacy with parents and carers is of a different quality and still contains a power imbalance. Therefore, although the type of relationship may be different, peer relationships are not generally all-encompassing and do not supersede family relationships. When specifically considering levels of self-esteem and life satisfaction, the quality of attachment relationships with parents is more influential than that with peers (Armsden and Greenberg 1987).

Attachment relationships with the family form the foundation for other social contacts. Indeed, the evidence suggests that young people explore their peer attachments from the secure base of attachment to parents (Feeney and Noller 1996). Adolescents who currently have or have experienced secure attachments are likely to be better adjusted and more socially competent (Rice 1990). The *quality* of relationship a young person has with their parents may also affect the *quality* of relationship they have with their peers. For example, a young person whose family relationships are characterised by conflict may have lots of arguments with their friends.

However, this association is not always exhibited. Some young people are able to make very strong friendships, despite the experience of troubled family relationships. As explored in Chapter 4, such friendships can contribute to resilience in the face of family difficulties. Of course, having the characteristics associated with resilience such as a good sense of self-esteem, helps with the process of making friends.

The interactions between parental and peer relationships are clearly complex and each individual case needs careful assessment. So, if a young person's family and peer relationships are both stressful practitioners will need to assess what is going wrong. Even if it seems too late to mend the family relationships, there may be scope for them to learn skills in making friends. They may benefit from the chance to reflect upon their habitual responses to others and change them. For example, if a young person finds that they often feel criticised by others they can practise monitoring whether they are over-sensitive. Role-play and groupwork can be useful methods of helping young people to experiment with different ways of responding to others.

Interestingly, sexuality is the one area where parent-adolescent communication is less effective and where young people turn to their peers. Moore and Rosenthal (1993) give details of studies into teenage sexuality. For example, parents are able to make fairly accurate estimates about the norm for teenage sexual behaviour, but consistently underestimate the level of their own child's sexual behaviour (Collis 1991, unpublished cited in Moore and Rosenthal). Parental discussions, communication and monitoring appear not to have a significant effect on the level of adolescent sexual activity, although there does appear to be some inhibiting influence on daughters (Moore, Peterson and Furstenberg 1986). Therefore, parents who say that their teenage children won't listen to their warnings about engaging in sexual activity are probably right!

Activity 8.2

Can you think of a young person with whom you work whose relationships with their peers seem to be affected by the type of relationships they have at home?

Examine the quality of the different relationships the young person has and list which aspects are similar and which are different.

However, parental behaviour does appear to influence adolescent sexuality. For example non-authoritative (see Chapter 3) parenting is associated with boys engaging in sexual activity at a younger age (Kandel 1990). This suggests that when parents express concerns about their children's sexual activity, it would be helpful to assess the whole family's attitude towards, and early experiences of, sexual relationships.

Where do young people turn to for information about sex? One study showed that 69 per cent of 17- to 20-year-olds discussed sexual issues with their friends, 61 per cent got their sex education from peers in comparison with 33 per cent who turned to their mothers and 15 per cent who turned to fathers (Moore and Rosenthal 1991). This is important because frequently the information gained from peers about sex is inaccurate. It could be surmised that young people who have troubled relationships with their parents may be even less likely to discuss sexual issues with them.

Social workers, foster carers and key workers in residential units can play a vital role in counteracting some of the distorted sexual information gained from friends. The starting point has to be establishing the current level of information. It is easy to make assumptions about young people's knowledge about sex, especially in a group context where there may be reluctance to show ignorance or fear of being laughed at. Quizzes, or true or false questions, could be used. Young people then need accurate, straightforward information, which can be given by verbally and backed up with leaflets etc. It will not possible to 'do sex education' on a one-off basis, it has to be part of an ongoing process of social and emotional education and support. Although adolescents are more usually able to cope with abstract concepts than younger children, it is often not until an issue touches them personally that it will be seen to have real relevance. Therefore, they need plenty of opportunities to come back and ask questions at another time.

Activity 8.3

Can you give possible reasons as to why adolescents generally remain close to their parents, but do not tend to discuss sexual issues with them.

Message for practice

When presented with difficulties in family communication that have emerged during adolescence, it will be helpful to look for the continuities with earlier behaviour. Attachment theory suggests that the quality of family relationships develops from very early interactions between the child and his or her caretakers. Therefore, a problem in adolescence can be viewed as the expression of a well-established pattern of family communication rather than a symptom of adolescence itself.

If parents assume that there will be a generation gap they may miss the opportunity to use the positive aspects of their relationship with their children in dealing with difficulties. Parents may need to hear that adolescents can still value their views and opinions.

When there are communication problems, other significant adults can play a role, perhaps by acting as a mediator to help each person put over their point of view.

Social workers dealing with young people also need to avoid falling into the trap of attributing lack of communication purely to adolescence. It is not uncommon to encounter a young person in difficult circumstances who presents as surly and uncommunicative. Describing this as 'typical teenage behaviour' may mean that not enough time and care is taken to establish sufficient trust to move beyond the initial stages.

Hormonal surges?

Is it the case that adolescents are slaves to surges of hormones raging in their bodies which cause them to have violent and uncontrollable swings of mood?

Undoubtedly there are significant biological changes resulting from puberty, and these have been the basis for many influential theories about adolescent development. However, the evidence suggests that there is no simple connection between hormone changes and mood changes. Many other factors also influence mood. For example, one study suggested that although hormone swings affect mood to some extent, day-to-day changes in activity affect mood much more (Csikszentmihalyi and Larson 1984).

Contrary to popular belief, biological changes do not have a direct effect on the expression of sexuality. For girls, in particular, sexual activity is heavily influenced by what their peers are doing. Starting to 'go out' with or 'date' peers is related more to age than puberty. Clearly the social influences on young people are a powerful force. This is also illustrated by the finding that an increase in sex hormones is related to an increase in thoughts about sex in both sexes, but these thoughts are more likely to be acted on by boys than girls, reflecting perhaps the prevailing societal belief that male sexual urges are less controllable (Udry and Billy 1987).

Puberty does have an important effect on family relationships by distancing the young person somewhat from parents. The reasons for this could include the symbolism of puberty as a signal of the child growing up and also their need for more privacy (Steinberg 1993).

The changes in the body cannot be ignored by the young person themselves and again these changes will be greatly influenced by societal context. These influences are very different on girls and boys as studies cited by Moore and Rosenthal (1993) suggest. One study showed that out of 6000 girls aged 12 to 17, 70 per cent wished that they were thinner (Duncan *et al.* 1985). Similarly breast development is associated with a girl's satisfaction with her body while for a boy the more important aspects seem to be fitness, strength and the need to shave (Peterson 1989; Tobin-Richards, Boxer and Peterson 1983).

Unger and Crawford (1992) suggest that the meaning of menstruation for young women in our society is both positive and negative. The attainment of physical maturity for girls can be met with an ambivalence that is not so evident for boys. This can be attributed to a number of factors. While it is desirable to become adult, Western society places high value on youthful and slim bodies. As weight gain is a necessary part of maturation for girls, the concern about this can become a source of distress and lead to dieting. Boys, however gain muscle in puberty and this is seen by themselves and society as positive. Breast development can also be a cause of embarrassment; over half of the elementary or junior high school girls in a US study reported being teased about their developing breasts (Brooks-Gunn 1987, cited in Unger and Crawford 1992). There is also considerable secrecy about menstruation, coupled with implications of lack of cleanliness and embarrassment, 'Strategies for dealing with menstruation in school included putting the maxipad up a sleeve; tucking it into a sweatshirt; or slipping a tampon into a sock' (Unger and Crawford 1992, p.281). The younger a girl attains puberty the harder it can be for her to manage. It can also place her at risk of unwanted sexual advances and of seeking acquaintances among older girls who are already engaged in sexual activity.

Family attitudes have an important effect on a young person's security with their body. Their esteem can be lower in families that either over-stress the importance of looks; project their own anxieties about body shape onto their children; or who fear that their child's development is too fast or slow (Schonfeld 1969). These factors will be important when considering a client showing eating disorders, for example.

Message for practice

Frequently young people's difficult behaviour is attributed to uncontrollable urges and biological changes. This explanation could well mask the fact that a young person is suffering mood swings because of emotional distress. There is a complex interaction of hormonal and social factors. It is likely that such biological changes will be harder for a young person to manage if their esteem is already low and they lack secure attachments.

For example, a girl reaching puberty at a younger age than her peers may be vulnerable to feelings of embarrassment and confusion. These feelings can be exacerbated if she is in transition between placements and has no trusted female adult to turn to. In such circumstances it can sometimes be a school nurse who can provide support and advice

Time of crisis?

Is adolescence by definition a stressful time which is characterised by crisis and uncertainty?

A popular idea is that an 'identity crisis' occurs during adolescence. This was formalised by Erikson in his theory of human development. This sets out a series of psychosocial crises that must be resolved at each stage of development (Erikson 1959). In adolescence this involves the crisis of identity versus identity diffusion. That is, in adolescence a process of reflection occurs and choices are made about the different aspects that contribute to a sense of self. Erikson believed that adolescents gain information about themselves through interaction with others. For example, if they find that others tend to confide in them they may incorporate the notion of themselves as 'sympathetic' into their self-image. By the same token, young people whose interactions with others are characterised by abuse or neglect could well incorporate notions of themselves as unlovable and unworthy.

Erikson stated that this process of building a coherent sense of self must occur before the young person can move onto real intimacy. The evidence suggests that adolescents indeed benefit from having the space and time to consider their social, cultural, ethnic and gender identity and that this process can continue well into their early twenties (Steinberg 1993). Not all adolescents in all societies will have the luxury of space and time to consider identity, especially if they start work at a young age.

However, it is not necessarily quite so clear that identity development precedes intimacy and Steinberg suggests that the two should be seen as developing in tandem:

> Close relationships are used as a safe context in which adolescents confront difficult questions of identity; yet at the same time, the development of an increasingly coherent and secure sense of self provides the foundation upon which adolescents build and strengthen intimate relationships with others. (Steinberg 1993, p.325)

Younger children tend to describe themselves in terms of external character-istics, but as they move into adolescence they are more likely to describe themselves in terms of ideology, their beliefs, quality of relationships and personality traits rather than simply external characteristics (Montemayor and Eisen 1977). Such developments can parallel cognitive developments in which young people may move to what Piaget called the *formal operational* stage, in which logical thinking is more sophisticated.

Formal operational thinking involves the consideration of a number of possible solutions to a problem. When they have reached this stage, young people can construct hypotheses and check them out with reality before coming to a conclusion. They can also think in purely abstract terms (Flavell 1985).

However, the attainment of such thinking is not necessarily automatic and not all adults use formal operational thought. Many of the young people encountered in practice have problems with logical thought. Cognitive development, like other domains of development, needs to be nurtured, encouraged and supported by interested adults. Children who have been neglected or abused may enter adolescence without having moved through the cognitive maturation described in the previous chapter. However, the development of formal operational thinking can be supported by education and other opportunities to practise logical and abstract thought (Smith and Cowie 1991). Therefore social workers need to ensure that there is a careful assessment of cognitive skills during adolescence.

An influential approach to the study of identity formation is that of Marcia (1966, 1980) in which young people are rated on two dimensions, the degree to which they have made commitments to some specific role or ideology and the degree to which they are engaged in a 'crisis' in the sense of reexamination of values. He was able to place them into one of four categories or 'identity statuses':

- *Identity achievement*: achievement of a coherent sense of identity following questioning and commitment.

- *Moratorium*: being in a state of questioning or 'crisis' without commitment.

- *Foreclosure*: being in a state of having made commitments without a period of crisis or experimentation.

- *Identity diffusion*: being in a state of having made no commitments and experiencing no active experimentation or crisis.

Studying identity within such a framework has shown that a clear sense of identity is associated with authoritative parenting styles (as described in Chapter 3). It is also associated with psychological health and the ability to be intimate with others. The experience of secure earlier attachments is associated with successful transition through adolescence. Indeed, the more secure a young person is in their family attachments, the easier it is for them to cope with eventual separation from their family (Howe 1995).

It is not so clear that adolescents necessarily experience a crisis of identity, nor that identity issues are always addressed in adolescence, rather than in early adulthood (Bee 1995). Coleman (1980) argues that the majority of teenagers appear to move to adulthood without necessarily suffering identity problems and crises and that Erikson overstated the case for identity problems in adolescence. Indeed, self-esteem may increase slightly during adolescence as young people gain a sense of themselves as distinct individuals separate from their families. Girls are more likely than boys to have problems with self-esteem when they reach puberty. As described above, puberty is a time of mixed messages for girls, and the pressures about physical appearance can be associated with dissatisfaction with their bodies. However, overall global self-esteem is less likely to be affected (Unger and Crawford 1992).

As Steinberg sums up:

> The weight of the evidence ... suggests that identity status classifications made during adolescence and young adulthood probably represent short-term, temporary states, rather than long-term, enduring traits ... revising and maintaining one's sense of self-definition is a challenge that continues beyond adolescence.' (p.276)

Typically, the young people known to practitioners may have fewer opportunities for building a positive self-image than their peers. Many have difficult relationships with peers and family and their experience of interactions with others may frequently be negative. If Erikson is right and identity is formed primarily through interactions with others this suggests that they will have great difficulty in developing a positive identity. This provides a role for the practitioner in maximising opportunities for young people to experience positive feedback from those around them. Although the majority of young people do not have an 'identity crisis' as such, it is likely that young people whose family relationships have been troubled, particularly if they have not been living at home, will need support in exploring their identity as a family member.

Bearing in mind Marcia's four categories may help when assessing a young person's current identity. For example, a young person who is desperate to be accepted by an important family member may choose early on to identify with them, without any questioning, that is they may be in identity *foreclosure*. Another young person who is exposed to conflicting opinions of themselves, for example, a positive view from school teachers and a negative view from a parent, may be in a state of questioning without commitment or identity *moratorium*. Finally, it also worth noting the potential for young people to revise their self-identity after adolescence. This potential could be maximised if the young person moves to a situation where they receive positive experiences, perhaps in further education or in a successful relationship, or as a parent.

Coleman (1980) has proposed a 'focal' rather than 'crisis' theory of development which suggests that adolescents cope by tackling different issues at different times, rather than trying to change everything at once. Therefore, they may focus first on exams, and then on negotiating to stay out later. This model could also be helpful when considering troubled adolescents. For example, far from being able to tackle issues one at a time, young people looked after may often have to deal with many issues all at once. Indeed, many young people feel the need to leave accommodation and move to independence at a time when their counterparts are using their secure home base to explore issues of identity and sexuality. Also, some adolescents living at home in difficult circumstances are required to leave by one or both parents at 16. Facing the overriding issue of finding somewhere to live and coping with bills and so on is likely to force a young person to cope with too many issues all at once. The distress they feel can be expressed in ways that could be described as 'typical teenage moods'. If young people are exhibiting strong mood swings it could well be attributable to the stress they feel at being required to mature too quickly. There is role here for practitioners in planning transitions so that changes are paced and ensuring that issues can be tackled one at a time.

Coleman also suggests two other, linked aspects of adolescence development that could be of use in understanding some adolescent behaviour: the 'imaginary audience' and the 'personal fable'. They are based on the work of Elkind (1967) and explore the impact of cognitive development reaching a stage of formal operational thinking. Formal operational thinking allows the young person to reflect on their own thoughts and also to think about the thoughts of others. However, this process can lead to a new kind of *egocentrism* in which the young person may believe that other people are thinking about, and preoccupied with, the same things as they are. So, for example, if the young person is thinking about their appearance, they may assume that other people are also thinking about their appearance. This means that they can be preoccupied with anticipating the reactions of others who become, in a way, an 'imaginary audience'. Further, a preoccupation with the imaginary audience can be associated with an adolescent believing their own thoughts to be very special and unique. Thus a 'personal fable' is constructed:

> In essence this is the individual's story about himself [sic], the story he tells to himself, and it may well include fantasies of omnipotence, and immortality. It is not a true story, but it serves a valuable purpose, and is exemplified in some of the most famous adolescent diaries. (Coleman 1980, p.32)

An exploration of a young person's personal fable and the kind of thoughts they may attribute to an imaginary audience could be helpful in understanding some behaviour. For example, a young person who has been sexually abused in childhood and who is acting in a sexually inappropriate way towards others may have many thoughts about sex. They may then believe the 'imaginary audience' also to be obsessed with sex and attribute sexual connotations to interactions. This could be coupled with a personal fable of unique badness. This kind of approach is interesting because it considers the interaction of cognitive and emotional development in adolescence. It also links closely with the notion of 'coherent story' as introduced in Chapter 3 and some of the techniques described for working with personal stories could be used with adolescents.

Activity 8.4

Consider an adolescent living away from home. Using the 'focal' theory that suggests that adolescent issues can be tackled one by one over a period of time, consider what issues will need to be addressed by the young person. List these issues and then suggest how carers or residential workers can help the young person with them.

Hints for answers

For example, in selecting two issues you could consider the following:

Sexual relationships: good, informative sexual and relational education can help with these. An understanding and acceptance of the usual teenage sexual explorations is vital. Also carers need to tolerate the way in which intimate relationships can dominate the adolescent's time. Allowing them the space to explore their feelings in a relationship may help them to work out how to build relationships. As the ability to establish good intimate relationships can have a great influence on adult psychological adjustment (Rutter and Rutter 1993) this issue must be taken seriously and not dismissed as teenage experimentation.

Family relationships: as described below, the young person may, in a sense, 'take with' him or her difficult family relationships even if they move physically out of the home. At the same time the distance from home may help them to reflect upon the nature of the relationships. If they can be helped to make more healthy attachments to alternative adults they still have the potential to explore a different way of relating to people.

ETHNIC IDENTITY

Evidence suggests that ethnic identity is particularly important for young people from an ethnic minority and that although the development of this identity is not necessarily problematic it does require the young person to make decisions about how to operate within a culture of racism and how to deal with encounters with racism.

Chapters 6 and 7 describes some of the complexities involved in the development of ethnic identity. During adolescence ethnic identity can become very important for children in ethnic minority groups. Phinney (1993) describes three stages in the development of ethnicity. Before adolescence there is a lack of exploration of ethnic concepts, described as '*unexamined* ethnic identity'. During early adolescence there may be a period of 'ethnic identity *search*' in which previous attitudes are questioned and political consciousness is heightened. By late adolescence young people have a clear and confident sense of their own ethnicity, reflecting 'ethnic identity *achievement*'. Again, most young people successfully reach the latter stage. However, for those who do experience problems, Maxime (1986) suggests pointers for intervention with this age group. Her suggestions build on those described in Chapter 7, but add:

- exposure to situations that inspire pride in their racial origin
- if the young person does have a dialect it should not be condemned, but they also need support in understanding when formal language should be used
- workers need to avoid giving double messages, for example Black is Beautiful, versus black as negative
- workers must avoid having low expectations of these young people and of communicating these low expectations.

The development of identity in adolescents of mixed race has been studied by Tizard and Phoenix (1993). They interviewed about sixty young people with one white and one Afro-Caribbean parent, both boys and girls, from both working- and middle-class areas. They also interviewed similar numbers of black and white young people. They found that:

- Just under half the young people of mixed race defined themselves as black. The rest defined themselves as 'brown', 'mixed' or 'coloured'.
- Some 60 per cent had a positive racial identity, and this positive identity was not necessarily associated with a self-definition as black. In fact, three-quarters of those with a positive identity described themselves as 'mixed' and were proud of it.
- Young people of mixed race were more likely to report experiences of racism than the black sample. All the young people had formulated strategies for coping with racism. There was no difference in the ways that those living with a white or black parent dealt with racism, and the advice given by black and white parents was not different.
- School experience was very important and schools with clear and effective anti-racist policies could have a positive effect on the lives of both black and mixed parentage young people.

Katz (1996) interviewed members of interracial families and also observed two infants. His main interest was in how people construct and describe their own identities and those of their children. He points to the diversity of experience of mixed race children and their families and the complexity of their own constructions of their identity. His study showed that the families were 'actively engaged in the process of developing new conceptions of identity which transcend the old totalising categories of race, class and nation.' (p.195)

Katz advocates the use of the 'biographical' or 'life history' approach which aims to obtain a narrative or life story from someone and to 'make sense of the ways in which people view themselves in relations to their culture or society'. The resulting narrative is seen as an account, not of the objective truth, but of a subjective understanding of life events. There are clear links between the 'life history' and concepts of 'personal fable' and 'coherent story'. This approach could be very fruitful in work with adolescents experiencing difficulties with forming a 'coherent story' of their lives (as described in Chapter 3). Using non-directive, open-ended interviewing the young person could be asked to tell their own story. This story could then serve as a jumping off point for joint work on a number of issues, including identity.

There is, currently, considerable debate about the extent to which ethnic issues should be considered as a priority factor when planning for children needing to be looked after away from home. The current legislation in England and Scotland requires racial origin to be one of the considerations in such planning. Guidance from the British Agency for Adoption and Fostering suggests that:

> Families who share a child's heritage can offer an added dimension, over and above a loving environment, covering such things as continuity of experience, contact with a relevant community, understanding of and pride in the child's particular inheritance and, for children from minority ethnic groups, skills and support in dealing with racism. (BAAF 1991, as reproduced in Gaber and Aldridge 1994, pp.233–234.)

Parker *et al.* (1991) rely on the literature that indicates that transracial adoption placements will not necessarily have an adverse effect on self-esteem (Tizard and Phoenix 1989) propose that placement of a black child with white carers may be preferable to a prolonged stay in unsuitable residential care. This should not deflect attention away from the need to recruit and support sufficient numbers of carers from all ethnic minority populations to meet the needs of young people living away from home. The lack of enough appropriate placements clearly needs considerable attention (Aldridge 1994).

Again, as stated in Chapter 2, the young person must always be kept at the centre of any assessment. Identity can be defined both on an individual level and by membership of a group (Richards 1994). A young person needs to have the opportunity to explore their identity at both these levels and to be given the opportunity to continue this exploration whether living at home or elsewhere. As with all children it is important to involve all attachment figures in any planning for black and mixed race children and to strive to work in partnership with them.

Message for practice

It is important to remember that stress and crisis is not automatically a feature of adolescence and therefore other possible reasons should be explored when a young person seems isolated or very stressed. Also, as suggested in a later section, behaviour problems need not necessarily be considered to be uncontrollable.

However, it is the case that for many young people with troubled backgrounds adolescence will be a time when the difficulties may become more pronounced and intense. For example, it can be more difficult for a young person to experiment with increasing independence if they lack the security of a base from which to explore. Young people lacking such 'base camps' can be significantly disadvantaged in their transition to adulthood (Gilligan 1997).

Permissive sexuality?

Is it the case that adolescents today are sexually promiscuous and the number of babies born to teenagers is an increasingly worrying trend?

It is very difficult to make statements about what constitutes normal sexual development since it is so open to societal pressure and shaping. Definitions of sexuality depend on personal, familial and cultural values and beliefs. For example, children are undoubtedly sensual and this sensuality is expressed physically with hugs and kisses. It is part of normal development for young children to behave spontaneously in this way in an unselfconscious manner. However adults frequently interpret childhood sensuality in sexual terms, using such labels as 'flirting' and 'coy', or making statements such as 'is he your boyfriend?' and 'look they're kissing'.

Once children reach adolescence they start to be aware of sexuality and to put their own sexual interpretations onto actions. They are also subject to physical changes that force them to be aware of their own developing sexuality. What was a non-specific sexuality becomes directed by biology, society, family and peers.

Representations of sex surround us. Sex is used in advertising, films and television. The internet has provided young people with the opportunity to access a vast array of sexual images, including those that portray exploitation of and violence towards women and children. The onset of HIV and AIDS has had the dual effect of allowing much more explicit public discourses about sex, as well as expressions of moral judgements about sexual behaviour. Similarly, childhood sexuality, particularly that of girls, is used in advertising and film and television, while again the political message is one of moral concern about young people and sex. Young people are therefore likely to receive many mixed messages about sex and about expectations of their behaviour.

However, in the context of overall child development, adolescent sexuality can be seen as a vital part of the change from a situation where primary attachments are to parents and carers to a situation where intimate attachments to partners become increasingly important. Sexuality and intimacy are not always automatically linked of course, but the recognition of oneself as a sexual being is an important part of the development of personal identity and of identity in relation to others. In our society, the development of sexual relationships is one of the key ways to move on from dependence on the family to interdependence with partners. In a climate of low employment it could be seen as one of the most important ways of asserting independence from family, especially if the young person is not moving on to college or university.

DEVELOPMENT OF SEXUALITY

Aspects of sexuality begin in babyhood. Boys will get erections in early infancy and both sexes engage in genital play while babies. What could be construed as sex play with the same sex and the opposite sex is seen at around eight years. This could involve comparing and showing genitals. This obvious sex-play tends to reduce, most probably because of social pressure. Little is known about the extent of masturbation but self-report studies suggest that for over half of children it represents their first explicitly sexual experience and for two-thirds of boys will lead to their first experience of ejaculation (Katchadourian 1990).

So sex play among children is normal, as is masturbation in private. Public masturbation or children engaging in oral genital play, vaginal insertion and intercourse are unusual at these early stages of sex play. These kind of activities would indicate cause for concern, not necessarily because of the acts per se, but because they demonstrate that the child has some distortion of what this society accepts as proper boundaries, something which needs further exploration and assessment. (See below for further discussion of problematic sexual development.)

In a detailed and comprehensive book, Moore and Rosenthal (1993) cite many studies of adolescent sexuality and a summary of some aspects relevant for practice will be presented here. It is true that more young people begin partnered sexual activity at an earlier age than before and are more ready to admit to a range of activities. The lead time from 'petting' to full intercourse is also shorter. One study suggested that in the UK 40 per cent of young people have their first experience of intercourse at 15 or younger and 9 per cent at 13 or younger. By 17, 63 per cent are non-virgins (Ford and Morgan 1989).

If a person starts going out with someone in early adolescence they are likely to start having sexual intercourse earlier than those who start 'dating' at a later age. There is more likely to be sexual activity in a relationship that is seen as committed, especially for girls. Both girls and boys will cite loving, caring and affection as being important in relationships, although girls are more likely to define love as being the reason for having sex. Boys are more likely to cite the satisfaction of sexual urges as the reason for sex. Most adolescents tend to engage in serial monogamy. So for most adolescents sexuality is expressed in the context of a relationship. Interestingly the same opposite-sex relationship can be described by the girl as committed and by the boy as casual.

Despite the number of messages about safe and protected sex, between a third and two-thirds do not use a condom for their first sexual experience. A study in Canada showed that 34 per cent used contraception while 27 per cent never used any contraception at all (Meikle, Peitchinis and Pearce 1985, cited in Moore and Rosenthal 1993). Once a relationship is established the pressure is usually on the girl to use the pill. The reasons for non-use often relate to the 'nothing bad will happen to me' belief. Also choosing to use contraception requires a recognition of the risks, a sense of control and the choice and implementation of a particular contraceptive method. These are complex issues to negotiate in the early stages of adolescent sexuality.

Goldman and Goldman (1982) carried out a study into young people's sexual knowledge in Australia, England, North America and Sweden. In Sweden sex education begins at seven and is integrated into the school curriculum and includes information about contraception. Here sexual knowledge was the highest. In the other three countries knowledge was lower and young people said they would like more sex education in school. They also said that they would not trust teachers to give confidential advice and instead got their information from parents, books or the media.

Even where family relationships are close and supportive it may be difficult for sexual matters to be discussed. When family relationships are strained and confrontational this is even more likely to be the case. Young people who have difficult relationships with family may not feel able to seek help with sexual matters from parents. They may well also miss a lot of school and miss out on what sex education there is. Social workers could have a vital role in supporting young people in obtaining the information about sex that they need.

PROBLEMATIC SEXUAL DEVELOPMENT

Although sexual exploration is a healthy aspect of adolescent development, there are some aspects of adolescent sexuality that may result in problems in sexual and emotional adjustment.

Moore and Rosenthal (1993) cite several studies that suggest an association between a number of other problem behaviours and unusually early sexual encounters. Early sexual encounters seem to be associated with behaviours such as drinking, smoking and truancy and delinquency. The evidence tends to suggest that the transition to early sexual activity follows involvement in other problem behaviours. It is also associated with risk-taking in general and risky sexual behaviour in particular. It appears that young people engaging in such activities tend to show impulsive and sensation-seeking characteristics.

CHILDREN WHO ABUSE

For some young people, the sexual behaviour in which they engage could be defined as abusive. Gil and Cavanagh Johnson (1993) suggest five criteria that should all be used to help differentiate between age-appropriate sex exploration between children and an abusive situation:

1. *Age-Difference.* An age difference of greater than three years can be an indication of an abusive relationship, particularly if an adolescent initiates sexual activity with a child who is not yet an adolescent.

2. *Size difference.* If one child is much bigger and stronger than the other, then there is the possibility that undue force is involved in sexual encounters.

3. *Difference in status.* Status differences could include one young person being the babysitter for the other, the captain of a team they are both in and so on.

4. *Type of sexual activity.* Although there is a huge variety in the type of sexual play and exploration, development normally follows a progression from curiosity in one's own body, to curiosity about others, to increased experimentation and sexual activity with others. Sexual behaviour that does not follow this pattern may be an indication of problems.

5. *Dynamics.* Normal sexual exploration involves dynamics of 'spontaneity, joy, laughter, embarrassment, and sporadic levels of inhibition and disinhibition'. Problematic sexual behaviour may have dynamics that are 'agitated, anxious, fearful, or intense. They have higher levels of arousal, and the sexual activity may be habitual' (p.32). In these cases the sexual activity becomes habitual and the main focus of the young person's life.

The authors provide a comprehensive description of normal and problematic sexual activity in young people, as well as detailed guidance for intervention and treatment.

PROSTITUTION

Adolescent prostitution is also likely to be associated with problems in sexual and emotional adjustment. It is an issue that is important for practitioners because of its strong association with both problems in the family background and with childhood sexual abuse.

> The paths to prostitution vary, but a common characteristic is that the young girl is living in an environment which is unhappy, unrewarding or hostile. These young girls may have to cope with problems of family stress, poverty, crime, substance abuse, lack of education and/or

unemployment - any or all of these are likely to lead to prostitution as a means of survival. (Moore and Rosenthal 1993, p.170)

The factors leading to male prostitution are similar. For both sexes it may seem the best economic option, but is associated with many risks, including being the victims of violence and enforced drug-taking. The report of UK National Commission of Inquiry into the Prevention of Child Abuse (Mostyn 1996) suggests that there is currently a conflict between the need to protect young people involved in prostitution and the Criminal Justice System because children as young as ten can be prosecuted in England for prostitution-related offences. The report recommends that for young people, protection issues should take precedence while the 'emphasis of criminal proceedings should be placed on the identification and prosecution of clients and pimps who exploit children through prostitution rather than on the child' (p.53). Social workers can have a role in supporting young people involved in prostitution who are not helped by being treated as deviants or criminals, but who need access to good sex education and opportunities for furthering their wider education as well as support in developing supportive relationships.

TEENAGE PARENTHOOD

It is difficult to present a clear picture about teenage parenthood because of statistical, cultural, socio-economic and national variations. First, it is important to distinguish between pregnancy rates and birth rates. When looking at *birth* rates it seems that, contrary to popular belief, the proportion of births to teenagers as opposed to older women has *not* been rising over recent years. Most studies have indicated that the rate rose in the 1970's, but since then has been falling back to the levels of the 1950's (Bee 1995; Moore and Rosenthal 1993; Santrok 1994).

Birth rates vary considerably between countries. The US has the highest proportions of teenage births. The *pregnancy* rate for teenagers in the US is estimated to be one in ten, that is, about one million pregnancies a year. About half of these pregnancies lead to birth. This is over twice the pregnancy rate in England, France and Canada, three times the rate in Sweden and seven times the rate in the Netherlands (Santrok 1994).

Although the level of adolescent motherhood has remained steady, an increase in the *abortion* rate since the late 1970s suggests that the rate of pregnancy has increased. Young women who choose abortion are more likely to be contraceptive users, to be single, to have high educational or career aims, to have a higher socioeconomic status and to be influenced by religious belief and parental attitudes (Hayes 1987, cited in Moore and Rosenthal 1993).

What has dramatically increased is the proportion of teenage mothers who are not married, which is now over 70 per cent in Britain (Moore and Rosenthal 1993). The large majority of babies in these instances are born to young women who live below the poverty level. Again, contrary to popular myth, motherhood is rarely a choice for material gain. Indeed adolescent parents are distinctly economically disadvantaged (Phoenix 1991).

The fathers of children born to teenage mothers are not necessarily teenagers themselves and can come from a wide range of ages. In some cases they may be involved in an abusive and or incestuous relationship with the mother. In a longitudinal study of young mothers, Phoenix (1991), found that many relationships split up during the pregnancy, and that if the relationship continued the women frequently felt emotionally and materially unsupported by the child's father.

The implications for practice are many. Social workers are likely to be involved in supporting the teenage mother (and possibly the father) as well as assessing the probable impact upon the child if born. In addition, the concerns of many other people will need to be considered; for example, the young woman's parents, siblings, extended family, carers and residential staff.

- In the first instance the young woman will need access to specialised advice about her alternatives as *early* in the pregnancy as possible. The research about the impact of having an abortion during teenage years is limited, but it seems that it need not necessarily be psychologically damaging (Hayes 1987). Practitioners will need to help the young person obtain all the information she requires and encourage her to think through the consequences of all possible choices. She may then need help with presenting her choice to her family.

- Teenage mothers and their child have an elevated risk of complications during pregnancy and birth, probably attributable to poor antenatal care (Moore and Rosenthal 1993). Therefore, it is essential to ensure that the pregnant teenager receives good and prompt antenatal care. She is likely to need considerable support with the actual practical and emotional factors involved in attending clinics. For example, one young pregnant woman reported that she expe-

rienced disapproving looks and comments from other expectant
mothers at a clinic.

- The long-term consequences for teenage mothers can be to lose
  out on schooling, to have lower occupational achievement and to
  be economically disadvantaged. For some, school problems will
  have already been a feature before pregnancy. However, the most
  important message for practice is that the long-term negative effects can be ameliorated if the young woman can remain in education (Hayes 1987). The potential positive effects of school are set
  out in detail in Chapter 8 and here the message is reinforced: that
  resilience can be fostered by good educational experiences. Clearly
  there is a responsibility for all professions involved to make a con-
  certed effort to provide good educational opportunities for pregnant teenagers and young mothers.

- Assessing the likely impact upon the child is as complicated as assessing the impact upon the mother. Studies into the effect on a
  child of having a teenage mother have shown an increased risk of
  parental neglect, child abuse and abandonment. It has been suggested that teenage mothers are less responsive to their babies, and
  use less verbal interaction, which in turn may impede cognitive development. At school age, children born to teenage parents have
  been shown to have problems in cognitive functioning, social
  functioning and school motivation (studies cited in Moore and
  Rosenthal 1993 and Steinberg 1993). However, further research
  in Britain has suggested that these problems could stem as much
  from the *poverty* associated with having a teenage mother as from
  her youth (Phoenix 1991). The first message for practice is that
  the material circumstances of the young woman must be seen as a
  priority, and not just over the short term. The second message is
  that a protective network should be assembled around the child
  according to his or her needs. Often extended family members
  who have a difficult relationship with the mother can, nonetheless,
  be a resource for the child.

- Finally, for some young women who perceive themselves to have
  few career options, motherhood may be a positive choice (Unger
  and Crawford 1992). For some young women who have limited
  contact with their families because of being looked after away

from home, a baby may serve as a bridge to increased contact (Biehal *et al.* 1995).

- There is little research into the effects on a teenage man of father-hood. Similarly, there has been little investigation into the kind of support that may help a young man to take a meaningful role in the parenting of his child. Even though the parental relationship may break up, the practitioner could play a role in supporting a young father and/or his family in maintaining a relationship with the child. For example, while a young man may show some reluctance in acknowledging his fatherhood, his mother may experience strong feelings of attachment as a grandmother and offer the mother and child emotional and practical support.

Activity 8.5

Consider the implications for identity development for a young woman who has a child at the age of 15. Again it may be helpful to use the 'focal' perspective to identify ways in which many different issues have to be tackled at once.

SEXUAL ORIENTATION

Issues of sexual orientation can also be explored during adolescence. In one American study 26 per cent of 12-year-olds surveyed described themselves as having uncertainties about their sexual orientation. By 18 years 5 per cent still described being uncertain. By the end of adolescence about 92 per cent defined themselves as exclusively heterosexual. A third of the remaining 8 per cent defined themselves as exclusively homosexual with the others describing themselves as having both heterosexual and homosexual orientations (Remafedi *et al.* 1992). Self-report studies are obviously limited by what young people are prepared to admit to within a culture where homosexuality is stigmatised and considered deviant by many. Remafedi (1987) also found that 41 per cent of young men who saw themselves as homosexual had lost a friend because of it. Sexual *activity* need not necessarily be directly related to sexual *identity*. Young people who consider themselves to be homosexual may not engage in homosexual relationships for a number of reasons, and others may define themselves as heterosexual despite having homosexual experiences. Bee (1995) cites a study which suggested that 15 per cent of boys and

10 per cent of girls have at least one homosexual experience, with 2 to 3 per cent continuing in homosexual relationships (Dreyer 1982).

Those who define themselves as homosexual are not usually confused about their gender identity and show the same range of feminine and masculine characteristics as those who define themselves as exclusively heterosexual.

Explanations for the development of sexuality vary greatly and research continues into the forces acting on human expression of sexuality. Individuals give different personal accounts of the development of their homosexual identity, some cite biological factors, others personal or political choice, others cite love for a particular individual that transcends gender and others describe factors in upbringing and early experiences (Kitzinger 1986).

In practice, social workers need to recognise that adolescents may question their sexual orientation and may need support in resolving this process. Young men who have been sexually abused by men may also question their sexuality and will need support with their sexual identity development.

If young people define themselves as homosexual then they may well need support in coping with family disapproval and possibly rejection. They may also need help in developing a supportive social network. Support organisations for young people who are gay and lesbian can offer social, emotional and practical help.

SOCIAL INFLUENCES ON EXPRESSION OF SEXUALITY

There is significant evidence that the development of female and male sexuality is subject to different social forces. Boys' sexual urges are generally regarded to be more 'natural' and uncontrollable than those of girls. Girls are also expected to be the ones to control the extent of sexual activity and to be the ones who take responsibility for contraception, although, at the same time they are not supposed to anticipate the sexual event (Unger and Crawford 1992). Lees (1993) describes the extent to which a young woman's identity rests upon her sexuality. Interviews with teenage girls showed just how much their reputation rests on acting in an appropriate sexual manner, and on avoiding the label of 'slag'. This was summed up by one girl's statement;' "It's a vicious circle. If you don't like them, then they'll call you a tight bitch. If you go with them they'll call you a slag afterwards"'(p.27). Lees argues that for many girls the best defence against being called a slag is to have a 'steady' boyfriend. Those who choose sexual activity in casual relationships run the risk of being denigrated and those who choose not to engage in sexual activity can be called man-haters or lesbians. Lees also found that the young men were also limited by the social expectations on them as their masculine identity was based on dissociating themselves from anything 'feminine' and boasting of 'conquests'. She describes gender power differences as a 'force field' that traps both boys and girls.

Lees' work offers some insight into the situation of young people who already have a low sense of self-esteem stemming from early attachment problems. Young women may feel confusions about intimacy and sexuality and seek sexual relationships in the hope of finding intimacy. However, because of their difficulties with attachment they may find it hard to sustain relationships. If they then find themselves to be the victims of hostile social judgement, their self-esteem could be further undermined. Young men with a low esteem and a low sense of self efficacy may not be able to take part in the assertion of aggressive masculinity and therefore feel isolated from a male peer group. They may not have the self-confidence to feel secure in adopting a less traditional male identity.

Prevailing male/female power imbalances in sexual relationships do appear to operate amongst adolescents. An Australian study showed that boys still tend not to consider rape to be an important issue and do not relate their behaviour to it. One-third of those boys surveyed said that intercourse was acceptable if the girl 'led them on' and 23 per cent said it was okay if the girl consented initially, but then changed her mind (Roberts 1992). Twenty-three per cent of high school young women surveyed in the US described some form of unwanted sexual activity from dates or boyfriends, and 15 per cent described what is now known as 'date rape' (Klingman and Vicary 1992). The prevailing discourse about teenage sexuality is one of young women having to control the power and urges of young men. It is less common for young women's own sexual desires to be recognised and although there may be many messages to young women about saying 'no', there are fewer messages about how to say 'yes' (Unger and Crawford 1992).

Bee (1995) describes young men and women as engaging in different 'sexual scripts'. Thus young women are likely to have internalised a 'female' sexual script that associates sex with love, whereas young men have a 'male' script that condones their right to be sexually aggressive. There are a number of implications for practice with troubled young people, some of which are:

- Some young people will have grown up in households where the adult male was sexually aggressive towards the female adult and possibly towards them also. The exploration of their own sex-role identities are likely to be influenced by such experience and this should be explored with them. The impact of their own gender and the particular social pressure upon them should also be considered.

- Within mixed residential settings staff may find that young men and women adopt traditional sex-role stereotypes. There is potential for positive work with groups of young people during the time when they are exploring their own sexual identities to help both genders with the development of mutual and satisfying sexual relationships.

- Some young women who become the subjects of social work intervention do not follow the traditional 'female script' and may act in a sexually assertive or aggressive manner. Practitioners need to be alert to the possibility of such young women being subject to greater moral disapproval than young men engaging in similar behaviour.

SEXUAL ABUSE

Both adolescent girls and boys can be the victims of sexual abuse by adults. The effects will depend on the quality of their attachment relationships and the level of support available to them from family or carers. (See Chapter 5 for more details.)

Young people who have been abused may exhibit problems in expressing adolescent sexuality and engaging in healthy experimentation. Some may avoid sexual exploration, while others may enter into a number of unsatisfying sexual encounters. It is often during adolescence that young people who have been abused will need sensitive support and good, honest sex education.

Some of the problems exhibited by young people that are attributed to adolescence may in fact be the expression of the effects of childhood sexual abuse. These may include persistent running away, extreme hostility, family discord, low self-esteem, difficult peer relationships, involvement in prostitution and so on.

Summit's *accommodation syndrome* is a five-stage model that describes why young people often do not tell anyone about sexual abuse and accounts for some of the behaviour that they may exhibit (Summit 1983). Much of this behaviour may become particularly evident during adolescence when young people are forcibly aware of issues of sexuality and may be exploring sexual relationships with their peers for the first time. The five stages and their implication for practice are:

1. *Secrecy:* children do not expect to be sexually abused, and the secrecy surrounding abuse means that the child is dependent upon the abuser for explanations of what is happening. Considerable force or threat of force is frequently used to ensure secrecy, and the longer children keep the secret, the harder it is for them to speak out. Enforced secrecy, often involving threats, is likely to distort the development of trust in attachment relationships, especially if the abuser is a family member. Also, during adolescence, young people can develop close and intense friendships. Having to keep such a secret about their lives is likely to interfere with the process of shared confidences that forms a part of such friendships as they move through adolescence.

2. *Helplessness:* Adults have more power than children and abusers make full use of that power to reinforce the child's helplessness. Other adults may not pick up on messages that a child is trying to give. Or, worse, they may underestimate the power imbalance and blame the child for the abuse, or for not speaking out sooner. It is not hard to imagine how damaging it would be for a young person's self-concept as they reach adolescence to feel such powerlessness. As they enter teenage years they will have an increasing recognition of the inappropriateness of their experience and are likely to exhibit symptoms of low self-esteem and distress.

3. *Entrapment and accommodation:* If sexual abuse is an ongoing experience and if it is kept secret, then the child learns to accommodate to it by adapting and surviving. They may 'structure' reality to protect an abusing parent, often by defining the parent as 'good' and themselves as 'bad'. The process of systematic entrapment and the child's attempt to cope by accommodating to and incorporating the experiences into his or her life could affect several developmental tasks. For example, the child's cognitive processes must be

distorted by the attempt to view such distressing experiences as normal. Many young people (especially young women) develop self-harming behaviours, while others (especially young men) behave in an aggressive and antisocial fashion. As Summit points out 'Much of what is eventually labelled as adolescent or adult psychopathology can be traced to the natural reactions of a healthy child to a profoundly unnatural and unhealthy parental environment' (p.184). It would also be difficult for a child to develop a coherent system of moral understanding under such circumstances. Finally, if the child is being abused at home, the home cannot then act as a secure base from which to explore the world of school and beyond.

4. *Delayed, conflicting and unconvincing disclosure:* It is difficult for adults to believe that a young person would tolerate sexual abuse and it is also difficult for non-abusing parents to accept the enormity of a disclosure. If a young person is already behaving in a way that is causing difficulties, then there is more reason for adults to disbelieve them. If a young person is not believed by those he or she is close to then this could compound the process of distortion of cognitive, moral and emotional development.

5. *Retraction:* It is frequently the case that young people retract allegations of sexual abuse, especially if the reactions of the those around them confirm what they have been told by the abuser, for example, that they and possibly siblings will be taken into care, that their mothers will be deeply hurt, that they will be blamed and so on. It is therefore not surprising that retraction so often occurs. The trauma of being involved in a sexual abuse investigation can in itself cause great distress. In addition, children, and especially adolescents have a tremendous fear that their peers will find out and that they will be stigmatised.

Finkelhor and Berliner (1995) carried out a review of evaluation studies of treatment after sexual abuse and suggest that:

- structured abuse-focused treatment is the most effective, with both the parent and child receiving intervention
- behavioural management should be used for abuse-related problems

- cognitive-behavioural therapy is helpful for both internalised and externalised behaviours
- brief treatment can be effective
- both group and individual treatment can be effective.

Activity 8.6

Choose a case you know which involves the discovery or disclosure of abuse during adolescence or use the attached case study. Consider the extent to which these five elements apply in your case:

1. secrecy

2. helplessness

3. entrapment and accommodation

4. delayed, conflicted and unconvincing disclosure

5. retraction.

Each of the elements of the syndrome are likely to have a profound impact on this age group.

Again, thinking of your case or the case study, consider how the child could be helped to overcome the effects of abuse on the expected developmental processes at this age.

Take into account factors in the child's situation that may render them vulnerable to the effects of abuse and those elements of resilience that could be drawn upon.

They recommend *trauma-specific* treatment for child sexual abuse based on these research-based principles. It draws on the link between thoughts, feelings and behaviour as described in previous chapters. So, for example, a young woman who *thinks* that she was to blame for being sexually abused, may *feel* as if she is a bad person and then may *act* aggressively. Treatment involves uncovering thoughts and related feelings and replacing the thoughts with more appropriate ones. The aim is for the young person to be able to account for the events and to recall the events without undue distress. In other words, the aim is for the young person to have a 'coherent story' for the trauma they suffered. This treatment model is described in clear and precise detail in Deblinger and Hope Heflin (1996).

Message for practice

Developing a sexual identity is a normal part of adolescence. Being involved in sexual activity is not normally associated with psychological disturbance, unless it begins unusually early or is in the context of an exploitative or abusive situation. Parents frequently cite concerns over sexual activity as sources of extreme conflict with their children and they can be given as a reason for parents to eject children from the home or to request alternative care. Social workers could be influential in helping parents and alternative carers to consider the realities of adolescent sexual exploration and to set an individual's behaviour into context.

Adolescence may be a particularly difficult period for young people who have experienced, or are currently experiencing sexual abuse and they may need considerable support with issues of sexuality.

Delinquency?

Do adolescents pose a threat to society because of their involvement in general delinquent behaviour and crime in particular?

Researchers have found that problem behaviours tend to form two main clusters. One cluster is what is commonly characterised as 'acting out' and involves truanting, drug misuse, precocious sexual activity and aggression. Alternatively, problems may be expressed inwardly through depression and anxiety or through eating disorders. It is delinquency and associated criminal activity that causes most public anxiety. Again the stereotype contains some truth and some exaggeration. Only a minority of young people commit offences. Of those who do, many are one-off offenders. However, if a person is going to break the law they are most likely to do so during adolescence or early adulthood. In the US half of all property crimes are committed by those under 18 who make up a quarter of the population. Some 20 per cent of rapes and 30 per cent to 50 per cent of child sexual abuse are committed by adolescents. Also 50 per cent of committed adult sex offenders state that they began abusing during their adolescent years. Rates of violent crimes against people are increasing amongst the young. Finally, it is worth noting that although adolescents are involved in committing crime, they are also the most likely victims of theft, robbery, rape and assault. (Studies cited by Steinberg 1993.)

Self-report surveys in the US have shown that although black and white young people reported committing the same amount of crime, young people from ethnic minorities are far more likely to be arrested and to receive harsher punishment than their white counterparts. This, of course, distorts the picture of who is responsible for crime (Krisberg *et al.* 1986).

Young people who commit their first offence during their adolescence are most likely to be low-rate offenders and to 'grow out' of delinquency. They show no great different characteristics from non-offending young people. The main differences seem to be lower parental monitoring and the influence of a peer group involved in offending behaviour.

The small group who are a great cause for concern are those whose problems were identified well before adolescence, maybe as young as eight (Rutter and Rutter 1993). Persistent delinquency is associated with poor-quality relationships in childhood and poor social training. As noted in the introductory chapter, links between background and behaviour may not be causal, but the association is clear. It is in adolescence that the cumulative effect of adversities during childhood can be expressed. The effects of unhelpful aspects of parenting can also come to the fore at this stage.

Rutter and Rutter (1993) provide a detailed examination of child and adolescent aggression and delinquency drawn extensively from research material. Here is a summary of important findings to be considered for practice:

- Aggressive behaviour and conduct disorder tend to be persistent over time.

- Conduct disorders in *pre-school* years predict similar behaviour in *middle* childhood.

- Aggression in early and middle childhood is strongly predictive of later socially disruptive behaviour and delinquency, both non-aggressive and violent.

- Early *offending* is predictive of later delinquency.

- Most of those exhibiting persistent problems are boys.

A combination of factors is associated with early and prolonged delinquency:

- Material factors including poor housing, poverty and little oppor-tunities for constructive amusement.

- Family factors including large families and poor relations between family members and a lack of techniques for dealing with family crisis.

- parental criminality and weak family relationships

- Family discord.

- Self-perpetuation of behaviour by the child. As described in Chapter 7, children who end up involved in spirals of hostility often do not distinguish between intentional and accidental hurt to themselves and respond to all provocation, even accidental, aggressively.

- Ineffective supervision and discipline including lack of 'house rules', parental monitoring and consistent discipline or rewards; authoritarian parenting and discipline that is more to do with parents' tensions and angers than the child's actual behaviour.

- The experience of physical abuse.

- The young people themselves are likely to have had school problems for some years, to score low on IQ tests, to be unpopular with peers and to spend much time watching television.

However, Rutter and Rutter suggest that an underlying factor may be a '*hyperactive–impulsive–inattentive*' disposition. This can be a *vulnerability* that when associated with severe family *adversity* can be connected with problems like delinquency. Conversely, positive family circumstances can act as a *protective* factor.

Again, as discussed earlier, the interaction of all these factors is extremely complex and no assumptions should be made that a child experiencing some of these factors will necessarily exhibit delinquent behaviour. It is also the case that some difficult behaviour can be shown by adolescents who have been sexually abused as children and therefore assumptions cannot be made about the reason for such problems.

Message for practice

Delinquency is not a necessary part of adolescence. The majority of adolescents do not become involved in delinquent behaviour, or else do so only on a small scale and do not continue to offend as adults. The small minority who show serious and persistent behaviour problems in adolescence are very likely to have already had problems. Therefore a detailed assessment of preceding childhood experiences is essential. What is clear is that early intervention is crucial before adolescence with young people whose conduct raises concern.

Conduct disorders

Conduct disorders and aggression are factors associated with parents requesting support, parents requesting local authority care, a child being physically abused during chastisement, school problems or exclusion, involvement with the police and hearing system, distress for the child and parents and breakdown of placements.

Activity 8.7

In a study of 43 children on the child abuse register for physical abuse, (Pitcairn *et al.* 1993) it was found that:

1. a high proportion of them showed high levels of behavioural problems which were not being treated and

2. control and discipline in the majority of cases was rated as lax.

Does this mirror your experience? How might parents be helped to adopt the more effective authoritative parenting style described in Chapter 3.

Such problems therefore need detailed and careful and prompt intervention. Intervention also requires effective inter-disciplinary agreement. Any intervention needs to be consistent across all settings in which the child or young person operates. Intervention also requires good communication and partnership with the family, who need to accept and understand the rationale for that intervention.

Cigno (1995) argues persuasively for intervention based on behaviourist techniques, seeing it as consistent with partnership with, and empowerment of, parents, because behavioural intervention in the home requires:

- parents to be informed and involved
- parents to be partners in therapy
- specific, agreed goals
- a lack of mystique
- intervention that is task centred
- close attention to the to the detail of what parents are telling you
- a focus on the 'here and now' problems.

Social learning theory…concerns how children and adults learn patterns of behaviour, as a result of social interactions, or simply through coping with the environment…it suggests how to focus upon the practical rather than upon their weaknesses or shortcomings, and upon how to empower those with whom we work. (Sutton 1994, pp.5-6, cited in Cigno 1995, p.375)

Herbert (1987) has developed a detailed behavioural approach to the assessment and treatment of severe conduct disorders. Herbert uses a social learning approach which suggests that behavioural problems are a manifestation of the young person's attempts to cope with the environment they live in. In other words, behavioural problems are learnt in the same way that other behaviours are and that the child is not being a problem, but trying to solve one. The social learning approach as espoused by Herbert is not inconsistent with attachment theory as the behaviour is seen as developing within the context of close relationships. Indeed, a key to the theory is that parents or carers may well be (unconsciously) reinforcing difficult behaviour. Behaviour problems can thus be viewed as natural, but inappropriate, responses to adverse situations:

It is hypothesised that much of a child's behaviour is learned, maintained, and regulated by its effects upon the natural environment and the feedback it receives with regard to these consequences. Behaviour does not occur in a vacuum. It is a resultant of a complex transaction between the individual, with his [sic] inborn strengths and weaknesses, acting and reacting within an environment which encourages and sometimes discourages his behaviour. (p.5)

Some of his main points are:

- Attachment theory is used to describe the importance of early relationships for the development of appropriate behaviour, emphasising the fact that children essentially want to please and emulate those to whom they are attached. The atmosphere of the home therefore has a huge impact on the child's moral development.

- Serious conduct problems must be diagnosed as early as possible because of the strong links with later delinquency. Disruptive, aggressive or antisocial behaviour is particularly worrying.

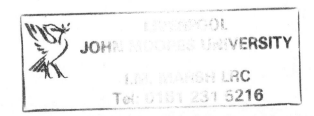

- Antisocial behaviour can be associated with having parents who provide insufficient supervision and discipline.

- Some children are temperamentally more difficult to discipline, being impulsive, unpredictable and unmalleable. If the parents are unable to establish effective controls at an early stage these children are likely to exhibit behavioural problems in adolescence. (See Chapters 2 and 6 for discussions about the interaction between child temperament and parenting.)

Put simply the social learning approach suggests an ABC model of the reinforcement of problem behaviour. First, there is an *antecedent*: for example, a parent might ask a young person to help with the washing up. This is followed by the *behaviour*: for example the young person flies into a tantrum, says they are expected to do everything and refuses. Finally there are the *consequences*: in this case the parent may feel too exhausted for a fight and to avoid the escalation will do the washing up themselves. The aim of intervention is to help parents or carers create an environment that both discourages the problem behaviour and encourages positive behaviours. Herbert provides a 12-step guide to the process of which the two main components are:

1. *Assessment*: A detailed, longitudinal, and functional assessment of the child and their behaviour in the context of the environment is fundamental. For behavioural treatment to work the initial assessment must be precise in identifying behaviour, its antecedents and consequences. The situation in which behavioural problems occur also needs to be specified. The assessment asks 'what' the child is doing, not 'why'. Aggression, non-compliance and hyperactivity are pinpointed as commonly presented problems.

2. *Behaviour modification*: If it is decided that the behaviour problems require treatment they are ranked in order of priority and the initial focus is on the one that most concerns the parent. A programme of treatment is negotiated with the parents and young person. Techniques will vary according to the individual situation, and include the use of rewards, punishment, modelling, skill training, cognitive approaches, groupwork and so on.

Much of the approach can seem like common sense. But there are factors that often undermine the common sense approach, for example:

- The *assessment* process is crucial. Intervention will not work unless considerable time has been spent on assessing the problems *in detail* and planning the programme *in detail.*

- People often underestimate the extent to which the target behaviour can *increase* before it decreases as the child escalates their attempt to get the desired response. The temptation may be to switch to another method, or give up, both of which *reinforce* the behaviour that was supposed to be reduced.

- Parents/carers, despite their best intentions may be *inconsistent* in their application of rewards and sanctions.

- There can be problems when people are required to reward a child for what may seem very small improvements.

- There can be difficulties if the parents/carers are not committed to the process, do not understand the rationale, or have doubts that it will be effective.

In summary this theory suggests that behaviour problems are a clear message that the young person is struggling to cope with their environment. However, the ways they have used to cope are antisocial and cause them more problems because they are not adaptive. In practice Herbert's work indicates that with detailed assessment it is possible to analyse what conditions are supporting the behaviour problems. With the use of various behavioural techniques it is possible for young people and their parents to learn new patterns of behaviour. If the children are accommodated away from home, alternative carers can instigate clear behavioural frameworks to change maladaptive behaviours. However, Fahlberg (1994) urges caution when planning rewards and sanctions for young people being looked after away from home. Children who have already been separated from those to whom they are attached may not respond well to sanctions involving further separation, for example, time out in a bedroom; instead time-out could be carried out in the same room as the adult. They also may not change their behaviour in order to gain a reward because they do not believe they deserve good things and because they do not have an attachment to the carer and therefore lack the urge to please them. She recommends that assessment is needed to understand the reasons for difficult behaviour, the focus should be then be on meeting the child's emotional needs and encouraging positive behaviours.

Looked after adolescents

Many young people received into care in adolescence have troubled relationships with their parents. Indeed it can often be during adolescence that attachment problems become most pronounced. As stated in earlier chapters, one of the important aspects of the attachment relationship is that it provides a secure base from which the child can explore the world. The lack of a secure base, or an insecure base will make the natural urge for the teenager to explore the outside world more complex and often frightening for the young person. If an adolescent is looked after away from home, they not only have to deal with the loss of what may be complicated and unsatisfactory attachment relationships, they also have to negotiate new relationships. As stated in the earlier chapters, attachment theory suggests that an internal working model of relationships develops from early relationships, which, in turn, influences later relationships.

Downes (1992) has written extensively about the ways in which foster carers can help adolescents with attachment disorders (see also the discussion of attachment in Chapter 2). She describes particular patterns of attachment behaviour which are stimulated by the threat of separation. Facing even brief separations across the family boundary, young people often demonstrate a particular pattern of attachment behaviour which illustrates the nature of their internal working model of relationships with the important people in their lives. Downes postulates that particular types of considered responses on the part of parents or carers can build and develop a young person's ability to use support effectively. These ideas mirror closely John Bowlby's work with very young children and underline the resonances of adolescent development with this earlier stage of maturation.

Secure attachment

This type of attachment relationship is characterised by the ability of the adolescent to use adult support appropriately at times of stress or challenge and in particular prior to or following brief separations, for example, visits to birth family, crossing the family boundary to school or college, etc.

Insecure/avoidant attachment

Typically the young person exhibiting this pattern of attachment seeks to avoid intimate contact with parents or carers and support needs to be offered in a very sensitive manner in order to allow the young person to make use of any benefits of nurturing. Often the young person will maintain emotional and physical distance from carers. They may be isolated with few friends. They may be either low in self-reliance, or fiercely self-reliant with problems with intimacy.

Carers need to help the young person experiment with being close by offering responses at times of crisis which allow for more intimacy, without scaring the young person away. For some carers though it can be more demanding to offer such unrewarded help than to deal with actual delinquency. They need to be able to cope with receiving little feedback from the young people.

Insecure / ambivalent attachment

The adolescent who has ambivalent feelings towards his or her attachment figure simultaneously both wants and fears closeness and support from adults. Typically, he or she will vacillate in their capacity to use the secure base and will appear to want nurturing but not to be able to use this in preparation for their explorations at school, college or in the community. Typically, this young person may attempt to sever the connection with carers prematurely in an attempt to establish their independence whilst clearly often demonstrating their inability to deal with the stresses they face.

The aim of the carer's work is to try to reduce the oscillating pattern and to enable the young person to pause between the feeling of the need to go and the going. Carers need to maintain a consistent stance without recrimination. They need to be able to welcome the young person back after an absence. However, the adolescent's behaviour can be very effective in achieving the aim of destroying those good relationships they may be establishing with carers. Carers therefore require considerable patience and understanding to cope with the undermining of their offers of support. Principally, they need to be able to resist falling into hostile patterns with the young people.

Insecure / anxious attachment

The behaviour which characterises this pattern of attachment is indicative of the adolescent's preoccupation with the presence or availability of adults or carers. The young person typically exhibits significant problems in separating with any feeling of security from their secure base and venturing into the adult world without displaying a high level of anxiety and distress.

If the carers are seen as the attachment figure then they need to be able to tolerate this kind of dependency upon them as a secure base and be available

---

Activity 8.8

Consider an adolescent with whom you are currently working and identify any particular pattern of attachment behaviour which you or the parents or the carers have observed which is their typical response to separation experiences across the family boundary. (This is not necessarily a traumatic separation but may be illustrated by any attempt on behalf of the adolescent to venture into the community, for example, leisure activity with peers, attendance at school or at college.)

Exploring the particular ideas of parental responses to particular types of attachment behaviour suggested above, identify ways in which these ideas may be translated into helpful responses to the adolescent's separations from the current family, whether parents or carers.

---

and reliable. The evidence suggests that this will not make the young person over-dependent; rather, the reassurance of the carer's availability will allow them to become more self-reliant.

If the parent or other family member is seen by the young person as the attachment figure then the carers will need to understand the ways this may affect their behaviour. For example, in times of stress they may go to great lengths to seek that person out. Carers need to resist entering into loyalty conflicts, and if possible maintain good communication with the young person's attachment figure.

Moving on

Another important developmental issue is that of moving to independence. For most young people this is a gradual and unproblematic process that builds from earlier experience so that: 'Adolescence does not usually involve some crude exchange of parents for peers as the key influence of support' (Gilligan 1997, p.16).

However, for young people who have experienced disruption, and particularly those who have been looked after by the local authority this process may not be straightforward. Many of these young people experience considerable difficulties with the transition to independence, one of their main problems being social isolation (Biehal *et al.* 1995; Stone 1989; Triseliotis *et al.* 1995). Attention to supporting the development of inter-dependency skills is therefore essential.

The difficulties for young people in establishing supportive networks when their attachments have been disrupted during childhood are well-known. For example, Stone (1989) describes the over-representation of care-leavers in prison and amongst the homeless and unemployed. She identifies some of the priority issues for care leavers as self-development and *social* and life skills. In her study of a number of leaving care schemes she showed that: 'There was no instance of young people building up or fitting into anything like a community network' (p.56).

Two more recent studies of young people in difficulty have explored these issues further. One (Triseliotis *et al.* 1995), found that in spite of disruptive experiences most of the 13- to 17-year-old young people in receipt of social work intervention they interviewed had important continuing relationships and felt close to one or more parent who acted as a main reference point, even if not in the same household. Friends also played an important part in their lives. A study of young people leaving care (Biehal *et al.* 1995) found a strong association between the quality of relationships with parents and the quality of friendship networks. Those who had poor friendship networks also tended to have poor relationships with parents while those who had good relationships with parents had good networks of friends. There was also an association between having good relationships (both family and wider) and a positive sense of identity, which was in turn associated with good self-esteem.

Both studies concluded that social workers were often not well informed about teenagers' social networks, and that policies for young people should take account of their need for a permanent social base and their need to develop a support network in order to cope with adulthood.

This suggests the need for more consideration of the friendship networks of vulnerable young people and, in particular, *how* they can actually be fostered. Those helping vulnerable young people need to help them to develop positive networks of support *despite* having experienced disruption in family relationships and should try to maximise their skills and opportunities for ameliorating adverse earlier experiences.

Conclusion

Rather than characterising adolescence as problem-laden, it is more useful to ask why concerns are raised once young people reach adolescence. Problems that may already have been present can become much more obvious and disturbing in teenagers. They may be manifested because of the growth in the

Activity 8.9

Read the case study and using the information you have been given in this and the previous chapters consider the questions that follow.

Case study

Paul is 14 years old and has been in residential accommodation for two years. His parents are both heavy drinkers and have had a violent relationship since Paul's early childhood. His reception into local authority accommodation was precipitated by a battle with his father during a marital row, Paul was hit by his father and ejected from the house. He is a tall, well-developed boy for his age, one of the earliest maturers in his school year. He is very conscious of his size and also of the fact that he closely resembles his father in appearance.

He has chosen to have no contact with his father but does see his mother regularly. These are very sad meetings when Paul takes on his mother's worries, he comes back to the residential unit burdened by anxiety about her. He has recently confided to a trusted staff member that he was sexually abused in an atmosphere of physical threat by a paternal uncle when he was at the prepubescent stage. This abuse began with threats and favours but later shifted to a relationship of intimidation.

This would fit with confusing accounts in the case notes of a worrying and sudden deterioration in Paul's school work in his late primary school stage. Paul thought he had tried to tell a member of primary school staff, but his communication skills are fairly poor and it is quite possible the disclosure was unclear. Paul is now extremely anxious about possible police action in relation to his disclosures and when anxious he can become very touchy and aggressive. He does have a guidance teacher in whom he is beginning to confide. Paul also has friends who have moved through primary into secondary schools with him. They are now puzzled by his aggressive behaviour and are beginning to withdraw from him at school break times. He is dependent on them for his social life as a number of the other residents in the unit are older than Paul or involved in trouble with the police in the local community.

Paul's father is outraged at the disclosures, but his mother has managed to convey her belief in him.

1. In what respect may Paul have experienced emotional abuse and neglect alongside the physical and sexual abuse?

2. How might maturational tasks he now faces be further complicated by his previous history and current circumstances?

3. What does he need to support him in the current crisis and who might offer this?

Hints for answers

For example, you should consider the effects of growing up in an atmosphere of family discord. The fact that Paul left the house rather than his father after being hit could lead him to feeling guilty for what happened and to his self-esteem being low. The fact that his attempt at disclosure was unsuccessful could further undermine his self-esteem and efficacy. At this age Paul could be expected to be exploring the outside world from the security of a home base. However, he may feel a lack of security from his home and from the alternative care. He may need help in exploring issues of sexuality. Finally, in considering positive aspects for intervention it would be important to build on his relationship with his mother, his friends and guidance teacher.

ability of the young person to challenge their parents, to make comparisons, and to articulate their thoughts better. Situations may be more frightening simply because adolescents are big and physical containment can no longer be a last resort (or first resort!) solution for parents. Finally, it is precisely because adolescents are so close to being adult that parents become so concerned and frightened about how they will cope when they are more independent.

An assessment framework is provided in Appendix 3. The framework is based on the main issues identified by Steinberg (Steinberg 1993) as affecting young people during adolescence and incorporates material covered in this chapter. The framework can be adapted for use in various practice situations. It focuses on looking for strengths within the situation which can be drawn upon when planning intervention with troubled young people.

Summary of developmental issues and considerations for practice

The *biological* changes of teenage years are overlayed with *social* meanings. 'Adolescence' is essentially a *social* construction and, as such, has different meanings in different countries and cultures. This forms the backdrop for the discussion of adolescent development.

From the perspective of attachment theory the main interest lies in the process of *transition* from childhood to adulthood and how well this process is supported by earlier experiences.

The developmental tasks of adolescence are often likened to those during toddler years. That is, like toddlers, adolescents are striving for more independence which may involve them in conflicts with parents. At the same time, they have a strong need for the secure base of close attachments while facing increasing demands from education, work, friends, relationships etc.

- The main message for practice is that during adolescence attachment networks are usually becoming wider, building on a base of family relationships and friendships. Family relationships remain essential to most young people. Even if they are not able to live at home, many young people retain strong ties to family members, including extended family. Careful assessment of the importance of family relationships is necessary without making assumptions about who is of importance.

- The finding that social workers often lack knowledge about young people's friendships acts as a reminder to pay attention to this area.

- All young people need a supportive network, which, if the family cannot provide, should be provided by others. The aim should be to help them to attain mature dependence on friends and family.

There is a complex interaction between *hormonal* and environmental influences on mood during adolescence.

- Young people require support with the physiological changes experienced during puberty.

- Young people who have experienced neglect or abuse may have difficulty with interpreting their own physiological indicators. For example, they may not accurately interpret feelings of hunger or tiredness. During puberty they may require extra support in attuning to their own internal states. Some may need accurate, clear information about puberty.

Adolescence can be a time for exploration of *identity*. As described, this need not lead to a crisis of identity for young people who have security and a positive self-esteem. As discussed in Chapter 7, self-esteem and self-efficacy are closely associated. Young people with a low sense of self-efficacy and poor self-esteem will be predisposed to experiencing identity problems.

- It could be helpful to explore the personal fables of young people with efficacy and self-esteem problems using self-narrative techniques described.

- If the family has been a site of conflict and distress the young person may feel a lack of family identity, and may actively reject values espoused by their family. In this situation other adults may be identified with, for example social workers, residential staff, parents of friends, teachers and so on.

- All young people, regardless of gender, race or sexual orientation have a right to a positive identity which is supported and reinforced by adults around them. Care must be taken to be sensitive to this; for example, criticisms of family of origin may be perceived as criticisms of self; derogatory comments about the part of town they come from may also be damaging. The expression of sexist, racist or homophobic opinions by people in positions of trust can be similarly undermining.

- As with younger children, all potential 'islands of competence' should be explored as avenues for boosting self-esteem and identity. Any interests, hobbies, skills should be encouraged and supported.

The development of *sexuality* is a process and is affected by biological and social forces. It does seem that teenagers are engaging in sexual activity at a younger age than did their parents' generation, but their values about the importance of the context of a committed relationship are not markedly different. Therefore, it is important to assess the behaviour of an individual adolescent within the context of that of their peers. This means not assuming that if a young person has sex at fifteen they are unusually precocious. On the other hand, just because 'everyone else is doing it' does not mean that the individual young person has the maturity to cope with a sexual relationship.

- All young people, whether they are involved in sexual relationships or not, should have access to clear, age-appropriate information about sex, relationships and contraception. Practitioners should ensure that each young person can identify one trusted adult that they would feel able to discuss sexual matters with. Carers may themselves need access to information and support if they are to adequately support and educate the young people in their care.

- Young people who have already been abused or neglected and who lack a secure attachment base are highly vulnerable to sexual exploitation, both within the context of relationships and commercially. Boosting resilience in these young people so that they have the confidence to withstand such exploitation is a challenge to practitioners. Examples of ways to intervene include role play to practise interpersonal skills, assertiveness training, same-sex groups which explore gender issues, couple counselling and support with informing the police about attempts at recruitment into prostitution.

Delinquent behaviour that springs out of nowhere during teenage years is unusual. As with other areas of adolescent development it is the *continuity* with earlier experiences that is most informative. Although some young people become involved in delinquent activities for the first time in teenage years, this usually wanes as they mature. When the roots of delinquency can be traced back to earlier conduct problems the need for intervention is strongly indicated. A combination of material, familial and peer group factors are associated with such problems, as is boredom, non-attendance at school and lack of opportunities for constructive activity.

- It can be easy for parents and professionals alike to feel despair in the face of persistent delinquent behaviour by a young person. The main message for practice is that it is highly likely that the young person is also distressed by their behaviour. This can be a good starting point in intervention and will involve including the young person in planning.

- If used thoughtfully and in conjunction with attention to the young person's emotional needs, behavioural approaches can be very effective. They are most effective if based on reward for positive change rather than punishment for failure.

- Helping the young person to find constructive ways to occupy his or her time has to be the main approach. Educational provision should be the first priority, both because it provides current occupation, and also because it can interrupt the trajectory towards more criminal activity in adult life. Other activities should probably, at least initially, be structured and supervised by adults, for example, schemes for young 'joyriders', outdoor activity schemes, sport clubs and so on.

- Overall, it may be necessary to set very small goals for improvement. Often young people are expected to make too many changes too quickly and with insufficient intensive support from adults.

Failure on these goals simply serves to reinforce their own belief that delinquency is the best choice.

Finally, the theme of continuity with earlier experiences is epitomised by the impact of *attachment history* upon adolescent attachment behaviour. Those faced with the challenge of caring for adolescents who cannot be looked after by their family know the extent to which inner working models developed in early childhood can impact upon current relationships.

- The key message for practice is that planning for the care of young people must be based on a bedrock of as much information as possible about their past. This does not mean just a list of family facts and of placements (although these are important), but detailed assessment of attachment experiences with all significant people in their life history.

Young people arrive at adolescence already some way along a developmental pathway. This pathway will have been influenced in different ways by many people. Some young people will have encountered continuous setbacks which have impacted upon their ability to respond to opportunities in adolescence. However, the direction of future pathways can be hugely influenced by constructive intervention by adults who rise to the challenge of seeking out and enhancing any areas of potential resilience both within and around the young people they care about.

CHAPTER 9

Conclusions

In this concluding chapter some of the key themes of the earlier text are revisited. The chapter addresses among other things the enormous significance of loss experiences in children's lives, the importance of attachment and our conceptions of who constitutes attachment figures, the importance of holistic assessments, the value of a strengths focus in assessment, and the relevance of developmental pathways and developmental outcomes in planning, and assessing the value of, interventions. The reader is reminded of the significance of these themes and is given some practice guidance tips.

Dealing with loss

Social workers should assume that any child client has been affected by loss in some way: loss by bereavement, loss by separation, loss by rejection, loss by betrayal of innocence, loss by failed expectations or dashed hopes. Serious loss of this kind can undermine a child's sense of belonging to people who care about her and thus her sense of her value and lovability. Much of the challenging behaviour of children, about which carers may complain to social workers, can be traced to unresolved losses in the child's life, and the knock-on effects of such losses. This framework of understanding related to the themes of loss and grief can be a most valuable frame of reference for the harassed social worker. Working in a manner sensitive to this issue of loss requires a number of things. It will require knowledge of the significance of attachment and loss in children's development; of likely reactions to severe and unresolved loss; and of likely influences on such reactions. In particular, professionals must never lose sight of the shattering impact of parental rejection for a child's sense of self-worth. Trying to empathise with a child's sense of loss, whatever its source, will also require workers to draw honestly on their own personal experiences of loss in order to try to sensitise themselves to some degree to the child's plight.

Practice points

How can a worker begin to prepare themselves for how to tap in to the depth of a child's sense of loss?

- Reflect on the impact of separations in the worker's own child-hood (due to hospitalisations, illness, death, summer holidays, summer camps, boarding school, parents' divorce etc.).
- Reflect on appropriate sources in literature, film, songs or poetry which address themes of loss.

Working effectively and sensitively with the child's loss will also require a comprehensive understanding of the child based on a thorough gathering of information about the child and a careful sifting/assessment of the significance of that information. It will also require a capacity to identify and negotiate with those adults in the child's life who are well placed to assist the child to begin to process unfinished business about past loss. This may involve helping a child to prepare for and carry out a visit to the grave of a departed relative. It may involve a carefully orchestrated setpiece meeting with a parent where the child hears an honest and fundamental explanation as to why the parent had been unable to care for the child and how this had led to the child entering the care system. Even more painfully, it may require the child being faced honestly and sensitively with the news that their future does not involve the realisation of any treasured fantasy about returning home, but in fact entails remaining in care, or placement for adoption. The importance of this focus on loss has implications not only for the priorities of social workers' own professional practice. It also raises issues for the quality of professional supervision available to them and for the quality of commitment which agencies have to the importance of these issues in the lives of their child clients.

Key questions for practice

- What major losses has this child suffered?
- How can information about these be gathered? (information from parents, key caregivers, agency records, hospital records etc.)
- At what developmental stage did these losses occur?

- What opportunities has this child had to process her reaction to these different losses?

- What are important sources of continuity in the child's life despite the losses?

- Are there ways in which the social worker can strengthen the connection to such threads of continuity?

- Does the child need to do any active work on grieving for losses at this point?

- And on a related point, does the child have a need for fuller or more accurate information concerning the circumstances surrounding any key past losses?

- If so, are there people of significance to the child who the child trusts and who may be able to help in the process of working through the loss?

- Are current caregivers properly briefed on the child's history of loss and the likely psychological reactions to such patterns of loss?

- Have the caregivers or other adults playing a significant role in the child's life (e.g. a key teacher) had a chance to have training and discussion about the precise nature of loss and its likely impact in the subject child's life?

The importance of attachments and a child's sense of having a 'secure base' from which to explore the world

A child's sense of attachment may have implications for many aspects of their functioning including their capacity to trust, learn, concentrate, play and socialise. Attachment relationships are important because they give children access to responsive adult care. That responsive care, in turn, helps children to form an internal working model of relationships as being potentially supportive and positive. In other words, through attachment relationships children can learn that it is positive and safe to trust and be close. As we mention below, however, it cannot be assumed that all attachment relationships yield safe, protective and supportive caring all of the time.

Social workers should always remember *attachment relationships are important*. A successful primary attachment may be especially important and ideally it should occur in the first year. A primary attachment figure is a person whom the child seeks out, and whose proximity and comfort can console the child in moments of extreme distress. However, it is not necessarily an 'all or nothing' scenario. If the child does not form a primary attachment to an adult in the first year it may still be possible, although more difficult, for the child to experience a primary attachment experience through a later relationship. It is important to bear in mind that attachments are not dependent on the gender of the carer, the quality of care, or the frequency of contact. Primary attachments may form with more than one adult. They may form despite abusive behaviour on the part of the adult. The context of the attachment relationship and the responsiveness of the attachment figure are two key factors in the nurturing of an attachment relationship. A child may thus form an attachment to an adult who abuses him or her in the absence of alternative attachment figures and because the abusive relationship also contains elements of warmth, responsiveness and support which the child desperately craves.

It is vital for social workers to realise that children are likely to have a hierarchy of attachment relationships to other important figures in their lives (Trinke and Batholomew 1997). It is profoundly unhelpful in our view to conceive of a child's attachment needs solely in terms of one or two precious or rarefied relationships. The frequent fragility of primary relationships in the lives of children enduring serious adversity such as life in care should surely highlight for us the importance of developing a cast of adults who may play different and important parts in the drama which is the child's life (Scales and Gibbons 1996). Children in care themselves seem to want such a range of adults with whom to relate (Sinclair and Gibbs 1996). Professionals should recognise children need people to whom they are special: carers, family members, teachers, social workers, sports coaches and so on. It is best not to put all the eggs into one basket in terms of such special relationships since we cannot guarantee individual people or relationships are forever.

Children may form a range of meaningful attachments with different people, and the degree of such attachment may vary. It may be helpful to think of secondary attachments as serving an important safety net function should any primary attachment(s) fail to materialise or should they collapse for some reason. A key professional task for social workers in work with children at risk is to ascertain which people make up their attachment network. This attachment network in a sense serves the child as a secure base from which to explore the world and to which to return in moments of crisis. This attachment can also usefully be considered as a potential 'safety net' which prevents the child falling deeper into difficulty in times of crisis.

Siblings are likely to be significant members of a child's attachment network especially in conditions of family stress. Siblings may be drawn together in their common struggle to cope with parental frailty and familial distress. The intensity of some sibling relationships in such circumstances may be double edged. Some sibling relationships may be unhelpful to both parties where negative family dynamics intrude and corrode the more positive tendencies often present in sibling relationships. Social workers may sometimes have to assess – and somehow regulate – the nature of sibling relationships where elements of emotional or other abuse have crept in. This question may be posed most sharply in whether to place certain siblings together, or in determining the extent of contact between siblings placed apart.

Key practice questions about children's attachment network

Who is important to the child or young person:

- at home
- in the extended family (grandparents, aunts, uncles, cousins)
- in school (teachers, ancillary staff, friends)
- in the neighbourhood (adult neighbours, friends, church members, shopkeepers etc.)
- in clubs (sports, cultural, musical)
- elsewhere (workplace or training centre)?

In working with children in distress it may be helpful to remember that the greater the distress and disruption, the greater the need for a sense of having a 'secure base'. In decision making about where children are to live professionals should strive to preserve threads and relationships in children's lives – the price of help should not be the severing or demeaning of past ties. Even where past ties contain negative elements, the professional challenge is to help the child to tap safely into the positive elements of such ties.

It is important in planning for children to establish which relationships are meaningful in 'secure base' terms by getting to know the child – children will tell you if you can listen to and hear all the messages. This will help the worker to identify and support those members of a social network whose relationships with the vulnerable person may provide a sense of 'secure base'. While attachments occur predominantly through relationships with other human beings it is also important to recognise how, in addition to relationships with people, memories, symbols, animals, stories, images, places, language, events can all contribute to a child's sense of having a 'secure base'. For children whose ties to attachments or whose sense of secure base is very tenuous because of the impact of adversity, symbols or objects which evoke connections to the past may assume special importance. Social workers need to be especially sensitive to this point in their practice with children in crisis or transition. It is also important to acknowledge that children may be deeply attached to people who have harmed them, wittingly or unwittingly. Attachment does not depend on the quality of care. The protection of the child must be secured in a way which remains sensitive to the meaning of that attachment relationship for the child

Practice points

What may enhance a sense of secure base for a child in crisis?

- bringing familiar objects from one placement or caregiver to another (toy, photograph etc.)
- having the endorsement of a valued attachment network member for a move
- having sight of comforting religious or ethnic symbols (where relevant and meaningful).

However tempting in the face of a child's pain and emotional void, it is inappropriate for a professional to serve as anything more than a transitional 'secure base' offering a relationship which in some instances may appropriately help a child 'cross the bridge' from one permanent carer to another. It is not feasible or appropriate for a professional to pose as a longer-term 'secure base', thus possibly obstructing or supplanting naturally occurring potential secure base relationships in the child's social ecology.

One of the most sensitive tasks in social work with children is the management of transitions from one caregiver to another, from one living arrangement to another. If one thinks of how much care is required to transplant a human organ or a young tree or plant, then one has a sense of the vulnerability of the child in transition and the care and attention to detail which should attend their move.

IMPORTANT ISSUES

Professionals should bear the following in mind.

A move is not just a logistical challenge – finding a placement, booking it and managing transport. It involves for the child loss of the familiar, and fear of the unknown. It may reawaken buried memories, fears and anxieties; it may tap into barely hidden emotional fault lines in the child's make up. Many questions will arise for the child: Will I see loved ones again? Will I ever get out of the new setting? How will I be treated? What will happen to me? Who will protect me if I get a hard time from other children or adults? What about contact with siblings? What about school etc. etc.? Children will need the opportunity to process over time the emotional and the practical effects of a move. It will be easier for the child to cope, the less that is unknown, the more they feel some influence or control, and the more that is familiar. Certain things may help the child to come to terms with what is happening: discussion and consultation about the new setting and practical arrangements; visits beforehand; handover by familiar adults; scrupulous adherence to arrangements (this symbolises certainty, order); bringing favourite toys, photographs, clothing (these symbolise continuity); visits back to previous setting, visits to/from familiar people. It helps for everyone to 'sing from the same hymn sheet', that is, for the adults – social worker, carers and family of origin – and the child to have a clear and common understanding of the *plan*.

Key practice questions

- Who are the people who serve as attachment figures in this child's life?
- Who does the child seek out for consolation in distress?
- Who has a partisan commitment to the child?
- Who might be said to be the people who make up the child's attachment network?

Holistic assessment

Each child is individual and each child's story is unique. Children each experience the world differently. They react to and act on it in their own way. Assessment must strive to help us know this child – and particularly her strengths. Assessment must seek to know and represent the whole child. Assessment of children and their needs must not be preoccupied only with deficits, problems or pathology. Too often, we would suggest, assessment is absorbed with the negative. It must instead adopt a rounded approach looking at both positives and negatives, strengths and weaknesses, resources and deficits, protective and risk factors. As two key American researchers in the field of resilience research put it, assessment must

> focus not only on the risk factors in the lives of these [vulnerable] children but also on the protective factors. These include competencies and sources of informal support that already exist in the extended family, the neighbourhood, and the community at large and that can be utilised to enlarge a child's repertoire of problem solving skills and self-esteem and self efficacy. (Werner and Smith 1992, p.208)

A satisfactory assessment must not only focus on problems as defined by somebody else or even by the child. It must not focus only on difficult behaviour or past failings. It must seek out qualities, interests and talents which the child has, and about which the child and other people feel good. A comprehensive assessment which attends to strengths as well as deficits will highlight resources not only in the child's own personal profile but also in their social ecology: people who care about them, take an interest, help them. An assessment must focus not only on the trigger for referral, it must also focus on the child. It must also address the ecology or social context within which the child has developed and within which problems have emerged or been defined.

Key practice questions

Seeking out strengths in assessment, consider the following:

- What talents does this young person have?
- What qualities does this young person have which other people find attractive?
- Which of the young person's qualities are helpful in dealing with adversity?
- Who are the people to whom this young person matters?
- What should be included in a list of this young person's social skills and accomplishments?
- Who or what constitute resources in assisting this young person to negotiate adversities and to make their way in the world?

Developmental pathways

A very hopeful message from developmental research is that children's fate or destiny is not cast in stone at conception, birth, or some other critical deadline in their development. What happens next is certainly influenced by what has happened earlier, but positive factors may emerge, sometimes unexpectedly, to counteract previously negative trends.

It may be useful to think of a child's developmental pathway as being rather like that of the intended course of a sailing yacht (see Figures 9.1 and 9.2). If conditions remain as predicted then the course will be close to that expected at the outset. The yacht's course will follow that plotted on the maps before the journey begins. Similarly the child's progress will follow the path predicted by the 'deal of the cards' at birth in terms of height, weight and temperament. What makes things interesting of course for sailors or people concerned with child development is that life is rarely that simple. Severe weather may occur, winds may blow the boat off course, the boat may suffer damage, a key crew member may be injured. On the other hand, adverse developments may be counterbalanced by favourable shifts in weather or winds which cancel out and outweigh earlier problems. Similarly, illness in the child or caregiver, stress in the home environment, unplanned separations may all adversely affect the child's progress. This may lead to the child 'underachieving' in terms of the expected path of progress. Children whose projected developmental trajectory is veering off course because of a surfeit of stress may be drawn back onto, or closer to, course by a critical moment or experience. A move to a supportive school, a relationship with an aunt who takes a new and deep interest, success at sport, the care of a foster carer may all be examples of how a child's progress may literally be turned around.

It may often seem puzzling that some children apparently exposed to the same adversity react differently. One child may seem permanently scarred in terms of loss of confidence and self-esteem. Another – even in the same family – seems to bounce back. There may be two sets of related reasons for the difference between the two children. First, the cumulative number of adversities experienced by the two children may be different despite their sharing at least one in common. There is various evidence to suggest that children may escape one or two adversities in their lives relatively unscathed, but that after the third, fourth or further adversities, the child begins to buckle under the pressure and their developmental progress and functioning becomes severely compromised. Children may also differ in their reaction to

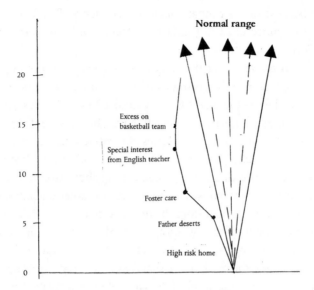

Figure 9.1 Key turning points in developmental pathways (1) (Gilligan, after Bowlby 1988)

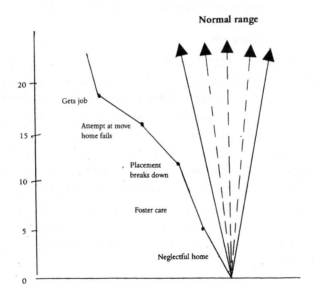

Figure 9.2 Key turning points in developmental pathways (2) (Gilligan, after Bowlby 1988)

stressors because of their innate quality of resilience. Resilience – this vital capacity to bounce back in the face of stress – is both constitutional and social in origin.

These two points about the weight of adversity and the importance of resilience are not merely abstract insights remote from the concerns of everyday social work practice. One may think of a set of scales where there is on one side an accumulation of negative weights representing stressors or adversities in the child' s life and a series of positive weights on the other side representing assets and protective factors in the child's life. Bearing in mind the importance of avoiding adversities creeping above two in number, it may be important for the social worker to be able to target one adversity which can be more easily removed from the negative side of the scales, or possibly indeed to add a new positive weight to the other side in order to cancel out the effect of the negative weight. While the constitutional element of resilience is beyond the reach of the social worker, it is possible that the social worker can influence the level of social resilience displayed by the child. Social resilience can be enhanced by secure attachments, self-esteem and a sense of self-efficacy. All of these may be amenable to influence by actions by the social worker or by other significant adults in the child's caring network who may be encouraged in this task by the social worker.

Developmental outcomes

Social workers need to remember what we are here for – improving the lot of the child. It is a modest aspiration – but let us at least try to ensure that the young person leaves our agency's supervision or care with somewhat fewer problems than when they entered. In our view a key message of the resilience paradigm for work with children in care is dealing with the small things as well as the big things. One of us has written elsewhere about the limitations of relying excessively on permanence as a guiding principle in this work (Gilligan 1997). It is a big idea, with many merits, but it also carries problems. Developmental outcomes depend on a perspective that bears developmental pathways and influences in mind, which emphasises care planning and which attends to the small details and the big picture. Some specific pointers are worth considering:

ATTEND TO THE VALUE OF EDUCATION AND SCHOOL EXPERIENCES

Success at school academically is invaluable for cognitive development, self-esteem, general social competence, social status and job prospects. But school is also an important source of opportunities to acquire friends, hobbies, sporting and cultural interests and general social skills and confidence. Thus the social worker should be alert to the importance of matters such as homework, reasons for school difficulties (possibly due to unidentified problems such as dyslexia, learning difficulties etc.), levels of literacy, numeracy and school attendance in children for whom they are responsible. Personal contact with teachers and close attention to school reports will help brief the social worker on the child's motivation, attainments and possible special tuition requirements relative to other children in the school. The value of fresh direct evidence from the school underlines the importance of school representation at set piece meetings such as case conferences and reviews.

REMEMBER THE THERAPEUTIC POWER OF THE EVERYDAY, THE ORDINARY, THE ROUTINE

We are too easily preoccupied with the 'problem' and too readily seduced by the idea that referral to some specialist service, some expert, some exclusive therapy will unlock 'the problem'. Meanwhile we blissfully ignore questions such as: Does the 'treatment'/placement/therapy or whatever work? Does the child want it? Does the specialist really understand the child's lived reality? Does referral generate stigma and thus resistance?

It is almost inevitable that a child labelled 'special' in some way will feel different and be seen as different. The sense of stigma resulting from this feeling of negative difference is very corrosive of self-esteem and social confidence. Referring on to specialist provision also risks ignoring the potential of naturally occurring resources within the child's ecology. Moreover, it does not face up to the problems of successful reintegration into the natural environment especially where intervention has meant full- or part-time withdrawal from same. We would suggest that social workers and other professionals should be much more ready to search out naturally occurring supports in a child's wider social habitat.

For example, the reassuring and familiar structure of a sensitively laid out and consistently managed primary school classroom and a warm relationship with a responsive teacher may do more for a child's craving for a 'secure base' than elaborate efforts around weekly one hour sessions of therapy. We must learn to recognise and value the therapeutic that is all around us. A child who has a talent for swimming recognised and encouraged may thrive in the structure and attention which regular daily or twice weekly coaching or training sessions offer. A child who loves horses may blossom through encounters with the thrill – and fear – of horseriding. The concentration, responsibility courage and discipline required will earn precious affirmation for the child and from people other than those who are not just professionally obliged to support the child.

REMEMBER THAT PROBLEMS USUALLY HAVE COMPLEX CAUSES, AND THEREFORE COMPLEX OR MULTI-FACETED SOLUTIONS

Beware simple answers to complex questions. The serious problems which prove most challenging usually have multiple sources and causes. Few are amenable to single responses. An effective intervention will require a sufficiently comprehensive plan which embraces a number of approaches and which also attends to a lot of the little details.

REMEMBER BEHAVIOUR IS OFTEN A CODED LANGUAGE ABOUT THE CHILD'S INNER WORLD AND THE (MIS) FIT BETWEEN THEIR NEEDS AND THE RESPONSES THE ADULT WORLD HAS MANAGED TO PRODUCE

When children behave in ways in which numbers of adults find difficult, it is most likely that the child is communicating distress. It is important for social workers to view behaviour as a form of communication which often contains many layers of significance and meaning. The challenge for professionals is not just to react to the surface behaviour but to discern the underlying meaning and pain behind the behaviour. Experience has taught this child certain messages about their own worth or the reliability of caring adults. A child's behaviour invites us to search out the messages which experience has taught a given child. Behaviour which is difficult is often a device for seeking attention, and for communicating emotional pain and distress. Heeding the underlying significance of difficult behaviour is vital. Appropriate attention to the child's unmet needs rather than to the challenging or provocative behaviour may be the most constructive strategy to adopt.

REMEMBER THAT SOCIAL EXPERIENCE AND DEVELOPMENT IS IMPORTANT BUT SO ALSO IS COGNITIVE DEVELOPMENT

Children's behaviour may reflect conclusions they have drawn about what has happened to them or who has done what to them. Or more accurately, behaviour may reflect the child's inner story or explanations of what they think has happened. It is important that children are helped to have a 'coherent story' (Dowling 1993) about the progress of their lives and the incidents and events which have shaped their destiny. It is important that children have a story which helps them know where they stand, where they have come from, and where they are going. It is important that they do not shoulder blame for the actions of others, or that they do not attribute wilful malice where in fact a problem such as alcoholism explains a parent's errant behaviour. A coherent account and understanding of what has happened will help the child more effectively to have a command of the experience. A firm grasp of a coherent story pulls fragments of experience into a more integrated whole and helps a child to make more sense of what has happened and what is happening. A child is lucky if their level of intelligence helps them more easily to interpret accurately what has happened, and to attribute causes and influences to their proper sources. But all children in such circumstances will need to have their own efforts supplemented with the assistance of sensitive adults attuned to the child's needs. Social workers should always be alert to the educational and therapeutic opportunities which enhance children's cognitive skills and which minimise barriers to their proper understanding and processing of emotional experiences.

ENHANCE THE YOUNG PERSON'S COPING AND SELF EFFICACY BY HELPING THE CHILD TO REHEARSE, OBSERVE AND DISCUSS PROBLEM SOLVING SKILLS AND STRATEGIES

Some of this strengthening of the young person's coping and self-efficacy can be done in an explicit and direct way. For instance, it might involve taking young people through a customised course on coping with life in care, or a course on dealing with being bullied. Other parts of it might be done through activities which indirectly achieve the desired effect. For instance, joining a project to develop a course about life in care or afterwards for other young people may help the course designers to grapple with and perhaps resolve more subtly issues which a full frontal course for them might not achieve.

Devices which allow young people in care simultaneously to meet other people's needs as well as their own seem likely to be very helpful. Examples of these might involve matching the needs of the young people and students where they both have complementary needs, e.g. journalism students working with young people in care to produce a newspaper or radio programme about life in care, drama students similarly in relation to a play about adolescence, photography students and a photo essay about young people's needs etc. In a different context health promotion workers might cooperate with young people in care in the production of health promotion materials, a process which might produce a valuable end product as well as much useful learning for the young participants.

It is clearly important to involve children in discussions about their needs and about their future. In one sense this is not something necessary to say to readers of a book such as this but it is still important to stress it. We must constantly work to find ever more effective ways of helping young people contribute to care plans and reviews. This entails giving clear information to the young person. It requires ensuring that the young person knows about (1) the reasons for their entering and remaining in care; (2) their rights while in care; and (3) future plans for the young person and how the young person can influence these. We need to regard young people as resources in the process of seeking solutions in their lives or milieux. We must encourage them to make choices and declare preferences in everyday living. We must coach young people in how to resolve conflict with peers without recourse to bullying or violence. These various opportunities and experiences can teach them that their opinions are of value and help them learn some of the skills of influence, negotiation and problem solving. Perhaps we have much to learn from the fields of negotiation and mediation. Skills from those areas could be very useful to caregivers in everyday living and could also be very valuable to consciously pass on to young people in their care.

Final practical tips for intervention

While it may be very difficult to alter the whole picture, it may still be possible to make a difference. Reducing by one the number of weights on the risk side of the scales and adding one or more weights to the protective side may have quite a dramatic effect on the functioning of a young person. Even more importantly it may alter the perception which the young person and those around her have of her potential for positive change and development. Some key changes prompted by skilful and targeted intervention may switch a vicious circle of gloom and despair into a virtuous cycle of growth and hope. These are as follows:

- Identify who is important to the child.
- Try to help build and sustain those relationships.
- Find who the child knew in the past who may still be willing to keep contact with the child.
- Try to find what interests and talents the child has.
- Try to encourage these.

- Find adults in the natural networks of the child who may be willing to play a mentoring role for the child in terms of talents or interests.

Accomplishment in some hobby, sport or cultural pursuit enhances the child's self-esteem, offers a constructive use of time and perhaps most importantly is likely to link a vulnerable child into networks of social relationships which may eventually endure and develop. Attend also to how important school is not only for academic learning but also as a site where vulnerable children may receive precious adult interest and support, where they may learn esteem-enhancing knowledge or skills and acquire friendships or the social skills and opportunities which promote them.

The final message of the book must be to underline yet again the child's social context as a source of decisive experiences and influences, and as a source of resources to assist the child, and the social worker seeking to help the child. Even in the most barren social landscape there are likely to be at least some resources and supports which can be tapped into. To the discerning and optimistic eye, the child's natural social context is a reservoir of informal supports and resources often lying ready to be tapped and mobilised (Gilligan 1999). To understand the child and their needs and history, and certainly to intervene effectively in their lives, it is vital that social workers – and child welfare professionals more generally – attend to the significance of the child's social ecology in the origin and resolution of needs and problems. Problems will make more sense when seen against the background of the child's social context. Solutions will seem more possible when seen in the light of the resources waiting in the same social context.

A Framework for Considering the Nature of Emotional Abuse and Physical Neglect and Effects on Development

This framework can be used to guide in the assessment of areas of vulnerability and resilience, as well as areas of adversity and protection for a child who appears to be emotionally and physically neglected.

The family and relationship context within which concerns about the child arise

It may be particularly relevant to consider the nature of the child's attachment to parents or carers.

What is the nature and strength of the adult bonding to the child?

1. What pattern of attachment do we see?

   a) Is the child, for example, able to explore in confidence from a base of security in the relationship?

   b) Is the child anxiously preoccupied with parents' availability or responses. In other words could the child be said to have an anxious attachment?

   c) Does the child show signs of both wanting and fearing closeness? In other words, may the child have mixed feelings about intimacy with adults and be, therefore, demonstrating an ambivalent attachment?

   d) Does the child avoid close contact with carers, demonstrating an avoidant attachment?

2. Can the child separate with ease from the parents? Some children have not separated in a healthy manner at all and could be said to have an enmeshed attachment to carers.

3. Is there any sign of enjoyment in the relationship in either the child or the adult's responses and behaviour?

What interaction do we observe?

It can be very helpful to observe detailed interaction between parents and children in order to explore any emerging recurrent patterns of initiation and response within the relationship.

It can be particularly helpful to observe the greeting and parting when children are separated and reunited, as well as observations of the parent and child when together for periods of time.

It is useful, additionally, to remember to observe the pattern of relationships between siblings. Are they mutually supportive, competitive or antagonistic?

When observing interactions and seeking to form a picture of attachment relationships, it is of value to focus on two particular areas.

1. Does the parent understand and respond to cues of the child's distress or need for support?

2. Does the parent reach out to the child in any way? It can be useful to observe whether or not the adult anticipates the child's wishes and is in tune with the child's likes and dislikes, their talents and abilities.

Areas of development – How the child is thriving with careful assessment of any delays or distortions and their likely causes

1. *Physical development:* We need to monitor, not only the child's growth in terms of height, weight and skull circumference, but also pay attention to issues such as visual problems, hearing impairments and poor dental care. For example, lack of attention to repeated ear infections may result in permanent hearing impairment. Poor dental care over time may be an indicator of generalised physical neglect. Consider the following:

   a) Is the child offered sufficient physical freedom in order to encourage the development of their sensory and motor skills?

b) When considering 'failure to thrive' in individual children, has the possibility of any organic cause for the lack of growth, for example coeliac disease (an abnormal intestinal immune response to gluten which can result in malnourishment) been investigated?

c) 'Catch-up' growth in different care settings needs to be monitored and evaluated. If this is relevant, how is it being monitored?

d) Recurrent problems of a physical nature, for example, soiling or vomiting may have a number of causes and hospital consultants or community paediatricians can be extremely helpful here.

e) Does/do the parent/s recognise that there is a need for concern?

2. *Social development:*

a) Does the parent nurture the child's opportunities for social contacts and what is their attitude towards this?

b) Does the child have social supports from other adults which may be protective? For example, extended family, neighbours, supportive group workers or individual therapists.

c) If the adult has no 'warm, confiding relationship', is this denied to the child also?

3. *Moral development:*

a) Is the child encouraged to develop a healthy conscience?

b) Is the child encouraged to take responsibility for his or her own actions?

c) Is there equitable management of sibling relationships, disputes, etc.?

d) Is the child learning about the consequences of his or her own behaviour in a balanced way?

4. *Emotional development:*

a) Is the child forced to take a particular role in relation to their parents, which is affecting their development? For example, are they the constant comforter for the parents, ally when the parent is in distress or scapegoat for family disputes?

b) Does the parent have some particular psychological illness in which they involve the child, for example, paranoid state or psychotic delusions?

c) Is the child able to express a range of feelings?

d) What is the parent's reaction to this? Do they respond? If so, how?

e) How does the child feel about him or herself?

f) Does the child express confidence in talents, abilities, capacities, or seem overwhelmed by self-doubt and self-blame?

g) Does the parent behave as though they are themselves the abused child, therefore eclipsing the child's needs?

h) Is the child allowed access to other supportive adults and peers?

5. *Cognitive or intellectual development:*

a) Is the child's intellectual development supported by a parent. For example, with very young children, do they appreciate the importance of play? For older children is their school work valued and supported at home?

b) Are the child's achievements, talents and potential recognised in any way?

c) Is the child encouraged to trust their own perceptions of the world?

d) What independent measures do we have of the child's progress, in relation to their potential?

e) We need close partnerships with colleagues to make a careful analysis of what factors might be interrupting the child's healthy cognitive development. For example, is there a specific learning difficulty?

f) What do nursery/school staff have to say? What are their observations of parental involvement and attitude, as well as the child's scholastic progress?

g) What observations can be made of the child's social behaviour at school?

The nature of any significant harm and its effects on the child's development

Bentovim (1991) offers us a definition of significant harm:

> significant harm is a compilation of events, both acute and long-standing, which interact with the child's ongoing development, and interrupt, alter or impair physical and psychological development.

He adds that being a victim of significant harm is likely to have a profound effect on the child's view of him or herself as a person and on their future life.

1. Is the child:

   a) rejected?

   b) isolated?

   c) corrupted?

   d) ignored?

   e) terrorised?

2. In relation to each of these questions, what *interaction* have we seen which demonstrates this dynamic?

It is important to reflect on these questions, whether or not the abusive treatment is deliberate and consciously meted out to the child or a consequence of understandable immaturity or illness in the parent.

We need to tune in to the meaning of parental behaviour and attitudes for the child and the effects, as well as the treatment itself.

What changes are required in order to meet the child's needs?

1. Does either parent perceive that there is a problem?

2. Is there evidence that reasonable efforts have been made to support parents in understanding the child's needs?

3. Does the parent understand the significance of their responses to the child's feelings and behaviour?

4. What must to change in order to meet this child's needs?

5. What signs of improvement do we hope to see?

6. How will we know that things have improved?

Parental capacity

1. Do the parents understand the current difficulties?

2. Are they willing and able to make the necessary changes?

3. Has a planned programme been attempted, working in partnership with parents, to help them understand any problems and develop strategies for meeting the child's needs?

4. If we are moving to compulsory measures of care, what conditions should be spelled out?

5. Are the expectations of change in parents' behaviour reasonable in the light of the child's needs and the parents' circumstances?

Can the changes be achieved without compulsory measures of care?

1. Outline details of attempts made and options considered to date for working with parents in offering them assistance.

2. Can they use the help offered?

3. What local resources may be adapted creatively to support parents in the care of their children?

4. In circumstances where we are considering the removal of children, serious attention needs to be paid to thorough efforts to work collaboratively before making orders to protect the child or to remove them to foster or residential care.

If compulsory measures are necessary, what might be the least detrimental alternative now?

1. What might be the realistic current alternatives for the care of the child? If we are considering removal of the child, how is the work of the placement to be planned in order to maintain as much collaborative and cooperative work as possible?

2. Why are we choosing this particular alternative? How will it meet the child's needs?

Who are the key people in a position to offer crucial observations/information and help in collaborative work?

1. Is there a teacher or other school-based professional who has information?

2. If the child is under five, what information does the health visitor have?

3. Is the family in contact with any voluntary agencies?

A Format for Considering a Young Child's Development

1. What patterns of attachment do you notice in this young child's close relationships? Does he/she:

   - seem preoccupied with adults' presence (anxious or insecure)?

   - show intense mixed feelings much of the time, that is, wanting to be close but finding it hard to tolerate (ambivalent or insecure)?

   - avoid close contact of any kind with familiar adults?

   - show healthy reliance on adults, e.g., ability to separate for brief periods with reassurance (healthy attachment or insecure/avoidant)?

2. Is this child able to seek adult support in times of stress? How does he/she do this?

3. Note down any details of separations or losses this child has experienced.

   - How old was the child when this occurred?

   - What were the child's reactions at the time?

   - What are the child's reactions now to change and uncertainty?

4. What range of emotional expression are you aware of in this child's daily interaction with:

   - parents on parting and greeting siblings. Does the child occupy a fixed role in the family system?

- other children – can this child co-operate in play, empathise with other children in distress, etc.?

5. Is there evidence of pleasure in the parent/child relationship?

6. How would you describe this child's play?

7. Does this child assert him/herself appropriately? How?

8. Is the child either:

   - overly passive?
   - overly aggressive?
   - how does this show itself?

9. What are the opportunities in the child's living situation for experimenting with age-appropriate assertion? e.g. choice?

10. Are there any indications of emotional abuse and/or neglect? How do they show themselves in

    - parent/child interaction?
    - the child's relationship with other significant adults?

11. How does this show in the child's behaviour/reactions?

12. Is there evidence of healthy emotional nurturing and protection from potential emotional harm in the home?

13. Are there any concerns about the child's physical growth/development? How is this monitored?

14. What supports are being offered to the child's parents. What is the precise focus of each supportive strategy?

15. Are the limits set for this child in the home setting appropriate to his/her age and stage?

16. What strengths or particular individual features do the key carers enjoy in this child?

17. Is there evidence that at least one adult is attuned to this particular child's temperament and needs?

Assessment of Adolescent Development

This is a framework for assessment based on issues identified as important in Steinberg (1993). The framework can be used for adolescents living at home or looked after away from home. The primary aim of the framework is to identify strengths in the current situation that can be harnessed when planning intervention.

Brief case summary

Fundamental changes

- Describe what you believe to have been impact of the biological changes of puberty on this young person and their relationships with family or carers and peers, for example, were they an early or late maturer?

- Is this young person seen to have a role (or potential role) in society by:

- themselves?

- their carers?

- their educators?

- Is the young person subjected to societal pressures or prejudices, for example, because of special needs, race or gender? What supports have helped or would help them to resist the negative effects of such prejudice?

Contexts of development

FAMILY

- If the young person has any ongoing family connections, describe the positive aspects they derive from these connections.

- Describe briefly and comment on the significance of the kind of parenting the young person received when not in local authority accommodation. Can you draw links between this care and their current emotional and behavioural state? Distinguish, if possible, between direct and indirect effects.

- Have there been other significant attachment figures in this young person's life and what has their impact been on their development? For example, what pattern of attachments do they demonstrate?

- What significant losses, separations or abuses has this young person experienced in their life to date and at what ages? What kinds of intervention or support have been helpful for the young person in making sense of these events:
  - at the time?
  - currently?

PEERS

- Similarly, describe important friendships and their positive aspects for the young person. If the young person appears not to have friends, suggest why this might be. Has there been continuity through their childhood in:
  - friendships
  - their ability to make friends?

EDUCATION

- What has the young person gained from schooling to date? This includes education, special contact, guidance staff etc., and how can their continued education be supported?

WORK/LEISURE

- What beliefs and attitudes does the young person have about their own work prospects. How have these been shaped by their caregivers through their lives?

Psychosocial issues

AUTONOMY

- Within their current situation is the young person demonstrating the ability to act in an increasingly interdependent rather than dependent way? To what extent are they susceptible to pressure from peers? If the young person finds it difficult to behave autonomously, what strengths do they have that can be built on to help empower them?

INTIMACY

- Explain the possible connections between the kind of attachment the young person experienced in early childhood and their current ability to form intimate relationships. What aspects of the current care situation contribute to their ability to make intimate relationships?

IDENTITY

- Has the young person developed a cultural identity that they feel comfortable with? How has their experience in care supported their connection with their culture of origin?

- Has the young person developed a gender role that they are comfortable with and how is this manifested? If they challenge traditional sex-role expectations how can they be supported in this challenge?

SEXUALITY

- In comparison with how adolescent sexuality is currently generally expressed are there aspects of this young person's sexuality that cause them or their carers concern? If so can you trace the possible origins of the difficulty? Similarly, if there are no concerns about sexuality, what factors supported this healthy development?

- If their experiences of sexuality have been in an abusive context, either from adults or peers, how can they be helped to find a positive way to express their sexuality?

PROBLEMS

- Does the young person express any of their problems outwardly with activities such as drug or alcohol misuse, criminal activity, aggression or precocious sexual behaviour? If so, give examples and try to link them with their previous experiences.

- Do they show signs of turning problems inwards, for example, are they depressed or suicidal, do they have eating problems or show anxiety problems? Again, give examples and try to link them with their previous experiences.

- Are there positive aspects of the current relationship with the carers that could be used to help the young person control their problem behaviours?

ACHIEVEMENT

- Does the young person have a sufficient sense of empowerment and control to see themselves as having choices in life? Are they able to weigh up the possible outcomes of different life choices?

- What aspects of their current relationships would help them to be able to attribute success or failure to their own abilities rather than fate or luck?

Bibliography

Aboud, F. (1988) *Children and Prejudice.* Oxford: Blackwell.

Ahmed, S. (1985) 'Black children in a day nursery: some issues of practice.' *Focus 33,* 17–20.

Ahmed, S. (1989) 'Protecting black children from abuse.' *Social Work Today* 8 June.

Ahmed, B. (1991) 'Setting the context: race and the children's Act 1989.' In S. MacDonald (ed.) *All Equal under the Act?* London: Race Equality Unit, Personal Social Services.

Ainsworth, M.D.S. and Bowlby, J. (1991) 'Attachments and other affectional bonds across the life cycle.' In C.M. Parkes, J. Stevenson-Hinde, J. and P. Marris, *Attachment Across the Life Cycle.* London: Tavistock/Routledge.

Ainsworth, M.D.S., Blehar, M. Walters, E. and Walls, S. (1978) *Patterns of Attachment.* Hillsdale NJ: Erlbaum.

Aldridge, J. (1994) 'In the best interests of the child.' In I. Gaber and J. Aldridge, (eds) *Culture, Identity and Transracial Adoption: In the Best Interests of the Child.* London: Free Association Books.

Alejandro-Wright, M.N. (1985) 'The child's conception of racial classification.' In M.B. Spencer, G.K. Brookins and W.R. Allen (eds) *Beginnings: The Social and Affective Development of Black Children.* Hillsdale, NJ: Erlbaum.

Angeli, N., Christy, J., Howe, J. and Wolff, B. (1994) 'Facilitating parenting skills in vulnerable families.' *Health Visitor 67,* 4, 130–132.

Argent, H. (1995) *See You Soon: Contact with Children Looked After by Local Authorities.* London: BAAF.

Argent H, and Kerrane, A. (1997) *Taking Extra Care: Respite Shared and Permanent Care for Children with Disabilities.* London: BAAF.

Armsden, G.C. and Greenberg, M.T. (1987) 'The inventory of parent and peer attachment: individual differences and their relationship to psychological well-being in adolescence.' *Journal of Youth and Adolescence 16,* 427–453.

Audit Commission (1994) *Seen But Not Heard: Coordinating Community Child Health and Social Services for Children in Need.* London: HMSO.

Baldwin, N. and Spencer, N. (1993) 'Deprivation and child abuse: implications for strategic planning in children's services.' *Children and Society 7,* 4, 357–375.

Baldwin, N., Johansen, P. and Seale, A. (1989/90) *Race in Child Protection: A Code of Practice.* Kirklees Social Services Department, UK: Race Equality Unit, Black and White Alliance.

Bandura, A. (1981) 'Self-referent thought: a developmental analysis of self-efficacy.' In J.H. Flavell and L. Ross (eds) *Social Cognitive Development.* Cambridge: Cambridge University Press.

Baumrind, D. (1972) 'Socialization and instrumental competence in young children.' In W.W. Hartup (ed.) *The Young Child: Reviews of Research, Vol. 2.* Washington, DC: National Association for the Education of Young Children.

Bee, H. (1994) *The Developing Child.* New York: Harper Collins.

Bentovim, A. (1991) 'Significant harm in context.' In M. Adcock, R. White and A. Hollows (eds) *Significant Harm: Management and Outcome.* Croydon: Significant Publications.

Berliner, L. (1990) 'Clinical work with sexually abused children.' In C. Howells and C. Hollins (eds) *Clinical Approaches to Sex Offenders and Their Victims.* London: Wiley.

Berliner, L. (1997) 'Intervention with children who experience trauma.' In D. Cicchetti and S. Toth (eds) *Developmental Perspectives on Trauma: Theory, Research and Intervention.* Woodbridge: University of Rochester Press.

Biehal, N., Clayden, J. Stein, M. and Wade, J. (1995) *Moving On: Young people and Leaving Care Schemes.* London: HMSO.

Binney, V., McKnight, I. and Broughton, S. (1994) 'Relationship play therapy for attachment disturbances in four to seven year old children.' In J. Richer (ed.) *The Clinical Application of Ethology and Attachment Theory*. The Association of Child Psychology and Psychiatry, Occasional Papers Services.

Booth, J. and Booth, W. (1993) 'The experience of parenthood: a research approach.' In A. Croft (ed.) *Parents with Learning Disabilities*. Kidderminster: British Institute for Learning Disability.

Bourguignon, J.P. and Watson, K.W. (1987) *After Adoption: A Manual for Professionals Working with Adoptive Families*. Springfield, IL: Illinois Department of Children and Family Services.

Boushel, M. (1994) 'The protective environment of children: towards a framework for anti-oppressive, cross-cultural and cross-national understanding.' *British Journal of Social Work 24*, 173–190.

Bower, M. (1978) *Family Therapy in Clinical Practice*. New York: Jason Aronson.

Bower, T.G.R. (1977) *A Primer of Infant Development*. San Francisco: W.H. Freeman and Company.

Bowlby, J. (1969) *Attachment and Loss, Vols. 1 and 2*. New York: Basic Books.

Bowlby, J. (1988) 'Developmental psychiatry comes of age.' *The American Journal of Psychiatry 145*, 1, 1–10.

Bradshaw, J. (1990) *Child Poverty and Deprivation in the UK*. London: National Children's Bureau.

Bradshaw, J. (1996) 'Family policy and family poverty.' *Policy Studies 17* 2, 93–106.

Briere, J. and Conte, J. (1993) 'Self-reported amnesia for abuse in adults molested as children.' *Journal of Traumatic Stress 6*, 21–31.

British Agencies of Adoption and Fostering (1991) *Practice Note 26 (Children Act 1989), Children and Their Heritage: The Importance of Culture, Race, Religion and Language in Family Placement*. London: BAAF.

Bronfenbrenner, U. (1989) 'Ecological systems theory.' *Annals of Child Development 6*, 187–249.

Brooks, R.B. (1991) *The Self-esteem Teacher*. Circle Pines, MN: American Guidance Service

Brooks, R.B. (1994) 'Children at risk: fostering resilience and hope.' *American Journal Orthopsychiatry, 64*, 4, 545–553.

Brown, G. and Harris, T. (1978) *Social Origins of Depression: A Study of Psychiatric Disorder in Women*. London: Tavistock.

Buss, A.H. and Plomin, R.A. (1984) *Temperament Theory of Personality Development*. New York: Wiley–Interscience.

Carpenter, V. and Young, K. (1986) *Coming in from the Margins*. Leicester: National Association of Youth Clubs.

Casey, M. (1987) *Domestic Violence against Women*. Dublin: Dublin Federation of Refuges.

Cassell, D. and Coleman, R. (1995) 'Parents with psychiatric problems.' In P. Reder and L. Lucey (eds) *Assessment of Parenting: Psychiatric and Psychological Contributions*. London: Routledge.

CCETSW (1991a) *The Teaching of Child Care in the Diploma of Social Work*. London: CCETSW.

CCETSW (1991b) *A Framework for Continuing Professional Development (Paper 31)*. London: CCETSW.

Ceci, S.J. and Bruck, M. (1993) 'The suggestibility of child witnesses.' *Psychological Bulletin 113*, 403–439.

Chess, S. and Thomas, A. (1977) 'Temperamental individuality from childhood to adolescence.' *Journal of Child Psychiatry 16*, 218–226.

Christiansson, S.A. (1992) 'Emotional stress and eye witness memory: a critical review.' *Psychological Bulletin 12*, 284–309.

Ciccheti, D. and Barnett, D. (1991) 'Attachment organisation in maltreated pre-schoolers.' *Development and Psychopathology 3*, 397–411.

Cigno, K. (1995) 'Helping to prevent abuse: a behavioural approach with families.' In K. Wilson and A. James (eds) *The Child Protection Handbook*. London, Philadelphia, Toronto, Sydney, Tokyo: Balliere Tindall.

Cohn Donnelly, A. (1997) 'Early intervention efforts to prevent physical abuse and neglect.' Paper delivered at the Sixth European Congress on Child Abuse and Neglect, ISPCAN, Barcelona.

Coie, J.D. and Dodge, K.A. (1983) 'Continuities and changes in children's social status: a five year longitudinal study.' *Merrill–Palmer Quarterly 29*, 261–282.

Coleman, J.C. (1980) *The Nature of Adolescence*. London and New York: Methuen.

Coleman, J.C. and Hendry, L. (1990) *The Nature of Adolescence, 2nd edition*, London: Routledge.

Coleman, R. and Cassell, D. (1995) 'Parents who misuse drugs or alcohol.' In P. Reder and L. Lucey (eds) *Assessment of Parenting: Psychiatric and Psychological Contributions*. London: Routledge.

Condry, J. and Condry, S. (1976) 'Sex differences: a study of the eye of the beholder.' *Child Development 47*, 812–819.

Conte, J. and Berliner, L (1988) 'The impact of sexual abuse on children: the empirical findings.' In L. Walker (ed.) *Handbook on Sexual Abuse of Children: Assessment and Issues.* New York: Springer Publishing.

Cooper, C. (1985) *Good Enough Parenting.* London: BAAF.

Cooper, D.M. (1993) *Child Abuse Revisited: Children, Society and Social Work.* Milton Keynes: Open University Press.

Coopersmith, S. (1967) *The Antecedents of Self-Esteem.* San Francisco: W.H. Freeman.

Cox, A.D., Puckering, C., Pound, A. and Mills, M. (1987) 'The impact of maternal depression in young children.' *Journal of Child Psychology and Psychiatry 28*, 917–928.

Cox, B. D. (1993) *Internalization through Re-interpretation of Spontaneous Intervention: The Examples of Mathematics, Instruction and Metamemory.* New Orleans: Society for Research in Child Development.

Crittenden, P.M. (1996) 'Research on maltreating families: implications for intervention.' In J. Briere, L. Berliner, J.A. Bulkley, C. Jenny and T. Reid (eds) *The APSAC Handbook on Child Maltreatment.* Thousand Oaks, CA, London, New Dehli: Sage Publications.

Crittenden, P.M. and Ainsworth, M.D.S. (1989) 'Child maltreatment and attachment theory.' In D. Cicchetti and V. Carlson (eds) *Child Maltreatment: Theory and Research on the Causes and Consequences of Child Abuse and Neglect.* Cambridge and New York: Cambridge University Press.

Csikszentmihalyi, M. and Larson, R. (1984) *Being Adolescent* New York: Basic Books.

Cummings, E.M. (1987) 'Coping with background anger in early childhood.' *Child Development 58*, 976–984.

Cummings, E.M. and Davies (1994) 'Maternal depression and child development.' *Child Psychology and Psychiatry 35*,73–112.

Cunningham, C. and Davis, H. (1985) *Working with Parents: Frameworks for Collaboration.* Milton Keynes: Open University Press.

Damon, W. (1988) *The Moral Child.* New York: Free Press.

Davey, A. (1983) *Learning to Be Prejudiced; Growing Up in Multi-ethnic Britain.* London: Edwards Arnold.

Davie, R. (1996) 'Partnership with children: the advancing trend.' In R. Davie, G. Upton and V. Varma (eds) *The Voice of the Child: A Handbook for Professionals.* London, Washington, DC: Falmer Press.

Deblinger, E. and Hope Heflin, A. (1996) *Treating Sexually Abused Children and Their Nonoffending Parents: A Cognitive Behavioural Approach.* Thousand Oaks, California, London and New Dehli: Sage Publications.

Dent, H. and Stephenson, G. (1979) 'An experimental study of the effectiveness of different techniques of questioning child witnesses.' *British Journal of Social and Clinical Psychology 18*, 41–51.

Department of Health (1989) *Principles and Practice in Regulations and Guidance.* London: HMSO.

Department of Health (1991) *Patterns and Outcomes in Child Placement: Messages from Current Research and Their Implications.* London: HMSO.

Department of Health (1995) *Looking After Children: Good Parenting, Good Outcomes.* London: HMSO.

Derman-Sparks, L. (1991) *Anti-bias Curriculum: Tools for Empowering Young Children.* Washington, DC: National Association for the Education of Young Children.

Devore, W. and Schlessinger, E.G. (1987) *Ethnic-Sensitive Social Work Practice.* Ohio: Merrill Publishing Company.

DHSS (1995) *Child Protection: Messages from Research.* London: HMSO.

Diaz, R.M. (1983) 'Thought and two languages: the impact of bilingualism on cognitive development.' *Review of Research in Education 10*, 23–54.

Dobash, R.E. and Dobash, R. (1984) 'The nature and antecedents of violent events.' *British Journal of Criminology 24*, 269–288.

Dobash, R.E. and Dobash, R. (1992) *Women, Violence and Social Change.* London: Routledge.

Dodge, K.A. (1980) 'Social cognition and children's aggressive behaviour.' *Child Development 51*, 162–70.

Donaldson, M. (1978) *Children's Minds.* London: Fontana.

Douglas, J. (1989) *Behaviour Problems in Young Children.* Tavistock: Routledge.

Dowling, E. (1993) 'Are family therapists listening to the young? A psychological perspective.' *Journal of Family Therapy 15*, 403–411.

Downes, C. (1992) *Separation Revisited: Adolescents in Foster Family Care.* Aldershot, Hampshire: Ashgate

Dreyer, P.H. (1982) 'Sexuality during adolescence.' In B.B. Wolman (ed.) *Handbook of Developmental Psychology.* Englewood Cliffs, NJ: Prentice-Hall.

Duncan, P., Ritter, P., Dornbusch, S. and Carlsmith, J. (1985) 'The effects of pubertal timing on body image, school behaviour and deviance.' *Journal of Youth and Adolescence 14,* 227–236.

Dunn, J. (1993) *Young Children's Close Relationships: Beyond Attachment.* Thousand Oaks, California, London and New Dehli: Sage Publications.

Dunn, J. and Kendrick, C. (1982) *Siblings: Love, Envy and Understanding.* Cambridge, MA, and London: Harvard University Press.

Dunn, J. and Plomin, R. (1990) *Separate Lives: Why Siblings are so Different.* New York: Basic Books.

Dunn, J., Brown, J., Stankowski, C., Teska, C. and Youngblake, L. (1991) 'Young children's understanding of other people's feelings and beliefs: differences in their antecedents.' *Child Development 62,* 1352–1366.

Dwivedi, K.N. (1996) 'Race and the child's perspective.' In R. Davies, G. Upton and V. Varma (eds) *The Voice of the Child: A Handbook for Professionals.* London, Washington DC: Falmer Press.

Edwards, J. (1998) 'Screening out men: or "has mum changed her washing powder recently?"'. In J. Popay; J. Hearn and J. Edwards (eds) *Men, Gender Divisions and Welfare.* London: Routledge.

Elkind, D. (1967) 'Egocentrism in adolescence.' *Child Development 38,* 1025–1034.

Elliot, M. (1995) *Child Sexual Abuse Prevention: What Offenders Tell Us.* London: Kidscape Charity for Children.

Erickson, M.F. and Egeland, B. (1996) 'Child neglect.' In J. Briere, L., Berliner, J.A. Buckley, C. Jenny and T. Reid(eds) *The APSAC Handbook on Child Maltreatment.* Thousand Oaks CA: London and New Dehli: Sage Publications.

Erickson, M.F., Egeland, B. and Pianta, R.C. (1989) 'The effects of maltreatment on the development of young children.' In D. Cichetti and C. Carleson (eds) *Child Maltreatment: Theory and Research on the Causes and Consequences of Child Abuse and Neglect* New York: Cambridge University Press.

Erikson, E. (1959) 'Identity and the life cycle.' *Psychological Issues 1,* 1–7.

Espinosa, M.P., Newman, C.G., Sigma, M.D., Binib, N. and McDonald, M.A. (1992) 'Playground behaviour of school age children in relation to schooling and family characteristics.' *Developmental Psychology 28,* 1188–95.

Fahlberg, V. (1988) *Fitting the Pieces Together.* London: BAAF.

Fahlberg, V. (1994) *A Child's Journey through Placement.* London: BAAF.

Farmer, E. and Owen, O. (1995) *Decision-Making, Intervention and Outcome in Child Protection Work.* London, HMSO.

Feeney, J. and Noller, P. (1996) *Adult Attachment.* Thousand Oaks, CA, London, New Dehli: Sage Publications.

Feldman-Summers, S. and Pope, K. (1994) 'The experience of "forgetting" childhood abuse: a national survey of psychologists.' *Journal of Consulting and Clinical Psychology 62,* 3, 636–639.

Finkelhor, D. (1986) *A Sourcebook on Child Sexual Abuse. Thousand Oaks, CA, London and New Dehli: Sage Publications.*

Finkelhor, D. and Berliner, L. (1995) 'Research on the treatment of sexually abused children: a review and recommendations.' *Journal of the American Academy of Child and Adolescent Psychiatry 34,* 1408–1423.

Finkelhor, D. and Bronne, A. (1985) 'The traumatic impact of sexual abuse: conceptualization.' *American Journal Ortho-Psychiatry 55,* 155–7.

Fivush, R. (1984) 'Learning about school: the development of kindergartner's school scripts.' *Child Development 55,* 1697–1709.

Flavell, J.H. (1985) *Cognitive Development,* (2nd edn). Englewood Cliffs, NJ: Prentice-Hall.

Fonagy, P., Steele, M., Steele, H., Higgit, A. and Target, M. (1994) 'The theory and practice of resilience.' *Journal of Child Psychology and Psychiatry 35,* 2, 231–257.

Ford, N. and Morgan, K. (1989) 'Heterosexual lifestyles of young people in an English city.' *Journal of Population and Social Studies 1,* 167–185.

Gaber, I. and Aldridge, J. (1994) *Culture, Identity and Transracial Adoption: In the Best Interests of the Child.* London: Free Association Books.

Gambe, D., Gomes, J., Kapur, V., Rangel, M. and Stubbs, P. (1992) *Anti-Racist Social Work Education: Improving Practice with Children and Families.* London: CCETSW.

Garbarino, J.M. (1980) 'Defining emotional maltreatment: The meaning is the message.' *Journal of Psychiatric Treatment and Evaluation 2*, 105–110.

Garbarino, J. and Garbarino, A. (1986) *Emotional Maltreatment of Children.* Chicago: National Committee for Prevention of Child Abuse.

Garth, A. (1995) 'Parents with learning disability.' In P. Reder and L. Lucey (eds) *Assessment of Parenting: Psychiatric and Psychological Contributions.* London: Routledge.

Gaudin Jr, J.M. (1993) 'Effective intervention with neglectful families.' *Criminal Justice and Behaviour 20*, 1, 66–89.

Geiger B. (1996) *Fathers as Primary Caregivers.* Westport, CN: Greenwood Press.

Gersch, I.S. (1996) 'Listening to children in educational contexts' In R. Davie, G. Upton and V. Varma (eds) *The Voice of the Child: A Handbook for Professionals.* London and Washington, DC: Falmer Press.

Gibbons, J., Gallagher, B., Bell, C. and Gordon, D. (1995) *Development After Physical Abuse in Early Childhood: A Follow-Up Study of Children on Protection Registers.* London: HMSO.

Gil, E. and Cavanagh Johnson, T. (1993) *Sexualized Children: Assessment and Treatment of Sexualized Children and Children Who Molest.* Rockville, MD: Launch Press.

Gilligan, C. (1993) *In a Different Voice: Psychological Theory and Women's Development* (2nd edn). Cambridge, MA, and London: Harvard University Press.

Gilligan, R. (1997) 'Beyond permanence? The importance of resilience in child placement practice and planning.' *Adoption and Fostering 21*, 1, 12–20.

Gilligan, R. (1998) 'The importance of schools and teachers in child welfare.' *Child and Family Social Work 3*, 13–25.

Gilligan, R. (1999) 'Children's own social networks and network members: key resources in helping children at risk' In M. Hill (ed.) *Effective Ways of Helping Children.* London: Jessica Kingsley Publishers.

Goldman, L (1994) *Life and Loss: A Guide to Helping Grieving Children.* Accelerated Development Inc.

Goldman, R. and Goldman, J. (1982) *Children's Sexual Thinking.* London: Routledge and Kegan Paul.

Goldsmith, E.B. (1990) 'In support of working parents and their children.' *Journal of Social Behaviour and Personality 5*, 6, 517–520.

Golombok, S. and Fivush, R. (1994) *Gender Development.* Cambridge, New York and Melbourne: Cambridge University Press.

Goodman, G.S. and Reed, R. (1986) 'Age differences in eyewitnesses testimony and behaviour.' *Law and Human Behaviour 10*, 317–332.

Goodyer, I.M. (1990) 'Family relationships, life events and childhood psychopathology.' *Journal of Child Psychology and Psychiatry 31*, 1, 161–192.

Gottman, J.M. and Parker, J.G. (1987) *Conversations of Friends.* New York: Cambridge University Press.

Gray, G., Smith, A. and Rutter, M. (1980) 'School attendance and the first year of employment.' In G. Gray, A. Smith and M. Rutter (eds) *Out of School: Modern Perspectives in Truancy and School Refusal.* Chichester: Wiley.

Grossmann, K., Fremmer-Bombik, E., Rudolph, J. and Grossmann, K.E. (1988) 'Maternal attachment representations as related to patterns of infant-mother attachment and maternal care during the first year.' In R.A. Hinde and J. Stevenson-Hinde (eds) *Relationships Within Families: Mutual Influences.* Oxford: Oxford University Press.

Grossman, K.E. and Grossman, K. (1991) 'Attachment quality as an organizer of emotional and behavioural responses in a longitudinal perspective.' In C.M. Parkes, J. Stevenson-Hinde and P. Marris (eds) *Attachment Across the Life Cycle.* London: Tavistock/Routledge.

Hakuta, K. and Garcia, E.E. (1989) 'Bilingualism and education.' *American Psychologist 44*, 374–379.

Harter, S. (1982) 'The perceived competence scale for children.' *Child Development 53*, 87–97.

Hartman, A. (1984) *Working with Adoptive Families Beyond Placement.* New York: Child Welfare League of America.

Hayes, C.D. (1987) 'Adolescent pregnancy and childbearing: An emerging research focus.' In S.L. Hooferth and C.D. Hayes (eds) *Risking the Future: Adolescent Sexuality, Pregnancy and Childbearing 2: Working Papers and Statistical Appendices.* Washington, D.C: National Academy Press.

Herbert, M. (1987) *Conduct Disorders of Childhood and Adolescence.* New York: Wiley.

Hess. P.M. and Proch, K.O. (1993) *Contact: Managing Visits to Children Looked After Away from Home.* London: BAAF.

Hester, M. and Pearson, C. (1993) 'Domestic violence, mediation and child contact arrangements: issues from current research.' *Family Mediation 3*, 2, 3–6.

Hester, M. and Radford, L. (1992) 'Domestic violence and access arrangements for children in Denmark and Britain.' *Journal of Social Welfare and Family Law 1*, 57–70.

Hester, M. and Radford, L (1996) *Domestic Violence and Child Contact Arrangements in England and Denmark.* Bristol: Policy Press.

Hetherington, E.M. (1989) 'Coping with family transitions: winners, losers and survivors.' *Child Development 60*, 1–14.

Hirst, M. and Baldwin, S. (1994) *Unequal Opportunities: Growing up Disabled,* Social Policy Research Unit, University of York.

Hoffman-Plotkin, D. and Twentyman, C.T. (1984) 'A multimodal assessment of behavioural and cognitive deficits in abused and neglected preschoolers.' *Child Development 55*, 794–802.

Holmes, J. (1993) 'Attachment theory: a biological basis for psychotherapy.' *British Journal of Psychiatry 163*, 430–438.

Howe, D. (1995) *Attachment Theory for Social Work Practice.* Houndsmill, Basingstoke, Hampshire and London: Macmillan Press.

Imrie, R.W. (1984) 'The nature of knowledge in social work.' *Social Work Jan.-Feb.*, 41–45.

Jewett, C. (1984) *Helping Children Cope with Separation and Loss.* London: BAAF.

Kandel, D.B. (1990) 'Parenting styles, drug use, and children's adjustment in families of young adults.' *Journal of Marriage and the Family 52*, 183–196.

Katchadourian, H. (1990) 'Sexuality.' In S.S. Feldman and G.R. Elliot (eds) *At the Threshold: The Developing Adolescent.* Cambridge MA: Harvard University Press.

Katz, I. (1996) *The Construction of Racial Identity in Children of Mixed Parentage: Mixed Metaphors.* London and Bristol: Jessica Kingsley Publishers.

Katz, P (1982) 'Development of children's racial awareness and intergroup attitudes.' In L.G. Katz (ed) *Current Topics in Early Childhood Education, Vol.4.* Norwood, NJ: Ablex.

Kelly, L. (1994) 'The interconnectedness of domestic violence and child abuse: challenges for research, policy and practice.' In A. Mullender and R. Morley (eds) *Children Living with Domestic Violence. Putting Men's Abuse of Women on the Child Care Agenda.* London: Whiting and Birch.

Kitzinger, C. (1986) 'Introducing and developing Q as a feminist methodology: a study of accounts of lesbianism.' In S. Wilkinson (ed) *Feminist Social Psychology.* Milton Keynes: Open University Press.

Klaus, M.H. and Kennell, J.H. (1976) *Maternal-Infant Bonding.* St Louis: C.V. Mosby Company.

Klingman, L. and Vicary, J.R. (1992) 'Risk factors associated with date rape and sexual assault of adolescent girls.' Poster presentation, Society for Research on Adolescence, Pennsylvania State University, March.

Kohlberg, L (1969) 'Stages and sequence: the cognitive-developmental approach to socialization.' In D.A. Goslin (ed) *Handbook of Socialization Theory and Research.* Chicago: Rand McNally.

Kosonen, M. (1994) 'Sibling relationships for children in the care system.' *Adoption and Fostering 18*, 3, 30–35.

Kosonen, M. (1996a) 'Siblings as providers of support and help during middle childhood: children's perceptions.' *Children and Society 10*, 267–279.

Kosonen M (1996b) 'Maintaining sibling relationships: neglected dimension in child care practice.' *British Journal of Social Work 26*, 809–822.

Kosonen M (1997) 'Sibling abuse: a hidden misery: children's perceptions of their relationships with their siblings.' Paper presented at BAPSCAN Congress. Approaching the Millennium: The Future Shape of Child Protection. Centre for the Study of Child and Society, University of Glasgow.

Krisberg, B., Schwartz, I., Fishman, G., Eisikovits, Z. and Guttman, E. (1986) *The Incarceration of Minority Youth.* Minneapolis: Hubert H. Humphrey Institute of Public Affairs, National Council on Crime and Delinquency.

Lees, S. (1993) *Sugar and Spice: Sexuality and Adolescent Girls.* Harmondsworth: Penguin.

Lewis, M. (1994) 'Does attachment imply a relationship or multiple relationships?' *Psychological Inquiry 1*, 47–51.

Lewis, M. and Feiring, C. (1989) 'Infant, mother and mother-infant interaction: behaviour and subsequent attachment.' *Child Development 60*, 831–837.

Lightfoot, C (1993) *Playing with Desire.* New Orleans: Society for Research in Child Development.

Littner, N. (1975) 'The importance of natural parents to the child in placement.' *Child Welfare 54*, pp.175–181.

Maccoby, E. and Martin, J. (1983) 'Socialization in the context of the family: Parent-child interaction.' In E.M. Hetherington (ed) *Handbook of Child Psychology: Socialization, Personality and Social Development.* Vol 4. New York: Wiley.

Maccoby, E.E. and Jacklin, C.N. (1987) 'Gender segregation in children.' In H.W. Reese (ed) *Advances in Child Development and Behaviour 20*, 239–287. New York: Academic Press.

Main, M. (1991) 'Meta cognitive knowledge, meta cognitive monitoring and singular (coherent) versus multiple (incoherent) model of attachment: findings and directions for future research.' In C.M. Parkes, J. Stevenson-Hinde and P. Marris (eds) *Attachment Across the Life Cycle.* London: Tavistock/Routledge.

Main, M. and Goldwyn, R. (1984) 'Predicting rejection of her infant from mother's representations of her own experience: Implications for the abused – abusing intergenerational cycle.' *Child Abuse and Neglect 8*, 203–217.

Maitra, B. (1995) 'Giving due consideration to the family's racial and cultural background.' In P. Reder and L. Lucey (eds) *Assessment of Parenting: Psychiatric and Psychological Contributions.* London: Routledge.

Malik, N.M and Furman, W. (1993) 'Practitioner review: problems in children's peer relations: what can the clinician do?' *Journal of Child Psychology 34*, 8, 1303–1326.

Mama, A. (1989) *The Hidden Struggle: Statutory and Voluntary Sector Responses to Women and Children Escaping from Violence in the Home.* Bristol: Women's Aid Federation England and University of Bristol School of Applied Social Studies.

Marcia, J.E. (1966) 'Development and validation of ego-identity status.' *Journal of Personality and Social Psychology 3*, 551–558.

Marcia, J.E. (1980) 'Identity in adolescence.' In J. Adelson (ed) *Handbook of Adolescent Psychology.* New York: Wiley.

Martin, F. (1998) 'Tales of transition: self-narrative and direct scribing in exploring care-leaving.' *Child and Family Social Work 3*, 1, 1–12.

Maxime J.E. (1986) 'Some psychological models of black self-concept.' In S. Ahmed, J. Cheetham and J. Small (eds) *Social Work with Black Children and their Families.* London: BAAF.

McDonald, S. (1991) *All Equal Under the Act: A Practical Guide to the Children Act 1989 for Social Workers.* London: Race Equality Unit.

McFadden, E. (1986) *The Child Who is Physically Battered and Abused.* Ypsilanti: University of Michigan.

McFadden, E. (1996) *Fostering the Child who has been Sexually Abused.* Ypsilanti: University of Michigan.

McGee, C. (1997) 'Children's experiences of domestic violence.' *Journal of Child and Family Social Work 2*, 1, 13–21.

McGibbon, A. Cooper, L. and Kelly, L. (1989) 'What support: An exploratory study of council policy and practice and local support services in the area of domestic violence within Hammersmith and Fulham Council.' In A. Mullender and R. Marley (eds) *Children Living with Domestic Violence: Putting Men's Abuse of Women on the Child Care Agenda.* London: Whiting and Birch.

Meadows, S. (1986) *Understanding Child Development.* London: Routledge.

Meikle, S., Peitchinis, J.A. and Pearce, K. (1985) *Teenage Sexuality.* London: Taylor and Francis.

Meisels, S. and Shonkoff, J. (1990) *Handbook of Early Childhood Intervention.* Cambridge: Cambridge University Press.

Modi, P., Marks, C. and Wattley, R. (1995) 'From the margin to the centre: empowering the black child.' In C. Cloke and M. Davies (eds) *Participation and Empowerment in Child Protection.* London: Pitman Publishing.

Montemayor, R. and Eisen, M. (1977) 'The development of self-conceptions from childhood to adolescence.' *Developmental Psychology 13*, 314–319

Moore, K., Peterson J. and Furstenberg, F. Jr (1986) 'Parental attitudes and the occurrence of early sexual activity.' *Journal of Marriage and the Family 48*, 777–782.

Moore, S. and Rosenthal, D. (1991) 'Adolescents' perceptions of friends' and parents' attitudes to sex and sexual risk-taking.' *Journal of Community and Applied Psychology 1*, 189–200.

Moore, S. and Rosenthal, D. (1993) *Sexuality in Adolescence.* London and New York: Routledge.

Mostyn, W. (1996) *Childhood Matters: Report of the National Commission of Inquiry into the Prevention of Child Abuse. London: The Stationery Office.*

NCB (1988) 'The father's role in the family.' *Highlight 78.*

NCH Action for Children (1994) *The Hidden Victims: Children and Domestic Violence.* London: NCH Action for Children

NCH Action for Children (1997) *Making a Difference: Working with Women and Children Experiencing Domestic Violence.* London: NCH Action for Children.

Naylor, B. (1989) 'Dealing with child sexual assault.' *British Journal of Criminology 29,* 4, 395–407.

Ogilvy, C.M., Boath, E.H., Cheyne, W.M., Jahoda, G. and Schaffer, H.R. (1992) 'Staff–child interaction styles in multi-ethnic nursery schools.' *British Journal of Developmental Psychology 10,* 85–97.

O'Hagan, K. (1993) *Emotional and Psychological Abuse of Children.* Thousand Oaks, CA, London and New Dehli: Sage Publications.

O'Hara, M. (1993) 'Child protection and domestic violence: changing policy and practice.' In London Borough of Hackney *The Links Between Domestic Violence and Child Abuse: Developing Services.* London: London Borough of Hackney.

O'Hara, M. (1994) 'Child deaths in contexts of domestic violence: Implications for professional practice.' In A. Mullender and R. Morley (eds) *Children Living with Domestic Violence: Putting Men's Abuse of Women on the Child Care Agenda.* London: Whiting and Birch

Olweus, D. (1993) *Bullying at School: What We Know and What We Can Do.* Oxford: Blackwell.

Parker, R., Ward, H., Jackson, S., Aldgate, J. and Wedge, P. (1991) *Looking after children: Assessing outcomes in child care.* London: HMSO.

Parton, N. (1995) 'Neglect as child protection: the political context and the practical outcomes.' *Children and Society 9,*1, 67–89.

Parton, N. (1997) *Child Protection and Family Support: Tensions, Contradictions and Possibilities.* London: Routledge.

Peterson, C. (1989) *Looking Forward Through the Life Span.* New York: Prentice-Hall.

Petersen, C. and Seligman, M.E.P. (1985) 'The learned helplessness model of depression: current status of theory and research.' In E. Beckham (ed) *Handbook of Depression, Treatment Assessment and Research.* Homewood, IL: Dorsey Press.

Phillips, M. and Dutt, R. (1990) *Towards a Black Perspective in Child Protection.* London: Race Equality Unit.

Phinney, J.S. (1993) 'A three-stage model of ethnic identity development in adolescence.' In M.E. Bernal and G.P. Knight (eds) *Ethnic Identity: Formation and Transmission Among Hispanics and Other Minorities.* Albany, NY: State University of New York Press.

Phoenix, A. (1991) *Young Mothers?* Cambridge: Polity Press.

Piaget, J. (1932) *The Moral Judgement of the Child.* Harmondsworth: Penguin.

Piaget, J. (1952) *The Origins of Intelligence in Children.* New York: International Universities Press.

Piaget, J. (1954) *The Construction of Reality in the Child.* New York: Basic Books.

Piaget, J. (1962) *Play, Dreams and Fun in Childhood.* London: Routledge.

Pitcairn, T., Waterhouse, L., McGhee, J., Secker, J. and Sullivan, C. (1993) 'Evaluating parenting in child physical abuse.' In L. Waterhouse (ed) *Child Abuse and Child Abusers: Protection and Prevention.* London: Jessica Kingsley Publishers.

Quinton, D. and Rutter, M. (1988) *Parenting Breakdown: The Making and Breaking of Inter-Generational Links.* Aldershot: Avebury.

Rashid, S.P. (1996) 'Attachment reviewed through a cultural lens.' In D. Howe (ed) *Attachment and Loss in Child and Family Social Work.* Avebury: Ashgate.

Reddy, V. (1991) 'Playing with others' expectations: teasing and mucking about in the first year.' In A.Whiten (ed) *Natural Theories of Mind.* Oxford: Blackwell.

Reder, P. and Duncan, S. (1995) 'The meaning of the child.' In P. Reder and L. Lucey (eds) *Assessment of Parenting: Psychiatric and Psychological Contributions.* London: Routledge.

Reder, P. and Lucey, C. (1991). 'The assessment of parenting: some interactional considerations.' *Psychiatric Bulletin 15,* 347–8.

Reder, P. and Lucey, C. (1995) *The Assessment of Parenting: Psychiatric and Psychological Contributions.* London: Routledge.

Remafedi, G. (1987) 'Male homosexuality: the adolescent's perspective.' *Pediatrics 79,* 331–337.

Remafedi, G., Resnick, M., Blum, R. and Harris, L. (1992) 'Demography of sexual orientation in adolescents.' *Pediatrics 89,* 714–21.

Rice, K. (1990) 'Attachment in adolescence: a narrative and meta-analytic review.' *Journal of Youth and Adolescence 19*, 511–538.

Richards, B. (1994) 'What is identity?' In I. Gaber and J. Aldridge (eds) *Culture, Identity and Transracial Adoption: In the Best Interests of the Child.* London: Free Association Books.

Richman, N. (1977) 'Behaviour problems in pre-school children.' *British Journal of Psychology 131*, 523–527.

Richman, N., Stevenson, J. and Graham, P. (1982) *Pre-School to School: A Behavioural Study* London: Academic Press.

Rickford, F. (1997) 'Mind games' *Community Care 23* 19 Jan., 18–19.

Ricks, M.H. (1985)'The social transmission of parental behaviour: Attachment across generations' in I. Bretherton and E. Waters (eds) *Growing Points of Attachment Theory and Research.* Monographs of the Society for Research in Child Development, 50, (1–2, Serial No. 209).

Roberts, G. (1992) 'Rape OK if led on, say third of boys.' *The Age*, Melbourne, 5, 6.

Robinson, J.L., Zahn-Waxler, C. and Emde, R. (1994) 'Patterns of development in early empathic behaviour: environmental and child contributional influences.' *Social Development 3*, 125–145.

Rogoff, B. (1990) *Apprenticeship Training.* New York: Oxford University Press.

Rowe, J., Hundleby, M. and Garnett, L. (1989) *Child Care Now.* London: British Agencies for Adoption and Fostering, Research Series 6.

Rutter, M. (1981) *Maternal Deprivation Reassessed* (2nd edn). Harmondsworth: Penguin.

Rutter, M. (1985) 'Resilience in the face of adversity: protective factors and resistance to psychiatric disorder.' *British Journal of Psychiatry 147*, 598–611.

Rutter, M. (1991) 'Pathways from childhood to adult life: the role of schooling.' *Pastoral Care* Sep. 3–10.

Rutter, M. and Quinton, D. (1977) 'Psychiatric disorder: ecological factors and concepts of causation.' In H. McGurk (ed) *Ecological Factors in Human Development.* Amsterdam: North Holland.

Rutter, M. and Quinton, D. (1984) 'Parental psychiatric disorder: effects on children.' *Psychological Medicine 14*, 853–880.

Rutter, M. and Rutter, M. (1993) *Developing Minds: Challenge and Continuity across the Life Span.* Harmondsworth: Penguin.

Rutter M, Tizard, C. and Reads, P. (1986) *Depression and Young People: Developmental and Clinical Perspectives.* Guildford Press: New York.

Rutter, M., Maugham, B., Mortimore, P. and Ouston, J. (1979) Fifteen Thousand Hours: Secondary Schools and their Effects on Children. London: Open Books.

Ryan, P. (1979) *Training Foster Parents to Handle Lying and Stealing.* Ypsilanti, MI: Eastern Michigan University.

Santrok, J.W. (1994) *Child Development.* Madison, WI; Dubuque, IA: W.C.B. Brown and Benchmark.

Save the Children (1997) *Out of the Frying Pan: The True Cost of Feeding a Family on a Low Income.* London: Save the Children.

Saywitz, K.J. (1995) 'Improving children's testimony: The question, the answer and the environment.' In M.S. Zavagoza Jr.; G.C.N. Graham; R. Hirschiman Hall, and Y.S. Ben Prath (eds) *Memory and Testimony in Child Witnesses.* Thousand Oaks, CA, London, New Dehli: Sage Publications.

Saywitz, K.J. and Goodman, G.S. (1996) 'Interviewing children in and out of court: current research and practice implications.' In J. Briere, L. Berliner, J.A. Buckley, C. Jenny and T. Reid (eds) *The APSAC Handbook on Child Maltreatment.* Thousand Oaks, CA, London and New Dehli: Sage Publications.

Scales, P. and Gibbons, J. (1996) 'Extended family members and unrelated adults in the lives of young adolescents: a research agenda' *Journal of Early Adolescence 16*, 4, 365–389.

Scarr, S. (1990) 'Mother's proper place, children's needs and women's rights.' *Journal of Social Behaviour and Personality 5*, 6, 507–515.

Schaffer, H.R. (1989) *Making Decisions about Children: Psychological Questions and Answers.* Oxford: Blackwell.

Schaffer, H.R. (1996) *Social Development.* Oxford: Blackwell.

Schaffer, H.R. and Emerson, P.E. (1964) 'The development of social attachments in infancy.' *Monographs of the Society for Research in Child Development 29*, (3, Whole No. 94).

Schlesinger, H.S. and Meadow, K.P. (1972) *Sound and Sign.* Berkeley: University of California Press.

Schofield, G. (1996) 'Attachment theory, neglect and the concept of parenting skills. Training: the needs of parents with learning disabilities and their children.' In D. Hare (ed) *Attachment and Love in Child and Family Social Work.* Aldershot: Avebury.

Schonfeld, W.A. (1969) 'The body and body image in adolescents.' In G. Caplan and S. Lebovici (eds) *Adolescence: Psychosocial Perspectives.* New York: Basic Books.

Seligman, M.E.P. and Peterson, C. (1986) 'A learned helplessness perspective on childhood depression: theory and research.' In M. Rutter; C. Tizard and P. Reads (eds) *Depression and Young People: Developmental and Clinical Perspectives.* Guildford Press: New York.

Semaj, L. (1978) 'Racial identification and preference in children: a cognitive developmental approach.' Ph.D. thesis, State University of New Jersey.

Sheinberg, M. and Penn, P. (1991) 'Gender dilemmas, gender questions, and the gender mantra.' *Journal of Marital and Family Therapy 17,* 1, 33–44.

Sinclair, I. and Gibbs, I. (1996) *Quality of Care in Children's Homes: A Short Report and Issues Paper* University of York: Social Work Research and Development Unit.

Sinclair, R.; Hearn, B. and Pugh, G. (1997) *Preventive Work with Families.* London: National Children's Bureau.

Smetana, J. (1989) 'Adolescents' and parents' reasoning about actual family conflict.' *Child Development 60,* 1052–1067.

Smith, G. (1992) 'The unbearable traumatogenic past: child sexual abuse.' In U. Varma (ed.) *The Secret Lives of Vulnerable Children.* London: Routledge.

Smith, G. (1995) 'Do children have the right to leave their pasts behind them? Contact with children who have been abused.' In H. Argent (ed) *See you Soon: Contact for Children Looked after by Local Authorities.* London: BAAF.

Smith, P.K. and Cowie, H. (1991) *Understanding Children's Development.* Oxford: Blackwell.

Social Services Inspectorate (1994a) *National Overview Report of Child Protection Inspections.* London: Department of Health.

Social Services Inspectorate (1994b) *National Inspection Report of Services for Disabled Children and Their Families.* London: Department of Health.

Sonuga-Barke, E.J.S.; Minocha, K.; Taylor, E.A. and Sandberg, S. (1993) 'Inter-ethnic bias in teachers' ratings of childhood hyperactivity.' *British Journal of Developmental Psychology 11,* 187–200.

Spieker, S.J. and Booth, C.L. (1988) 'Maternal antecedents of attachment quality.' In J. Bellsky and T. Nezworski (eds) *Clinical Applications of Attachment.* Hillsdale NJ: Erlbaum.

Sroufe, L.A. and Fleeson, J. (1988) 'The coherence of family relationships.' In R.Hinde and J. Stevenson (eds) *Relationships within Families.* Milton Keynes: Open University Press.

Stainton Rogers, W. (1989) 'Childrearing in a multicultural society' In W. Stainton Rogers, D. Hevey and E. Ash (eds) *Child Abuse and Neglect: Facing the Challenge.* London: Batsford in association with the Open University.

Stark, E. and Flitcraft, A. (1985) 'Women and children at risk: a feminist perspective on child abuse.' *International Journal of Health Services 1,* 461–493.

Steinberg, L. (1993) *Adolescence.* New York: McGraw-Hill.

Stevenson, O. (1996) 'Emotional abuse and neglect: a time for reappraisal.' *Child and Family Social Work 1,* 1, 13–18.

Stevenson, J., Richman, N. and Graham, P. (1985) 'Behaviour problems and language abilities at 3 years and behavioural disturbance at 8 years.' *Journal of Child Psychology and Psychiatry 26,* 215–230.

Stone, M. (1989) *Young People Leaving Care: A study of management systems, service delivery and user evaluation.* Westerham, Kent: The Royal Philanthropic Society.

Stopford, V. (1993) *Understanding Disability: Causes, Characteristics and Coping.* London: Edward Arnold.

Summit, R. (1983) 'The child sexual abuse accommodation syndrome.' *Child Abuse and Neglect 7,* 177–193.

Sutton, C. (1994) *Social Work, Community Work and Psychology.* Leicester: British Psychological Society.

Swadi, H. (1994) 'Parenting capacity and substance misuse: An assessment scheme.' *ACPP Review and Newsletter 16,* 237–46.

Swift, K.J. (1995) *Manufacturing 'Bad Mothers': A Critical Perspective in Child Neglect.* Toronto: University of Toronto Press Inc.

Thelen, E. (1989) 'The (re)discovery of motor development: learning new things from an old field.' *Developmental Psychology 25*, 946–949.

Thompson, R. (1995) *Preventing Child Maltreatment Through Social Support.* Thousand Oaks, CA, London, New Dehli: Sage Publications.

Tizard, B. and Phoenix, A. (1989) 'Black identity and transracial adoption.' *New Community 15*, 3, 427–437.

Tizard, B. and Phoenix, A. (1993) *Black, White or Mixed Race? Race and Racism in the Lives of Young People of Mixed Parentage.* London and New York: Routledge.

Tobin-Richards, M.H. Boxer, A.M. and Peterson, A.C. (1983) 'The psychological significance of pubertal change: sex differences in perceptions of self during early adolescence.' In J. Brooks-Gunn and A.C. Peterson (eds) *Girls at Puberty.* New York: Plenum.

Trevarthen, C. (1975) 'Early attempts at speech.' In R Lewin (ed) *Child Alive.* London: Temple Smith.

Trevarthen, C. (1977) 'Descriptive analyses of infant communicative behaviour.' In H.R. Schaffer (ed.) *Studies in Mother-Infant Interaction.* London: Academic Press.

Trevarthen, C. (1991) 'Cognitive and co-operative motives in infancy.' Symposium, Crete, Early Development: Current Theories and Research Findings.

Triseliotis, J., Borland, M., Hill, M. and Lambert, L. (1995) *Teenagers and the Social Work Services.* HMSO: London.

Trinke, S. and Batholomew, K. (1997) 'Hierarchies of attachment relationships in young adulthood.' *Journal of Social and Personal Relationships 14*, 5, 603–625.

Udry, J.R. and Billy, J. (1987) 'Initiation of coitus in early adolescence.' *American Sociological Review 52*, 841–855.

Unger, R. and Crawford, M. (1992) *Women and Gender: A Feminist Psychology.* Philadelphia: Temple University Press.

Utting, D. (1995) *Family and Parenthood: Supporting Families, Presenting Breakdown.* York: Joseph Rowntree Foundation.

Utting, W. (1997) People Like Us: the Report of the Review of the Safeguards for Children Living Away from Home. London: Department of Health/Welsh Office.

van der Veer, R. and Valsiner, J. (1991) *Understanding Vygotsky: A Quest for Synthesis.* Cambridge, MA, and Oxford: Blackwell.

Vaughn, G.M. (1964) 'The development of ethnic attitudes in New Zealand school children.' *Genetic Psychology Monographs 70*, 135–175.

Watson, G. (1989) 'The abuse of disabled children and young people.' In W. Stainton Rodgers, D. Heavey and E. Ashe (eds) *Child Abuse and Neglect: Facing the Challenge.* Milton Keynes: Open University.

Wattam, C. and Woodward, C. (1996) 'And do I abuse my children? No.' In *Childhood Matters*, Vol. 2, National Commission of Inquiry into the Prevention of Child Abuse. London: HMSO.

Werner, E. (1990) 'Protective factors and individual resilience.' In S. Meisels and J. Shonkoff (eds) *Handbook of Early Childhood Intervention.* Cambridge University Press.

Werner, E and Smith, R, (1992) *Overcoming the Odds: High Risk Children from Birth to Adulthood.* Ithaca: Cornell University Press.

Whiting, B.B. and Edwards, C.P. (1988) *Children of Different Worlds: The Formation of Social Behaviour.* Cambridge MA: Harvard University Press.

Williams, L.M. (1994) 'Recall of childhood trauma: a prospective study of women's memories of child sexual abuse.' *Journal of Consulting and Clinical Psychology 62*, 3, 1167–1176.

Wise, S. (1985) *Becoming a Feminist Social Worker.* Studies in Sexual Politics No. 6, University of Manchester: Sociology Department.

Women's Aid Federation England (1993) *Briefing Paper – Domestic Violence and Child Abuse: Some Links.* Bristol: Women's Aid Federation.

Yates, C. and Smith, P.K. (1989) 'Bullying in two English comprehensive schools.' In E. Roland and E. Munthe (eds) *Bullying: An International Perspective.* London: David Fulton.

Zahn-Waxler, C., Radke-Yarrow, M. and King, R.A. (1979) 'Child-rearing and children's prosocial initiations towards victims of distress.' *Child Development 50*, 319–330.

Zimmerman, R.B. (1988) 'Childhood depression: new theoretical formulations and implications for foster care services.' In *Child Welfare 67*, 1, 37–47.

Subject Index

Author Index